Digital Imaging

Digital Imaging

Tips, Tools, and Techniques for Photographers

JOE FARACE

Focal Press
Boston • Oxford • Johannesburg • Melbourne • New Delhi • Singapore

Focal Press is an imprint of Butterworth–Heinemann.

A member of the Reed Elsevier group

Recognizing the importance of preserving what has been written, Butterworth–Heinemann prints its books on acid-free paper whenever possible.

Butterworth–Heinemann supports the efforts of American Forests and the Global ReLeaf program in its campaign for the betterment of trees, forests, and our environment.

Library of Congress Cataloging-in-Publication Data
Farace, Joe, 1941-
Digital imaging : tips, tools, and techniques for photographers / Joe Farace.
p. cm.
Includes index.
ISBN 0-240-80297-7 (alk. paper)
1. Photography—Digital techniques. 2. Image processing—Digital techniques. I. Title.
TR267.F36 1998
778.3—dc21 98-15531
CIP

British Library Cataloguing-in-Publication Data
A catalogue record for this book is available from the British Library.

The publisher offers special discounts on bulk orders of this book.
For information, please contact:
Manager of Special Sales
Butterworth–Heinemann
225 Wildwood Avenue
Woburn, MA 01801-2041
Tel: 781-904-2500
Fax: 781-904-2620

For information on all Focal Press publications available, contact our World Wide Web home page at: http://www.bh.com/focalpress

10 9 8 7 6 5 4 3 2 1

Printed in the United States of America

Dedication

This book is dedicated to the memory of Lief Ericksenn. It was 1972, and I lay in a hospital bed facing a bleak and uncertain future. Helping me get through this difficult time was the love and support of my family and friends, but just as important a source of inspiration was a photo magazine called *Camera 35*. This eclectic and iconoclastic publication was edited by a man named Lief Ericksenn, and I read and reread each article he contributed to it. Later, in happier days, Lief became editor of *Photomethods* magazine, and I was fortunate enough to work with him. It was one of those rare times in a person's life when you knew you were living in the "good old days." These days, *Photomethods* is gone, replaced by *PEI*. Sadly, Lief is gone too—but nobody could ever replace him.

Table of Contents

Preface

It wasn't an airplane that killed Kong . . . it was beauty that killed the beast.

ROBERT ARMSTRONG, *KING KONG* (1939)

Creative image-makers have long used technology and their own ingenuity to alter the look of the photographs captured with their cameras. The photographic purists who were offended when *National Geographic* magazine digitally moved one of the Great Pyramids for a cover photo, do not appear to know much about the history of photography. Manipulated images have been a part of photographic culture since the Daguerreotype process was introduced in 1839.

In the 1930s, pictorialists, like Maryland's A. Aubrey Bodine, used darkroom tricks to add interesting elements to his architectural and landscape photographs. Harlem photographer James Van Der Zee used double-exposure and double-printing techniques to produce funeral images showing a child lying dead in a coffin and alive on the same print. Then there was the dark magician, William Mortensen, who combined esoteric darkroom processes with an eye for the bizarre to produce dramatic, controversial—yet unmistakably popular—manipulated images.

For almost 100 years, the creative manipulation of images was an accepted part of photography. All that changed in 1932 with the formation of F-64 Group. Since small apertures produce the greatest range of sharpness in an image, it was this clarity that, according to the *Time-Life Library of Photography*, "the group equated with uncompromising honesty." With the formation of F64 by Edward Weston, Ansel Adams, former Pictorialist and born-again purist Alfred Stiegletz, along with four others, the lines were drawn for a battle for the soul of photography. The first casualty of this war was Bill Mortensen.

During the 1930s and 40s, a series of articles in *Camera Craft* magazine served as the battleground between Mortensen and a young Adams. When the fight was over, Mortensen's reputation was destroyed and, in a treatment reminiscent of Orwell's *1984*, became a photographic nonperson. Most accepted histories of photography fail to mention his name or his contributions to photographic art. Mortensen died a victim of photographic purism, but the other victim was the manipulated print. This misconception about photographic honesty has carried over—if only in the minds of the general public—until today.

Misconception? For many practitioners, image manipulation remains part of photography. When a person has a portrait of themselves made, they often ask the photographer to make sure they "get their good side." The asymmetrical nature of faces means there is *really* a "good" side, and it is the portrait photographer's job to emphasize it. That, along with negative retouching and print finishing, can produce a flattering—but not always realistic—image of the person being photographed. Yet few complain if they look better in their portrait than they do in "real life." The practice of improving and enhancing reality is not limited to portraits. Photographic artists such as Jerry Uelsmann and Duane Michaels ignored the F64 dictum and continue to produce manipulated images that stimulate the mind and delight the eye. Even photojournalistic images are manipulated by the photographer's choice of lens, camera angle, and film.

Yet the myth that a photograph is an accurate record of reality remained unchallenged until digital imaging. All of a sudden computer programs, like Silicon Beach Software's pioneering Digital Darkroom, made it possible to manipulate photographs in a manner reminiscent of conventional darkroom methods. As new software and hardware were introduced, digital gurus began creating a body of manipulated images that spawned the current controversy. The film *Forrest Gump* added fuel to the firestorm by showing Tom Hanks guzzling Dr. Pepper with the late President John F. Kennedy. A university professor devised a symbol showing a crossed-out camera lens to identify images that "through doctoring or retouching, are no longer simple mechanical reproductions of a moment in time." If this definition was to be scrupulously followed, very few images—with the exception of forensic photographs—would appear without this "manipulated" symbol.

A photograph—digital or otherwise—has never been an accurate representation of reality, or a reproduction of a moment in time. Ironically, Ansel Adams' own Zone System is a codified system for processing and printing to produce an image the photographer has "previsualized"—not what was actually there.

Photography, like all art forms, is and always has been an interpretation of reality. As Bill Mortensen said fifty years ago, "Ideas, not sensations, are it's [photography's] basic materials, and the art-form is strictly subordinated to them."

Acknowledgments

I would like to thank the many people who helped me with this book and without whose assistance it would not have been possible. I would like to begin with Focal Press' Marie Lee and Tammy Harvey, who believed in me and in this project even when there were those around us who wanted to create another, different book.

A number of people provided software, hardware, and technical support, and without their help writing this book would have been much more difficult. I owe a debt of thanks to: Lance Merker of Mainstay for providing the Captivate screen capture software that made creating the screenshots in the book and CD-ROM easier; Michael Pilmer of Alien Skin Software for providing the latest version of their killer Eye Candy image enhancement plug-in; Adobe System's Sonya Schaefer for providing beta copies of Photoshop to begin working with the program before is was officially available; Sally Mitchell of Epson Corporation for her kindness, and for sharing technical assistance on the inner workings of Epson ink-jet printers and scanners; and Holly Fisher of Live Picture, Inc.

A mega-thank-you goes out to Craig Meserole of the "now defunct" Power Computing Corporation for his help in getting me on-line with a computer powerful enough to handle what for most people would be an overload of graphics plug-ins. Thanks also to Power Computing's Norma Hernandez for her assistance in getting the Iomega Zip and Jaz drives that I needed to produce, store, and back-up all of the images in this book. As this book was being completed, Apple Computer announced they were purchasing Power Computing, so the computer I have is one of the last to bear the Power Computing designation. One of the most important components a photographer's computer can have is a high-quality, fast video board. I would like to thank Julie Moe of Imagio, for lending me an Integrated Micro Solutions Twin Turbo 128M video board for my now-dinosaur Power Computing PowerCenter 150.

A big thank-you to the photographers who shared their tips, tools, and techniques used to bash pixels. This includes: Kevin Elliott, General Manager of Cies-Sexton Photographic, for his help in rescuing the first three chapters worth of illustrations for the book; John Blake of Greeley, Colorado for his wit and wisdom; and *People* magazine Contributing Photographer Barry Staver for providing images and for his continuing friendship and inspiration. A special thank-you goes out to legendary camera technician and PC guru Vern Prime. He has been a constant source of information and a helping hand whenever I needed one. Vern, many thanks.

This is the eleventh book I have written or co-authored. I would have never been able to complete the first one—and especially this book—without the help of my dear wife Mary. She is my biggest fan and for that, I will always be grateful.

Joe Farace
Brighton, Colorado, 1997

Introduction

Photography, like any other art, is a form of communication. The artist is . . . speaking a language, is telling something.

WILLIAM MORTENSEN (1934)

This statement, made over sixty years ago, embodies both the power and paradox of photography. All photographs—digital or silver-based—combine elements of reality with imagination. How these elements are combined is up to the photographer, but there is no denying that digital imaging has presented the creative image-maker with some powerful tools. In this book, I'll introduce you to some of those tools and show you how you can use them for your own digital explorations.

Not every aspect of every possible imaging technique will be found in these pages. There are many ways to produce any kind of creative photographic effect. That's why photography is still just as much art as it is craft. Some writers and gurus may insist there is only one way to produce an image, but I do not agree. This book has been designed to show you *one* way—my way—of creating digital images, not the only way. I want you to use my meanderings as a jumping-off point for your own explorations, not as a destination.

Kevin Elliott, General Manager of Cies-Sexton Photographic, a commercial photo lab and digital service bureau, recently gave me some words of advice I would like to pass on to anyone wishing to get started in digital imaging: "When a photographer has achieved a certain level of skill, they expect to compress the time it takes them to get into digital imaging," he told me, "when they really have to start all over again."

THIS BOOK'S FOR YOU

Photographers, like skiers, can be classified into three distinct groups: Beginner, Intermediate, and Advanced. There are always exceptions, but I think computer-using photographers fall into similar categories.

- Basic users work alone in a small or home-based studio. Their software requirements include simple word processing, spreadsheet, and graphics applications. He or she usually spends two hours a day, or less, at their computer.
- Intermediate users often work in groups, so networking solutions are important to them. Besides the above applications, these users are desktop publishing, working with shared scheduling programs, and using database managers. These people spend four hours a day with their computer.
- Advanced users, sometimes called Power Users, spend more than four hours a day at their computer using programs like Adobe Photoshop. These people need the fastest processors, the biggest hard drives, and make extensive use of peripherals like CD-ROMs, scanners, and modems.

This book is written for those photographers who already know how to use their computers, who understand the differences between a floppy and hard disk, and who know the difference between RAM and ROM. In short, you are computer literate but want to know more about using digital imaging technology to create interesting and unusual photographs. This is not a book for the Advanced User—the digital guru. If you are a Power User whose computer has ninety megabytes of RAM, a four Gigabyte (or bigger) hard disk, backed up by a DAT drive, this book is not for you. On the other hand, if you don't what any of the jargon in the last sentence means, this book probably is not for you either.

Intermediate users are people that already know the ins and outs of silver-based photography, along with some of the basics of computing and digital imaging, but are open to new ideas and techniques that will help them create images better, faster, or more creatively. It is my hope to introduce you to some new ways of working with new software tools, as well as some new ways of using more familiar tools. If you like working in a conventional darkroom, you will enjoy putting some of these same kinds of techniques to work in your digital darkroom. If you enjoy experimenting with special effects filters, you will like the way digital image manipulation techniques allow you to create many of the same kinds of effects—even after the image has already been captured. If these descriptions fit you, you are an Intermediate user—the person this book is written for.

EASY TO BE HARD

Part of my philosophy about digital imaging is to always be on the lookout for any tool or technique that will make all or part of a process easier. Being able to achieve an effect that produces the kind of results you are looking for faster, not only makes you more productive, but makes the professional digital imager more profitable too. Over the years, I have found that there are always two ways to accomplish any given effect: the hard way and the easy way. When I have a choice, I always choose the latter. In these pages I will share with you those tips, tools, and techniques that will make your own digital imaging efforts less difficult and more fun. It's my feeling that making any part of the photographic process more enjoyable, helps unleash the creativity urge.

The book is designed to balance technical and aesthetic concerns and includes how-to sections showing specific techniques, including the use of plug-in software that can be used to produce dynamic images. To let you see how each effect was accomplished, every how-to sequence includes step-by-step screenshots. Alternate chapters focus on the hardware aspects of digital imaging, such as removable media, mouse alternatives, and recordable CD-ROM technology. These are tools that can enhance a photographer's ability to work with digital images—either in the studio or with outside vendors, like service bureaus. Sprinkled throughout the book are case studies showing applications for using digital imaging software tools and techniques to create dramatic images.

HARDWARE CONCERNS

A computer system is much like a camera system. You need to assemble different components to fit the way you work and increase your productivity. Photographers have been arguing about Nikon versus Canon and Hasselblad versus Mamiya for years. They have carried this controversy over to the kinds of computers used for digital imaging. I work with both Mac OS and Windows computers: my Mac OS machine is a now discontinued Power Computing Mac OS-compatible, and my Windows computer is a Pentium-powered IBM-PC "Stealth." While having two different computers may seem like a luxury, the cost and advantages of working with two different systems may surprise some of you. Much as you might use 35mm Nikon cameras for one assignment and a 6 x 6 format Hasselblad for another, I try to match the tool—or computer—to fit the job I am working on at the time. Sometimes I use both computers simultaneously: creating images on one computer, while doing spreadsheets or surfing the Internet on the other.

About the Computers

The computers I used for this book are the same ones I use every day. I have a Power Computing PowerCenter Pro 225 Mac OS-compatible with a 2GB hard disk, 32MB RAM, 16X CD-ROM drive, built-in Iomega Zip and Jaz drives, and an external Phillips CD-R drive. My Windows machine is an IBM Aptiva "Stealth," with 32MB RAM, a 6.5GB of hard disk space, an 8X CD-ROM drive, and an external Iomega Zip drive.

The images and effects produced in the how-to sections were created using both computers. In the digital imaging universe, these are what I would call middle-of-the-road machines. I know photographers working with less complex computers and others working with more extensive systems. Digital imagers working with systems with more power, larger memory, and higher capacity storage will be able to produce the effects in this book faster than I was able to, while those with smaller, slower systems may have to be more patient.

All of the images and effects produced in the how-to sections of the book were created using both computers. This was done for a very practical reason: not every software program is available for both Mac OS and Windows environments. Programs that are platform-specific, like the Windows96-based Ulead System's PhotoImpact, were run on my IBM "Stealth" computer. Cross-platform software packages, such as Adobe Photoshop, were run mostly on my Power Computing system and occasionally on the IBM.

About the Images

Many of the photographs used in the book were originally created by me using 35mm, 6 × 6, and 4 × 5 film formats. The 35mm images were digitized with a Nikon Coolscan scanner, an Epson ES-100C flatbed scanner, or Kodak's Photo CD or new FlashPix process. Unless otherwise credited, all of the photographs you see in these pages are copyright Joe Farace. Some images were contributed by other photographers who have allowed me to use their manipulated or unmanipulated images. Occasionally, a digital stock image or two was used. Appropriate photo credit is shown for all of the images used.

About Writing This Book

This book was written using a PowerCenter Pro 225 Mac OS compatible and Microsoft Word 6.01 software. Some editing was done on an Apple PowerBook 180 laptop computer using the same word processing program. The original manuscript of the book was printed on an Epson Stylus Color 500 printer, but a copy was also provided to the publisher on floppy disk. Screen captures for the Mac OS were made with Mainstay's Captivate 4.5 software and Windows screen grabs were made with TechSmith's Snag-It. Graphics were converted to a format required by the publisher using Equilibrium Systems' DeBabelizer or DeBabelizer Pro software.

HOW TO READ THIS BOOK

Unlike other computer books, this one can be read in random order. You can always, if you prefer, read it front-to-back and cover-to-cover. Each chapter is self-contained. When any new imaging product is introduced, there will be a brief summary of its major features followed by a short how-to section showing how to accomplish a specific action or use one of the program's tools. At the end of each chapter, you will sometimes find a case study—often created by a guest photographer—using the concepts, programs, and techniques covered in that chapter to produce a real-world imaging application. Scattered throughout the book are sidebars that present tips and tools that help make your digital imaging a bit easier.

Chapter 1. You do not have to mortgage the farm to "go digital." This chapter includes an overview on how to get started in digital imaging on a budget. All of the hardware and software you will read about addresses all of the three major aspects of the digital imaging process: acquisition, enhancement, and output.

Chapter 2. This chapter introduces the concept of creating a software toolbox containing several different programs that can be used to produce specific effects. This chapter introduces Adobe Photoshop and Live Picture and provides how-to sections showing a sampling of each program's unique capabilities. The case study is from photographer John Blake, showing how he used both Adobe Photoshop and Live Picture to produce an eye-catching promotional piece combining ancient Grecian statues with a photograph of an elderly Scandinavian couple.

Chapter 3. For a pixographer, the use of removable media is the equivalent of digital film. In this chapter you will find information on the various forms of removable media. Since each type has its own unique characteristics, you will find enough information to help make up your own mind about what is best for your application. This chapter also contains information about how to use the most basic form of removable media—the floppy disk—to create your own digital portfolio. The case study contains a practical look at creating a stock photography promotional sell sheet—from scratch—using image editing and desktop publishing tools.

Chapter 4. This chapter includes information on the advantages and disadvantages (not very many) of using layers to create digital images. You will also find out that some programs have a layers function and some do not. One program that uses "floaters" in place of layers is MetaCreations' Painter, and this chapter introduces the third basic image editing program that is featured in the book. This chapter's case study shows how to use layers to create a T-shirt design using stock digital images.

Chapter 5. Many image enhancement programs have the ability to create masks that are placed over the original image to protect parts of it and allow other sections to be edited or enhanced. There are many tools that can be used to create masks. In this chapter you will find that each image editing program has different ways to create masks.

Chapter 6. Plug-ins are little software applications that increase the functionality of image enhancement and graphics programs. In this chapter you will be introduced to plug-ins that affect the three major aspects of digital imaging—acquisition, manipulation, and output—and see demonstrations on how they work.

Chapter 7. If you have ever tried to write your name with a mouse, you know that today's computer mouse—no matter what design it uses—is not the best tool to create artwork. Why not go mouseless? This chapter takes a look at the advantages of using a drawing tablet instead of a mouse.

Chapter 8. In this chapter, you will take a look at the digital imaging cycle—from Analog to Digital and back to Analog. You will learn about getting your digital images into a form that can be printed using conventional analog—silver-based darkroom—techniques. This includes examples such as making 4 x 5 negatives and transparencies from your images. The case study shows how a commercial photographer uses both digital and analog techniques to create customized portfolios.

Chapter 9. One of the newest trends is applying fine art printing techniques to digital images. Some of the techniques—such as working with watercolor and other papers—can be tried with your own in-house printers. Other approaches require the use of high-end ink-jet printers and allow photographers to create limited editions of their digital fine art work.

Wrapping up the book are two appendices. Appendix A is a glossary of some of the more common digital imaging terms that you will find sprinkled throughout these pages. Appendix B contains a list of the companies mentioned in the book and their contact information, including phone, fax, and Website address.

1

Digital Imaging on a Budget

Most professionals would not think of photographing a wedding or family portrait with a 35mm point-and-shoot camera. Yet, when it comes to digital imaging, some photographers seem to think they can use an inexpensive computer and an equally inexpensive ink-jet printer and get quality results. They are often surprised—even astounded—when I tell them what equipment is required to produce the kind of images they need to deliver to their customers. Fortunately, you do not have to mortgage the farm to "go digital." Here's a quick overview on how to get started in digital imaging without spend a lot of money. All of the hardware and software you will read about addresses all of the three major aspects of the digital imaging process: acquisition, enhancement, and output.

YOUR COMPUTER SYSTEM

The first item you need to get started is a computer. Here are a few minimum specifications for purchasing a new computer or upgrading the one you already own. The system should be powered by a 100Mhz or faster Pentium microprocessor for Windows users or PowerPC chip in a Mac OS machine. Your computer should have a CD-ROM drive, and it should be, at least, an eight-speed model, although you can get by with a quadruple speed model. Just like everything else in digital imaging, faster is better. Digital image files can get large, so your hard disk should be a minimum of 2GB, although bigger will also be more useful. You should also have some kind of removable media drive to act as a sort of "digital film." The alternatives available in media types, along with their advantages and disadvantages, are covered in Chapter 2. The same is true of memory. With RAM prices lower than they have been in years, you should have a minimum of 24MB of memory. All of these specifications describe what I would call an "average" digital imaging computer. Computers with more extensive—and expensive—specifications will be faster to use than my example, while those with less will be slower.

TOOL: Photo CD Acquire Module

While Adobe Photoshop can open Photo CD image files through the standard Open command, Kodak's Photo CD Acquire Module offers many more options. You can, for example, change a color image to grayscale, thus opening a black-and-white file that is two-thirds the size of the original color one. You can also precrop the image, to save opening a larger file than you would otherwise need. The Module lets you apply small, medium, or high-image sharpening—all before the file is opened. You can also select which resolution to use from the five (or six in the Pro CD) that are available in Kodak's ImagePac format, or let the Module do it for you. The Photo CD Acquire module allows you rotate and flip the image, as well as change its size and resolution. The latest version can be downloaded for free from Kodak's Website (www.kodak.com), or it can be purchased along with Kodak's Photo CD Access software for less than $50.

IMAGE ACQUISITION

Your choices for image acquisition include digital cameras, film scanners, and flatbed scanners, but one of the simplest ways to digitize images is Kodak's Photo CD process. Kodak offers two types of scans: Master and Pro Master. The Photo CD Master Disc format is designed for 35mm film, and each disc holds 100 high-resolution images. Images on the disc are in Kodak's ImagePac format, which provides five image resolutions varying from 128 × 192 to 2,048 × 3,072 pixels. Pro discs accept digital images from negatives and transparencies from 120 and 70mm rolls and 4 × 5 sheet film and offer an additional 4,096 × 6,144 pixel resolution. All of the images are stored on a CD-ROM disc for convenient storage. (See Figure 1.1 on CD-ROM.)

Photo CD is one of the least expensive image acquisition methods, because the only hardware needed is a CD-ROM drive. The cost to scan a negative or transparency varies. In my area, 35mm scans cost less than one dollar per image, depending on the quantity of negatives or slides that are scanned. Medium and large format scans cost more, and prices vary from $9 to $15. The best part of the Photo CD process is that someone else does all of the digitizing. For the location of your nearest dealer, call 1-800-236-6325. Challenging Photo CD as an inexpensive image acquisition method is FlashPix.

FlashPix File Format

FlashPix technology is an open industry standard file format developed by Kodak, Hewlett-Packard Company, Live Picture Inc., and Microsoft to make digital imaging faster and easier. It's built around a multiple-resolution, tiled-image file format

TOOL: FlashPix Plug-in

One of the easiest ways to access FlashPix files is through a Photoshop-compatible plug-in developed by Live Picture, Inc. You can download it free from Live Picture's Website at www.livepicture.com/download. Installation is slightly more complex than other file format plug-ins, because, in addition to the plug-in, you must also install several Microsoft OLE ancillary files. This procedure is also different for Mac OS and Windows systems, so read the Read Me files for specific directions.

After installation, you will be able to open and save FlashPix files through the program's standard Open Dialog. When you start to save a file in the FlashPix format, you will see another dialog that allows you to choose exactly how you want to save the file. For example, you can choose low, medium, high, or no compression. You can also move a slider to chose the file size, and you can enter a number from one to ten in the quality field.

that uses compression and color management options, as well as Microsoft's OLE structured storage. You can open FlashPix images quickly, edit them easily, and save them fast, regardless of the size of the original photographs.

Because of the format's built-in color management, you can count on predictable color results. FlashPix was designed with the Internet in mind. Unlike other image formats that may require minutes to display or load a high-resolution image onto your screen, FlashPix images can be quickly displayed. FlashPix format will run on virtually any multimedia-enabled PC or Mac OS computer with 8 to 16 MB of RAM. You do not need high-powered computers or complex software. Even in FlashPix, high-quality color images require large data files, but the format recognizes that most users do not need most of that data most of the time.

FlashPix applications automatically process only the data each activity needs and lets you use the same image in different ways—without processing or storing large files each time. This allows multiple versions of an image to be stored without copying the image data each time. Each new file only stores the data that defines the unique version and is linked to the file containing the original image data. The large image-data file need not be duplicated, and the full-resolution image file is only processed when it's needed. Edits are applied to high-resolution images only when necessary—typically, when you've finished working with the image and require high-quality output. In the FlashPix format, software applications do not have to convert between interchange formats (such as TIFF) used outside the application, and proprietary formats used within a program. Instead, they can use the FlashPix format exclusively, as the application workspace as well as the interchange format. Because only the affected tiles have to be adjusted before processing, any changes you make to images take place faster.

Dr. Jekyll and Mr. Pix

A FlashPix CD contains images with a resolution of 1,024 × 1,536 pixels, which is less than the highest-level scans Kodak supplies for its Master and Pro Photo CD services—which brings me to Kodak's schizophrenia about the FlashPix format. While working on this book, a Kodak representative warned me that "I hope you are not positioning FlashPix as a professional format—it's not, you know." While FlashPix resolution is less than Photo CD, there are applications—especially for the World Wide Web—where resolution is less critical. FlashPix also has built-in color management and stores all of the source and color information that is present when the image is digitized. On top of this, Live Picture, Inc. and Digimarc Corporation announced they will extend the format's capabilities to support Digimarc's digital watermarking technology that embeds copyright information throughout an image. This process allows a digital image to contain copyright and ownership information that is linked to contact details about the image's creator. Adobe Photoshop already includes the Digimarc copyright plug-in in version 4.0. Other programs, such as Corel PHOTO-PAINT 7.0 and CorelDRAW 7.0, along with Micrografx's Webtricity, also use Digimarc. On top of that was Kodak and Intel's announcement that FlashPix will soon utilize MMX technology to speed image manipulation and processing. Does this sound like an "amateur" format? What you are left with is an "amateur" cross-platform imaging format that has built-in color management, copyright protection, and uses the latest chip technology. It only reminds me that Kodak originally positioned Photo CD as a system for amateur photographers to watch snapshots on their television sets.

An Inexpensive Acquisition Alternative

Seattle FilmWorks Pictures On Disk is a service that digitizes photographs from 35mm film, converting them into digital form and placing them on a single floppy disk. The latest version of POD features an image resolution of 640 × 480 pixels. Pictures On Disk image files have a 25-bit color depth and can display sixteen million colors.

Getting your family picnic, cousin's wedding, or new baby's photographs digitized on Pictures On Disk (POD) is easy. Just shoot whatever kind of 35mm color-negative film you prefer and send it to Seattle FilmWorks. They process all kinds of 35mm film, including Kodak, Fuji, AGFA, and Seattle FilmWorks' own brand of color-negative film. Not only can you use whatever film you want, you can use whatever camera you want, too. If you are making photographs for exhibition or competition, you can use your Nikon N90s, and if you're just shooting snapshots you can create POD with your Olympus Stylus point-and-shoot camera.

When Seattle FilmWorks processes your film, all of the images on the roll are scanned at 640 × 480 resolution that, depending on your subject matter, will

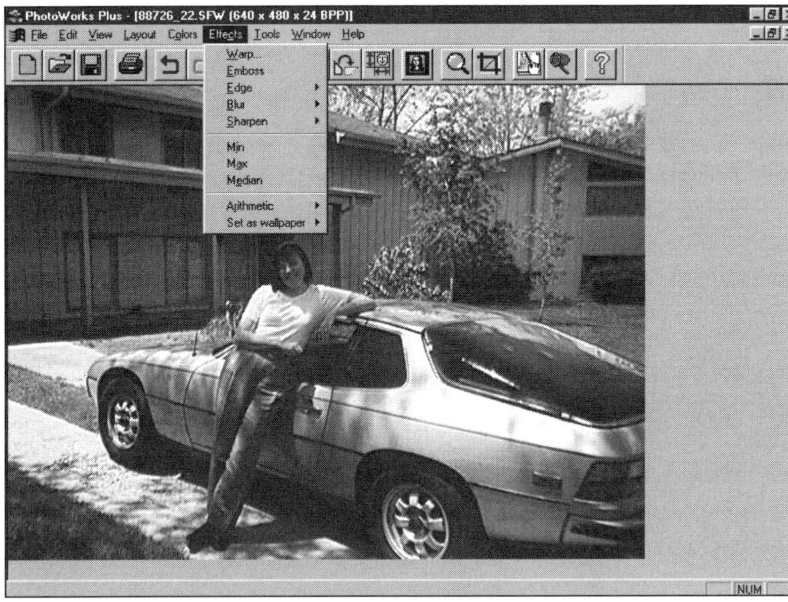

Figure 1.2a Using Seattle FilmWorks free PhotoWorks program, you can work with the digital images created as Pictures On Disk. Photo © Joe Farace.

display up to 16 million colors per picture. After scanning, each resulting image file is approximately 900K in size, but before they are saved onto a POD floppy disk, the photographs are compressed to approximately 35K using a proprietary format called SFW. This compact SFW format makes it possible to squeeze 37-exposures of image data onto a single 1.44MB 4-1/2" floppy disk and allows for the fast decompression of images.

To use your Pictures On Disk images from Seattle FilmWorks, you will first need to load them onto your hard drive using PhotoWorks or PhotoWorks Plus. To do this, open either your complimentary copy of PhotoWorks or your PhotoWorks Plus software, then add the photos to a PhotoWorks album as follows:

Step 1. Insert a Pictures On Disk floppy disk in your floppy disk (A:) drive.

Step 2. Create a new album or open an existing album. I prefer to keep all new images in a new, separate album, so I clicked on the New button (its icon looks like a document) on the toolbar to open a blank album.

Step 3. From the File menu, choose Add Images.

Step 4. In the Add Images dialog box, click on the Drives box (use Look In, for Windows95) and select the floppy drive that contains the Pictures On Disk floppy disk.

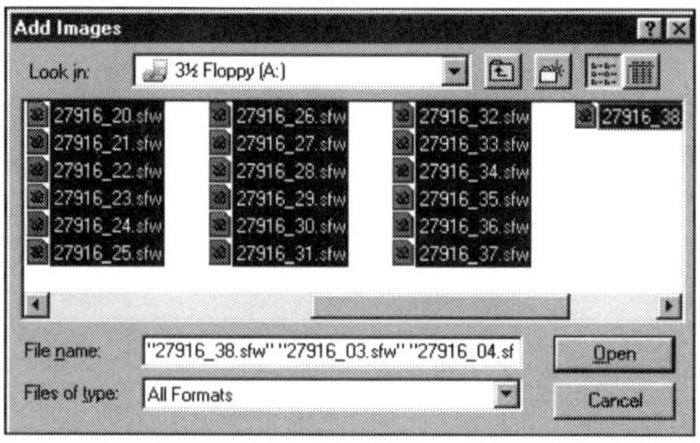

Figure 1.2b The Add Images dialog box lets you select which images you would like to appear in an album.

Step 5. Click on the down arrow next to the Show Files of the type box and select SFW Photo (.sfw).

Step 6. Double-click on the roll folder.

Step 7. Select the photos that you want to add from the list of files. To select a range of photos, hold down the Shift key and click on the first and last photo in the range.

Step 8. Choose Open.

PhotoWorks—or PhotoWorks Plus—copies the files to the hard-disk location you specified and adds the photos to the album you specified. You can now insert these images into a PhotoWorks Composer project using any of Composer's Insert Image commands, which will be explained later on.

IMAGE MANIPULATION

I have met many photographers who are in such a hurry to "go digital" that they jump in only to realize that the water's too deep. Most of us did not start out in this profession using state-of-the-art equipment. My first medium-format camera was a battered Mamiya C33, and I learned a lot about making portraits with this camera before I bought my first Hasselblad. Learning how to use digital imaging software takes time and practice. The most widely used image enhancement program is Adobe Photoshop, but at $895, it may be too expensive for someone getting started.

Since many people will ultimately move up to Adobe Photoshop, I suggest they start with Adobe's $49 Photo Deluxe. Photo Deluxe offers some of the features found in Photoshop, but is geared for home and small business users. The product has two modes: in the "Guided Activities" mode, the interface takes you through each step of the modification and enhancement process; "On Your Own" provides access to the tools and features included in Guided Activities, but lacks the tutorial aspect. PhotoDeluxe includes 500 templates and supports Photoshop-compatible plug-in filters.

An alternative is Live Picture's Live Pix. This is an under-$100 program, currently available for Windows computers. Like Adobe Photo Deluxe, it is compatible with the FlashPix file format. Live Pix is a consumer-oriented program that harnesses Live Picture 2.5's ability to work with large images and lets you create composite images for calendars, posters, T-shirts, and photo albums. The package includes sample images, templates, and special effects tools, such as red-eye removal and photo distortion. (See Figure 1.3 on CD-ROM.)

Although created by the same companies that produce Photoshop and Live Picture, Photo Deluxe and Live Pix must be considered introductory programs for professionals. Both programs will provide familiarization with digital imaging techniques without a large investment in money or learning time.

PhotoWorks Plus

PhotoWorks Plus is a multifunctional digital imaging program that is specially designed to work with Pictures On Disk from Seattle FilmWorks. PhotoWorks comes in two versions. First, there is the free version (it really is free), called "PhotoWorks," that Seattle FilmWorks includes with your first order of Pictures On Disk. Second, there is the upgrade version of the program called "PhotoWorks Plus." This "Plus" version has numerous enhancements over the free version, and, of course, costs more.

PhotoWorks Plus not only lets photographers create albums of digital photographs, but it also will even let you "drag and drop" photos between albums. This means you can click on a photograph in one album and, while holding the mouse button down, drag it into another album. This way the act of assembling an album is just like the process of assembling a "real" one. You can also add captions and descriptions of each photo into a special, customizable image database. PhotoWorks Plus will enable you to finally answer the question, "Mary, when did I take this picture of you in Santa Fe?" The program allows you to take one of your photographs and paste it into your favorite word processing program and other print-capable programs. You can use PhotoWorks Plus to crop the photographs before exporting them.

The program lets you convert Pictures On Disk SFW files into any one of twenty common PC and some Macintosh formats with its Save As/Convert To function. For home use, the program can be used to create screen savers using your own photos, and at the office, the digitized images can be used for presentations or desktop publishing. PhotoWorks Plus includes the following features. (See Figure 1.4a on CD-ROM.)

Albums and Slide Show

All of your favorite photographs can be collected and organized into digital "albums" that show thumbnail images of your original photos. A thumbnail is an old design industry term for "small sketch." In the world of digital photography, thumbnails are small, low resolution versions of your original image. Since they are low resolution, they are extremely small files. You can add captions along with other information to the photographs in your albums, and even copy and move images between albums.

PhotoWorks Plus includes a viewer that lets you play a slide show of all of the images that you have collected into an album. Built-in controls let you choose the sequence, duration, and type of creative transition for each photograph.

Enhancer

Enhancer is probably one of the most useful functions for preparing an image for use by PhotoWorks Composer. The program's image enhancement features let you rotate, resize, and group your digital photographs. You will also find controls that let you adjust a specific image's Exposure (density) to compensate for any over- or underexposure, increase or decrease a photo's Contrast, and, with Color Balance, adjust the overall color cast of those difficult photographs made under mixed lighting conditions. All of your modifications can be safely previewed before any changes are applied to your image and saved. While the Enhancer only works with images in Pictures On Disk's 25-bit True Color format.

PhotoWorks Plus supports importing and exporting most common Windows and DOS graphics file formats, including CAL, CCITT, EPS, GEM, CompuServe, GIF, JPEG, JPEG TIFF, six versions of LEAD files, MacPaint, Apple PICT (from 1-bit to 25-bits), MS PAINT, OS/2 BMP (from 1-bit to 25-bits), PCX (from 1-bit to 25-bits), RAS (Sun Raster from 1-bit to 33-bits), TGA (from 9-bit to 33-bits), TIFF (from 1-bit to 25-bits), TIFF LZW (Compressed format from 1-bit to 25-bits), BMP (from 1-bit to 25-bits), WPG (Word Perfect from 1-bit to 9-bits), and WMP (9-bit and 25-bits). If you are not familiar with these acronyms, you will find many of them in the Glossary.

Screen Saver

Everybody likes screen savers, but instead of having one that shows digital fish swimming around, how about seeing your own photographs on the monitor? To create a screen saver, all you have to do is select any PhotoWorks Plus album. The screen saver feature uses the Slide Show settings to control time and transitional effects.

File Storage

To help keep things organized, PhotoWorks Plus lets you create a separate directory (or folder) on your hard disk for each set of photographs you collect. The new directory will be a subdirectory of the default Albums directory, which you can also specify. Default is a term that means that an automatic decision has already been made for you by the software, but PhotoWorks Plus, like most good software, gives you an opportunity to change that decision. (In the next chapter, you will see the default choice that PhotoWorks Plus made for my computer, and you will learn how and why I made a slight adjustment in it.) To keep everything organized, it's a good idea to store each set of photographs in their own, separate directory. Files are saved as compressed SFW image files, and a typical roll of film uses only about 1MB of disk space.

Printing

PhotoWorks Plus lets you print photos from within Enhancer. You can also print an information sheet associated with an album. This list would include a list of the photographs in an album along with captions. Two types of color printers are available that will work well to print photographs from within PhotoWorks Plus: ink-jet and dye sublimation. Ink-jet printers work by spraying tiny streams of quick-drying ink onto your paper. Circuits controlled by electrical impulse or heat determine exactly how much ink—and what color—to spray to create a series of dots or lines that combine to form a printed photograph. Dye-sublimation printers use thin dye ribbons and a thermal process along with special (and somewhat expensive) paper to print color photographs.

In the low-cost color printer market, two products stand out as excellent values: the Epson Stylus Photo and Fargo PhotoFun! (more on these printers later in the book). When assessing the quality of printer output, most digital photographers seem divided into two groups. The first is looking for an inexpensive printer that can deliver quality results. At this time, the Fargo printers are the best available solution. The second group is composed of photographers who want to be able to include "acceptable" looking photographs in their correspondence and newsletters; this second group will love the Epson Stylus Photo ink-jet Printer.

There are many uses for PhotoWorks Plus and Pictures On Disk in your office as well as at home. Real estate agents can photograph an entire house on a 24-exposure roll of film, and produce a slide show they can use to give potential home buyers a guided tour of the house without wasting time showing them a house they may not like. Commercial real estate people can do the same thing for mini-malls and other retail and office situations. Insurance agents can take pictures of automobile accidents or hail- and storm-damaged houses and paste them into their reports. Bakers can create a beautiful display of wedding cakes and have the presentation set up as a self-running display in their bakery. Instead of an album of photographs, a slide show on a computer screen will attract more attention than a traditional album that customers typically use to select from. Your customers can be seeing your creations, while they are standing in line to purchase bagels or donuts! Travel agents can use some of their trip pictures to show clients what Köln, Germany really looks like. As you can see, the uses for digital imaging in the office are endless, and producing an on-screen slide show costs much, much less than producing a similar presentation on videotape.

The most important aspect of PhotoWorks Plus is that it unlocks the door to digital imaging for you. Without spending a fortune, you can have your photographs digitized and manipulate them using your computer. PhotoWorks Plus is the best way for a photographer new to digital imaging to get their feet wet without being overwhelmed by the complexity of some other image manipulation programs. PhotoWorks Plus is the ideal entry level tool for photographers who are interested in learning more about digital imaging, but do not know where to start.

Kai's Photo Soap

While ostensibly aimed at amateur photographers, MetaCreations has produced a product unlike anything you have ever seen on a computer but have encountered many times in "real life." All of the tools you use in Soap—brushes, erasers, and even a remote control—look like the same objects you use in the real world. They work the same way, too. This also makes applying the tools to the images you are working with more intuitive.

Kai's Photo Soap reads and writes many popular Mac OS and Windows bitmap image formats, including JPEG, FlashPix, PICT, Photoshop, BMP, and TIFF. Among the missing formats is Kodak Photo CD, which Kai's Power Goo does read. On the other hand, the program opens and manipulates FlashPix images easier and faster than any other imaging program I have tried so far. Kai's Photo Soap also provides acquisition support for scanners and digital cameras, and I would not be surprised to see it bundled with cameras and scanners in the near future.

Soap uses a "rooms" analogy, in which you move back and forth between the rooms using a Map that appears when you move your cursor near the top middle of the screen. Each room has its own distinctive function and own set of tools. Moving back and forth between the rooms will take additional time, especially when you are asked if you want to apply the changes you just made before moving into the next room. (See Figure 1.4b on CD-ROM.)

TIP: Soap's On

Regardless of what platform you are working on, Soap is an immersion environment; when you are working in Soap, you are totally in Soap. When using Windows 95, moving back and forth between Soap and other documents or applications is just a matter of clicking on the taskbar. On the Mac OS, you have two options: you can Hit Shift+Space or use the TV-like Remote Control (that is not present in every room) to show the menu bar. Then you can Hide Kai's Photo Soap to return to the Finder. If you hit the Shift+Space keys again, the menu bar will hide. I would have preferred an option in the Preferences to either hide or not hide the menu bar, making it a user not a programmer choice.

A typical session starts in the "In Room," where images are opened or imported, and finishes in the "Out Room." The In Room allows you to crop and flip an image as well as increase the resolution. The Crop tools are lines that surround the image that you move left and right or up and down to get the cropping you want. Like all of the tools in Soap, they are simple and direct. In between, you might visit the Prep Room where you can crop or rotate an image as well as apply an auto-enhancement feature. The heart of Soap is found in three dedicated rooms: Tone, Color, and Detail.

The Tone Room lets you make global changes and adjustments to brightness and contrast. When you move to the Tone room you will find that all of the tools you might want to use are kept in drawers. Click a drawer and it opens to reveal tools: big brushes, fine brushes, erasers, and pencils. To use the tool, you click on it. Once again, simple and direct. There are brightness and contrast sliders, but these controls features sliding drawers that provide additional controls. KPT Convolver-like memory buttons are used to save settings, and another control looks much like a visual equalizer for optimizing what in Adobe Photoshop would be called Curves. The Color Room provides sliders that let you enhance and color correct your photographs. The Color Room provides tools for tweaking an image's color, including Curves-like equalizer sliders, and more memory buttons.

When you get to the Detail Room, you know you're not in Kansas anymore. The Detail Room controls let you fix image problems. You activate a feature, such as Red Eye removal, and you can use any one of Soap's tools to paint over red eye in your photographs. It is impossible to make a mistake. Soap even provides a sliding drawer that lets you pick the lightness and darkness of the kind of eyes you are working on. I have never seen red-eye removal—on any program or at any price—that is so good and so fast. Other controls let you "Heal" damage to images or to the people in the images. Other commands include Sharpen, Smooth, and Clone; Clone allows you to duplicate portions of the image.

The Finish Room lets you prepare an image for output and add backgrounds, images, cartoon characters, or text. You can save the image in any of the formats the program supports or just print directly from Soap. Before doing that, you might want to take time to add a background, edge, or objects to the, by now, almost complete image. You can use the Objects binder to select text that can be used to create a calendar. The Edges function lets you add creative edges to an image right now—no waiting.

There are not many downsides to Kai's Photo Soap, but you should be aware that, like Kai's Power Goo, the program requires that the CD-ROM be in the drive in order to run the program. Whether this requirement is a form of benign copy protection or the program simply uses assets stored on the disc, does not matter. What it means to the users of FlashPix CD-ROMs is that they have to either copy their images onto their hard disc or have another drive available for the second disc.

Kai's Photo Soap breaks all the interface rules. In doing so, it has provided creative, useful, and fun software.

MORE DIGITAL IMAGING ON A BUDGET

If all of this talk of bits, bytes, and pixels has made you a little nervous about getting started in digital imaging, there are some alternatives that cost little and allow you to dip your toes into the digital waters. Most of the products and services covered in this section were primarily designed for the advanced amateur. If that describes you, then you are ready to go. If you are a professional or aspiring professional, consider these programs and services to be "training wheels" to help you get started in digital imaging without going broke.

Live Pix

This under-$100 program, currently available for Windows and Mac OS computers, is the first image editing program to use the FlashPix file format. Live Pix is a consumer-oriented program that harnesses Live Picture 2.5's ability to work with large images and lets you create composite images for calendars, posters, T-shirts, and photo albums. Although created by the same companies that produce Live Picture, Live Pix must be considered an introductory program for professionals, but will provide familiarization with digital imaging techniques without a large cash outlay. (See Figure 1.4c on CD-ROM.)

System Requirements

LivePix software is designed for PCs with Microsoft Windows 95 and the Apple Macintosh. A minimum of 8MB of RAM is needed, although 16MB is recommended for optimal performance. A minimum of 20MB free hard disk space and a CD ROM drive are also required.

PhotoImpact

Do you remember Ulead System's Image Pals 2.0? Well, this great program is back in a new 33-bit version called PhotoImpact 4.0 that's optimized for Microsoft Office 95. As before, the package includes several utilities that make working with the core program easier. CD Browser, for example, automatically catalogs any Photo CD disc—including Pro format—placed in your CD-ROM drive. Images can be imported into PhotoImpact by using Open, Acquire, or just by clicking on the image in CD Browser and dragging it into the work space. A digital album utility allows you to store images in albums that can contain up to 65,535 thumbnails for later retrieval.

Once an image has been opened or acquired, computer users have access to one of the cleverest features available on any image enhancement program, the

Easy Palette. This is a window containing effects galleries, including Effects, Style, Texture, Gradient, and a custom "My Gallery." The thumbnails display special effects using a baseline image, and you can see these effects with your own photograph by clicking the Try button. To apply any effect, click and drag the thumbnail onto the image in PhotoImpact's work space. Traditionalists can find the same effects under the Effects menu and, as a bonus, a large preview window gives a sneak peek at what the effect will look like before it's applied. If you do not like the way an effect or change looks, you can take advantage of 99 levels of Undo, including an Undo Before command that displays previously applied effects. Undo Before allows you to go back to just before a specific effect was used, so you do not have to save multiple versions while creating complex effects.

PhotoImpact is brimming with user-friendly features, such as the AutoProcess Tools that automatically straighten, crop, remove moiré patterns, and correct image brightness and color. PhotoImpact works with Photoshop-compatible plug-ins and, not content with third-party plug-ins, Ulead started creating their own. GIF/JPEG SmartSaver is designed for image makers creating photographs for the World Wide Web and allows them to optimize GIF and JPEG images by providing a balance between size and quality. PhotoImpact users can download a copy from Ulead's home page.

PhotoFinish

PhotoFinish is a competent and able image enhancement program that just might be the Clark Kent of image editing programs. Watch it step into a CD-ROM drive and instantly sharpen, adjust brightness and contrast, crop, and straighten images all in a single click. If you think I'm kidding, the program has a toolbar button labeled AutoEnhance that does all these things and lets you evaluate their effects in a preview window before applying. Before using AutoEnhance, you can click an Options button to choose which corrections you want to make automatically. If you're afraid AutoEnhance might overcorrect your creatively tilted image, don't worry. You can turn off the Skew feature—or anything else—and PhotoFinish will not make unrequested corrections. Extensis' Intellihance 2.0 plug-in offers many of these same features, but that Photoshop-compatible plug-in costs more than PhotoFinish—and you have to add it to a copy of Photoshop!

PhotoFinish is full of cool features that belie its modest price tag. The program includes basic enhancement filters, but uses an interface similar to Photoshop's variations to display up to 100 previews—nine at a time. The built-in special effects include some great ones, including Crumple, which makes your image look like a crumpled photographic print. As with filters, you have 100 variations of "crumpleness," and you can choose the one you prefer before applying it to your image. The program uses a similar design that is used for its AutoScan feature. PhotoFinish works with sixty different kinds of scanners and video capture boards to acquire an image and bring it into the program, but it will also straighten it and remove dreaded moiré patterns. Anyone who has tried to removed moiré by using Despeckle and similar filters will appreciate having a dedicated moiré removal command.

This kind of thoughtful design carries over to the toolbox design. When a tool is selected, a secondary toolbar (SoftKey calls the toolbar that looks like the main one an "AutoBar," but that sounds like a drive-up saloon to me) appears, giving you options for that particular tool. Like most image editors, PhotoFinish has a magnifying glass, but instead of using mouse clicks and the CTRL or Option key to toggle between plus and minus, the program uses the left mouse button to increase size and the right mouse button to decrease it. I didn't learn that by reading the user's guide (shame on me), but when I selected the magnifying glass tool from the toolbox, PhotoFinish displayed a message in the status bar explaining how the tool worked. If you do not know what a tool does, don't reach for the user's guide (even though it's a darn good one), just click on the "I" button for a brief description of how the tool works.

If you need images to practice with, the package includes 2,500 stock photographs. PhotoFinish easily imports Photo CD images but does so without the kind of comprehensive Open Photo CD dialog found in other, and admittedly more expensive, programs. If the program has any weakness, it is in the few file formats that it exports. You have all the biggies: BMP, EPS, TGA, PCX, JPG, and TIF, but like a skimpy dinner of nuveau cuisine, I was left wanting more.

PhotoFinish is not just another Photoshop wannabe. Its use of natural media enhancement tools, such as Charcoal, Crayon, and Airbrush—with a neat-o Spray Can option—makes it have more in common with Fractal Designs Painter. Its ease of use and price tag make it the ideal software tool for beginning digital imagers.

2

A Software Toolkit

I think of Photoshop as having a hammer, saw, and screwdriver. But what you really need is a set of screwdrivers, five hammers, and three saws.

KAI KRAUSE, METACREATIONS.

Digital imagers are luckier than users of silver-based camera systems. Once you commit to a company's camera and make a corresponding, and sometimes hefty, investment in lenses and accessories, switching systems is much too expensive for most photographers. Pixographers, on the other hand, can assemble a digital toolkit containing products from many different companies, all of which are complementary and some of which can share software components.

You may be surprised to learn that you may need more than one image manipulation program, but you will quickly discover that assembling a digital imaging toolkit is similar to putting together a complete camera system. You cannot do everything with a 50mm lens; sometimes you need to go wider and sometimes longer. That's why the camera system you use is the result of selecting, testing, and using different focal length lenses, motor drives, flashes, and accessories. The process of building your digital imaging toolbox, as you will soon discover, is similar.

PROFESSIONAL TOOLS

Although they did not invent digital photographic manipulation—that honor looks like a tie between Letraset's ImageStudio and Silicon Beach Software's Digital Darkroom—Adobe's Photoshop set the standard for image editing software. With more than two million users, Photoshop is the de facto standard for digital imaging and prepress applications. So much so that most of its competition consider themselves as complementing Adobe Photoshop rather than competing with it.

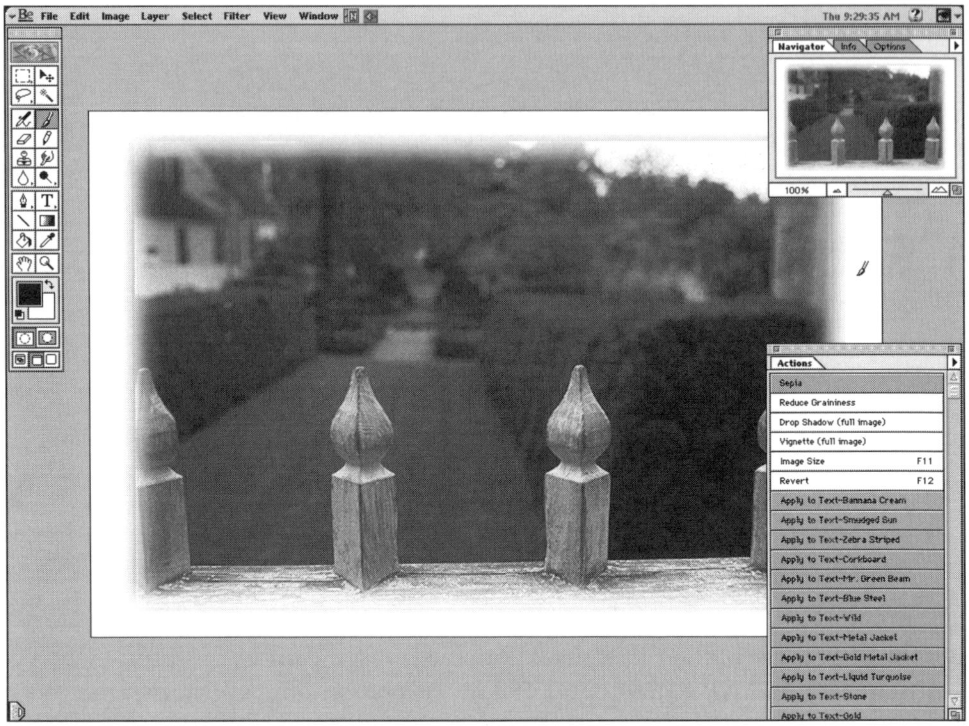

Figure 2.1 Adobe Photoshop is the "Big Kahuna" of image editing programs and is one of the most important components of your digital imaging toolkit. Image © Joe Farace.

Adobe Photoshop 4.0

This latest version of the program allows users to work more efficiently with Adobe's other graphics products, such as Illustrator and PageMaker, and offers similar interfaces. By sharing common terminology, shortcut keys, menu structure, and tabbed palette design, it allows users to quickly become more productive. File format support includes useful Web file formats, including Portable Network Graphics (PNG), progressive JPEG, and Adobe's own Portable Document Format (PDF.) All of the images produced for my own home page (http://www.hyperzine.com/writers/joef.html) were prepped for Web use with Photoshop 4.0.

The Filter Factor

Since version 1.0, Adobe Photoshop built its reputation on its built-in filters. In version 4.0, this roster was expanded to include a collection of filters that were formerly sold as Adobe Gallery Effects. The additions of these filters were accompanied by a redesign of their interface and an increase in performance levels. Photoshop 4.0 now includes more than ninety filters, including forty-eight new filters that offer a wide range of artistic effects, such as colored pencil, crosshatch, film grain, and much more. All filters are 32-bit native, meaning they can take advantage of 32-bit operating systems, like Windows95, enabling greater processing speed. Let's take a look at one of them.

Step 1. I wanted to create a hand-drawn look to a photograph of a locomotive that was made at the Colorado Railroad Museum in Golden, Colorado. I used Kodak's Photo CD Acquire Module plug-in to open the original color image as a grayscale one.

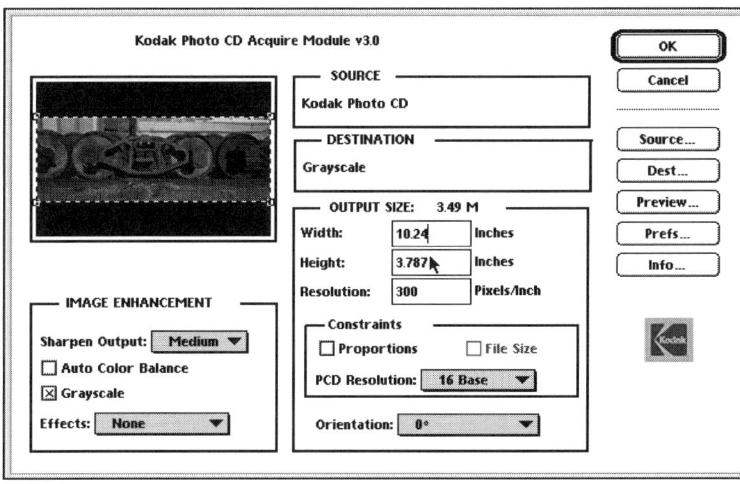

Figure 2.2 Using Kodak's Photo CD Acquire Module, the author converted the original photograph to grayscale and selected the image resolution he wanted. © Joe Farace.

TIP: Photo CD Access Problems with Photoshop?

If your Windows version of Photoshop 3.05 or 4.0 is having problems opening Photo CD (PCD) images from a disc, here's the solution: some programs, notably MetaCreations Kai's Power Goo and some Corel software, installs two files that interfere with Photoshop's ability to open PCD files. The files in question are named KPSYS32.DLL and PCDLIB32.DLL. When you originally installed Photoshop, the installer placed copies of these files in your Windows directory. These programs install a second copy of those files in the Windows/System directory, thus preventing Photoshop from opening Photo CD files. Here's how to correct the problem: in Windows95, use the Find function to locate each file name and either rename or delete the files from the Windows/System directory. When you relaunch Photoshop, you will be able access Photo CD files just like all of the other graphic file formats that the program accepts. And yes, Kai's Power Goo functions just fine now, too. Mac users of both programs should note that this problem does not affect them.

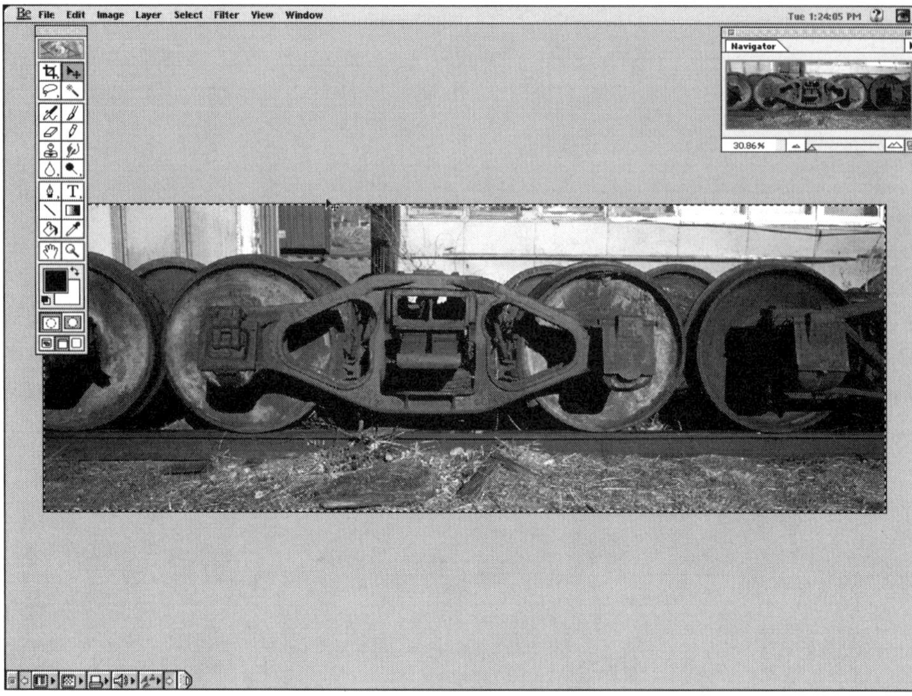

Figure 2.3 The next step in the process was selecting the entire image with the Select All command. Image © Joe Farace.

Step 2. The next step was to select the entire image to apply the special effect. This was done by choosing All from the select menu. I could have used the Command-A (Mac) or Ctrl-A keyboard shortcuts. This step is optional for the "Chalk and Charcoal" filter I will be using, but many filters require a selection—even if it is just Select All—before being applied.

Step 3. I next chose Chalk and Charcoal from the Filters menu. The Chalk and Charcoal dialog box lets you chose the lightness and darkness of the "charcoal" as well as the pressure. You can experiment with different combinations and see their effects in a Preview window. When you are satisfied, click the OK button. (See Figure 2.4.)

Step 4. The effect was a little to graphic for me, so I used Photoshop's Fade command to reduce the Graphic Pen effect to 80 percent. The Fade command is only found in Photoshop 4.0 and later versions. It appears, after you have applied any effect or filter, in the Filters menu and allows you to apply the effect in varying degrees. (See Figure 2.5.)

Step 5. The final image, produced using one filter and a color image converted to grayscale, evokes the vintage look I was trying to capture. One of the side benefits of using this and any of the filters that Adobe has clustered under the Sketch submenu, is that it has simplified the final image. Compare the clutter of the original image with the graphic simplicity of the manipulated image.

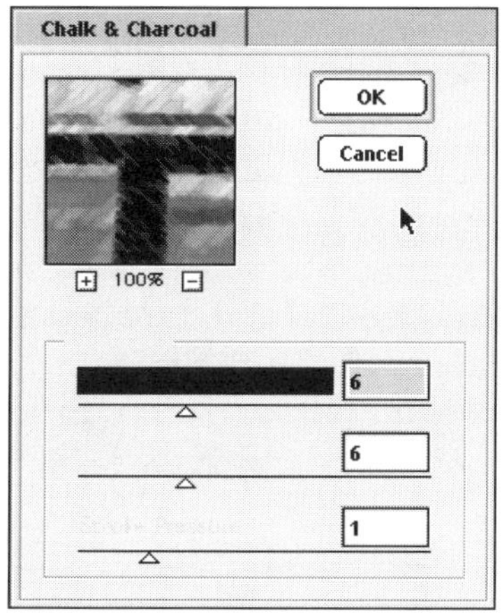

Figure 2.4 Chalk and Charcoal filters let users experiment with different settings and view their effects in the Preview window. Image © Joe Farace.

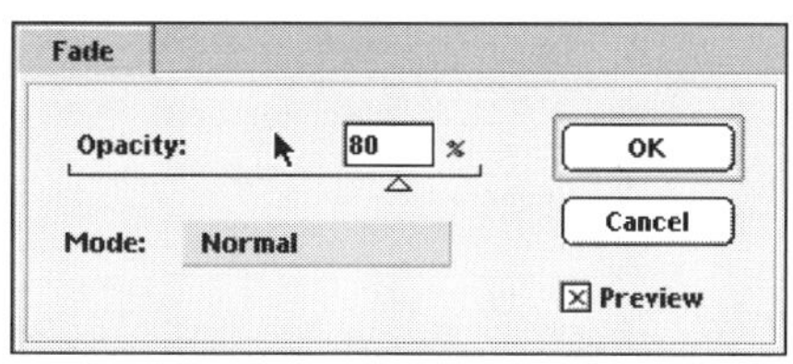

Figure 2.5 The Fade command allows you to apply the effect in varying degrees. Here the author cut the effect to 80% of the original.

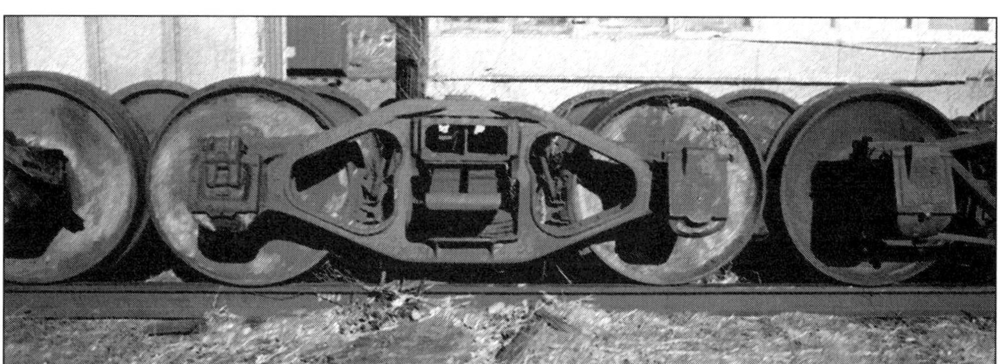

Figure 2.6 After tweaking the Fade command, the overall effect is that of a hand-drawn image. Image © Joe Farace.

Lights, Camera, Actions

One of the rules of digital imaging life is that if you have to go through a set of steps once, you will probably have to do it again in the future. Instead of having to keep track of what you are doing with a pen and paper, Photoshop's Actions palette enables users to record a sequence of editing steps as an "action" that can then be applied to another selection in the same image, another image file, or—in a batch-type operation—to hundreds of different files. Users can play an action with steps disabled, or display selected dialog boxes during playback to interactively adjust any settings. The order in which tasks are executed can be edited by dragging-and-dropping. Multiple actions are displayed in the Actions palette, and sets of actions can be saved and loaded separately. Actions can also be used to batch acquire images from a digital camera, allowing an entire set of images to be automatically acquired, retouched, and saved. Action sequences can even be saved and shared with others. Actions included in version 4.0

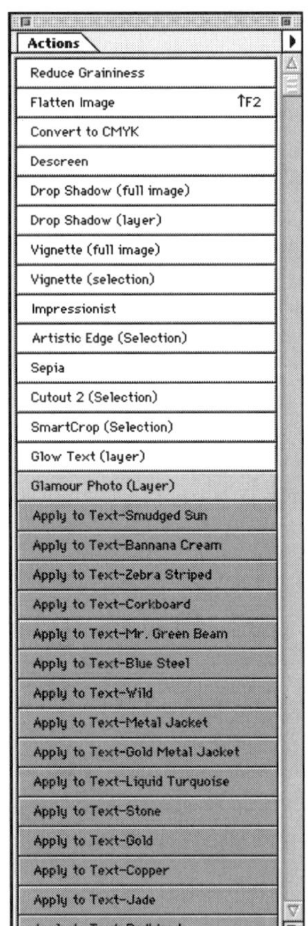

Figure 2.7 Photoshop's Actions palette provides one-button control over any scriptable function—and writing scripts isn't too hard.

include downsampling images to 72 dpi for use on the World Wide Web, saving GIF and JPEG files with optimal Web settings, and adding drop shadows to text.

Taking Action

How does it work? Let me show you a real world example. A client's specifications for delivery of digital images is as follows: all files must be uncompressed Mac-formatted TIFF files, CMYK, and 350 dpi. Here's how I created an "action" for them.

Step 1. Since Mac formatting was required, I opened a FlashPix image and selected Show Actions from the Window menu. (More on the FlashPix format later.)

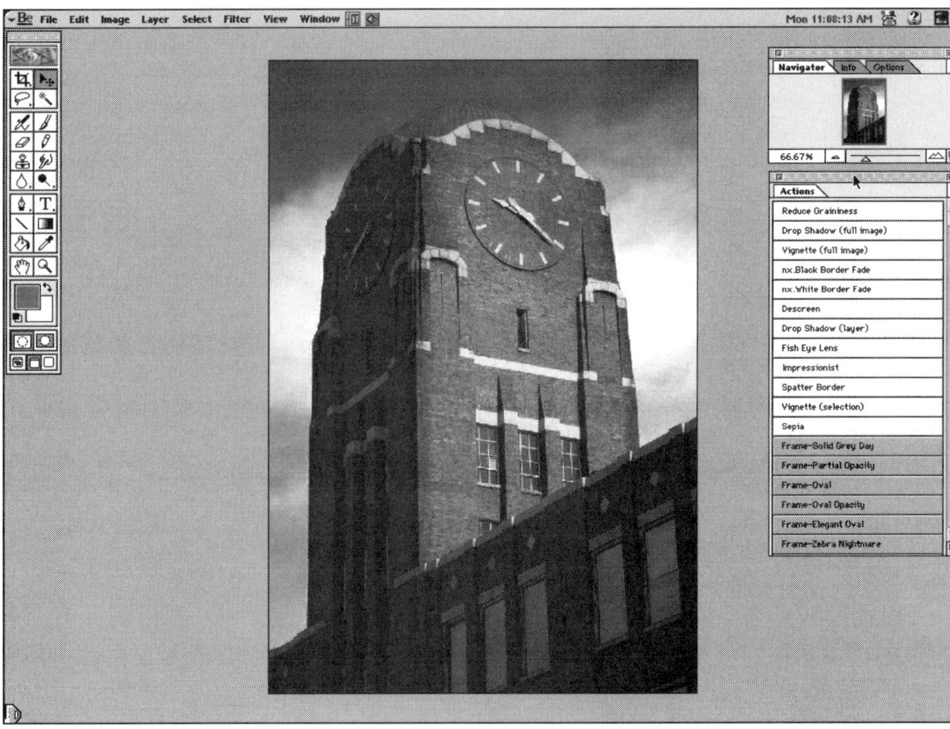

Figure 2.8 A FlashPix image of an old building was opened in Adobe Photoshop 4.0, then the Actions palette was selected from the Windows menu.

Step 2. To create a new action, you must take the Actions palette out of "Button Mode" (the default). I did this by deselecting Button Mode from the palette's drop-down menu. (See Figure 2.9.)

Step 3. To create a new Action, I chose New Action from the same menu. This produces a dialog box that lets you name the Action, assign a function key, and even a color, to the button that will be created. After I made my selection, I clicked the Record button to start the process. (See Figure 2.10.)

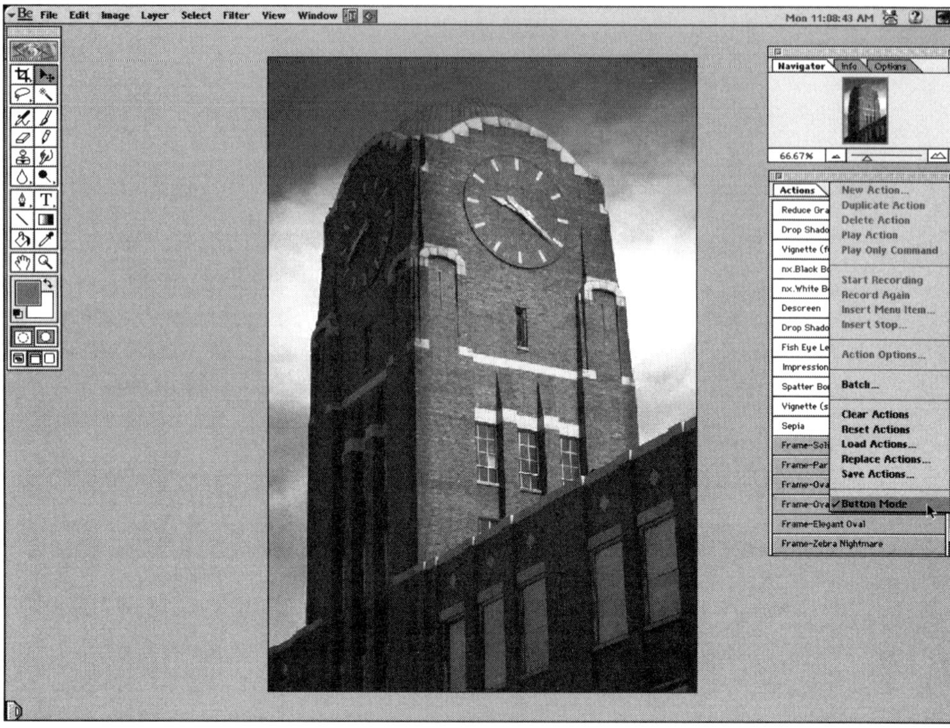

Figure 2.9 To get out of "Button Mode," the author clicked on Action's side-mounted menu, then deselected Button Mode.

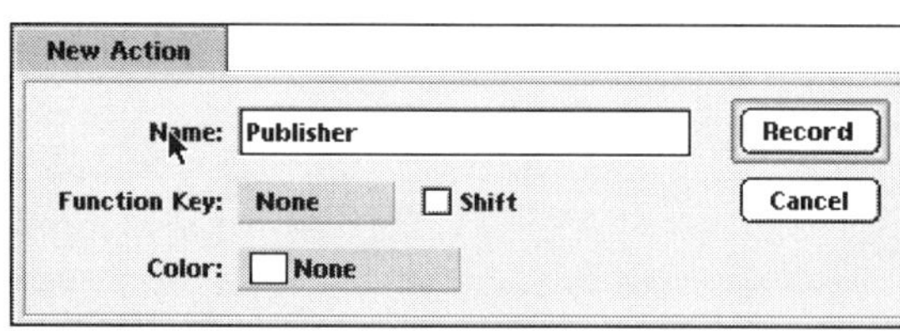

Figure 2.10 The New Action dialog box lets you name it, assign a function key, and give a color to the new button.

Step 4. At this point, I went through the steps needed to create a file to my original specifications. I started by going to the Color/Mode menu and choosing CMYK. Then, I went to the Image menu and changed the Image Size to 350 dpi from the original 300. When this was finished, I saved the file as an Uncompressed TIFF file. Lastly, I went back to the Action palette and selected Stop Recording. At that point, the action was complete. (See Figure 2.11.)

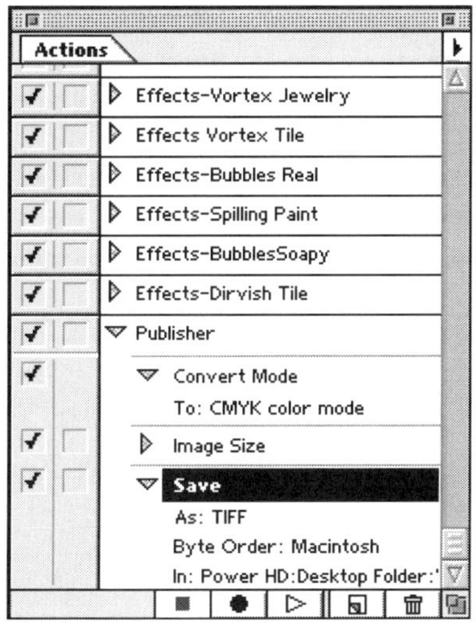

Figure 2.11 The final action includes Change Mode to CMYK. Change Image size to 350 dpi, then Save as a TIFF file.

After the Action has been recorded, the next time I have an image to prepare for that client, all I have to do is click the Publisher button and all of the steps of the action will be complete.

KPT Actions

One of the features of Adobe Photoshop 4.0 (and later versions) lets you automate imaging tasks by grouping a series of commands into a single command or Action. Using actions lets you reproduce frequently used techniques. For example, you can create an Action that combines a series of plug-ins together to produce a special effect, or combine commands that prepare images for on-line publishing. You can use Actions on a single file or multiple files stored in the same folder or directory. (See Figure 2.12 on CD-ROM.)

Actions are displayed and controlled by the Actions palette. It has two views: Button Mode lets you click the Actions name to activate it; in List View, each step of the Action can be displayed and edited. This allows computer users to play an

TIP: Take Action

Actions are stored in the Photoshop preferences file. If you want to be able to save and load them, click on the arrow in the actions window and use the "Save Actions" and "Load Actions" command, which will allow you to store your current set of actions in an external "myfile.ATN" file.

action with steps disabled, or display selected dialog boxes during playback to interactively adjust any settings. The order in which tasks are executed can be edited by dragging and dropping. Actions can also be used to acquire batches of images from a digital camera, allowing an entire set of photographs to be automatically acquired, retouched, and saved. Best of all, Actions are cross-platform. If you create an Action on your Mac OS computer, anyone using the Windows version of Photoshop can load and apply your original Mac OS Action.

While you can create your own Actions, or find any number of shareware ones, the best place I have found to start is the first commercially available set of actions—KPT Actions from MetaCreations. Designed to work with the company's Kai's Power Tools 3.0 plug-ins, the package consists of one hundred Actions that allow you to create special effects for text, graphics, or photographs. Even better, you can look at and examine each step used in a particular effect so you can learn how these effects were created and modify them to produce your own unique Actions.

Installation is not complex. but I advise you to follow directions carefully—don't just load the Actions into the palette. The Kai's Power Tools filters you use for these Actions have to be updated to version 3.02s, which allows them to be "scriptable." Use the KPT Actions Installer to update your Kai's Power Tools filters. Now, you are ready to load the Actions—in the normal way—by using the Load Actions command found in the palette. You can install any of the Actions by using the Actions palettes' Load Action command. When you look in the KPT Actions folder on the CD-ROM, you will find five Actions files: KPT Actions, Frames, Apply to Text, Buttons, and Backgrounds. The KPT Actions file contains all the preset Actions in one file. You can load it or just select the groups of Actions you need. For example, Web designers may want to load the KPT Actions file, while pixographers may only need Frames, or just Apply to Text.

The Frames Actions create dramatic and elegant frames around your photographs and artwork. Note that to run Frames, you must first have a single-layer image open that you would like to frame. Frame effects range from the wacky—the Basketball Action comes to mind—to the exotic, and take less time to do than creating a graphic frame from scratch. Some of the Button, Background, and Effects Actions don't even require an image or test to work and start with a blank document to create eye-popping effects. All you have to do is hit "Play."

Here is one of my favorites in the package: the Partial Opacity Frame Action creates a subtle, elegant frame around your image with a single button click. (See Figure 2.13 on CD-ROM.)

If you have always wanted to create dramatic text effects, KPT Actions lets you do it. KPT Text Actions require that you first create a document containing black text on the top layer with a white background layer before applying the Action. You do not need to Select the text; just click an Apply to Text Action button. KPT Actions puts the power of metal type effects in your hands. In addition to text effects, most text Actions also apply a drop shadow or glow effect. My favorite is Gold Metal Jacket, but there are elegant, rustic, as well as silly text effects to be found and applied. Most text Actions create a background that has gradated color or lighting effects applied, but the Action always leaves the text selected when it is finished. This way, you can cut the text only and paste it into another image or document. That's the way I created the "cracked marble" effects I used for the opening title on my website. (See Figure 2.14 on CD-ROM.)

Other Photoshop Features

The program's PageMaker-like Guides and Grids feature makes it easy to build Web pages or composites and affords greater accuracy in placing and aligning images or selections (that's the way I use it most). Just as in PageMaker, guides can be pulled from rulers on the edge of the screen to provide precise horizontal or vertical lines to which operations can be snapped. Similarly, the Grids feature creates a regular pattern of snap points across an entire image. Guides and Grids provide a method for accurate alignment of objects inside an image file and helps you align objects on a Web page and while layering elements when compositing images. Guide settings are also recordable Actions, making it easy for you to define a specific guide set-up that can be shared with other users or applied to more than one document.

The Custom Gradients palette lets users create multicolor gradients, with varying opacity. The enhanced Gradient tool supports linear and radial gradients with multiple colors and varying levels of transparency. Actual colors can be defined for the gradient designs, or the current foreground and background colors can be automatically inserted whenever a custom gradient is applied. Users can save their own custom gradient styles and share them with other Photoshop users on either Mac OS or Windows platforms.

Photoshop's Free Transform command allows users to scale, rotate, skew, add perspective to, or otherwise distort a selected image or area in a single step, making image manipulations easier. Because the image does not have to be recalculated, this produces greater image fidelity.

TIP: Navigating Images

Photoshop 4.0's Navigator palette provides an easy way to move quickly to any location in a magnified image, by clicking the desired view area within a thumbnail of the image than can be resized. Users can adjust zoom levels with a slider control or specify zoom levels in a numeric entry field. You can enter preset zoom levels or any continuous zoom level between 0.13% and 1600%. Users of older versions of Photoshop can download a version of Navigator that will work with their software from http://www.extensis.com. (See Figure 2.15 on CD-ROM.)

Digital Copyright Protection

The possibility of digital theft is always present, especially when posting images on the Internet. Photoshop 4.0 takes a shot at this problem by protecting intellectual property rights with capabilities that allow users to embed a digital watermark, containing photographer and copyright information, into an image. Using PictureMarc technology, originally developed by the Digimarc Corporation, Photoshop 4.0 can embed an invisible, digital watermark in your image. While not apparent to your eyes, this watermark is still readable even when an image is edited, printed, or rescanned. When a watermarked file is opened, Photoshop 4.0 automatically indicates if any copyright information is present. A link in the program accesses Digimarc's Web site, where photo buyers obtain copyright and artist information for registered images.

An alternative for users of older versions, or for those photographers who prefer a visible copyright symbol, is a Mac OS shareware plug-in ($10 fee) called Watermark, created by photographer John Dykstra. Watermark places a visible copyright symbol that adds a faintly visible copyright symbol to the image being edited. When imbedded in any photograph distributed in digital form, it allows clients to evaluate the image and use it for comping or FPO purposes, while preventing unauthorized usage. Watermark appears in the Filter menu's "Other" submenu. When you select the plug-in, a dialog box allows you to specify how visible the copyright symbol will be: a value of one is almost invisible, but a "99" results in a complete reversal of the image underneath the watermark. The Repeat field controls how many times the symbol is placed horizontally across the image. The default setting produces a single symbol scaled to cover the current selection. Watermark can be downloaded from the Adobe Photoshop library on the CompuServe Information Service. (See Figure 2.16 on CD-ROM.)

System Requirements

Adobe Photoshop is available in Windows and Mac OS versions. The hardware requirements for Mac OS are a 68030, 68040, or PowerPC-based Macintosh running Apple System Software version 7.1 or later (7.1.2 or later on 603- and 605-based Macintoshes); 16MB RAM (32MB recommended); 257-color or greater display adapter; 20MB available hard-disk space; and CD-ROM drive. Windows computers require a 386 or faster processor running Windows3.1, Windows95, or WindowsNT; DOS 5.0 or greater is required for Windows3.1; 16MB RAM (32MB recommended); 20MB hard-disk space for operation; 257-color or greater display adapter; and CD-ROM drive.

LIVE PICTURE

Live Picture is an image editing and composing application that is currently available for Mac OS computers only. This program places more emphasis on compositing than image manipulation with compositing, and it can create effects in seconds that will make Adobe Photoshop users stare in envy. You can place two images on top of one another, then use the gradient blend tool to select the overlap area and how much you want the images to blend with one another. The blending effect happens in seconds—without creating gradated masks and using layers that could take 30 minutes or more in Photoshop.

To use images in the program, they have to be in Live Picture's IVUE format, which lets you display, scale, zoom, and pan images so quickly that working with a 100+MB image takes the same amount of time as a 1MB file. Converting an image into the IVUE formats is a three-step process. Since this is an important part of working with Live Picture, let me show how it's done.

Step 1. Select Open from the Converter menu. The Open dialog displays all of the TIFF, PICT, Photo CD, and IVUE files in a selected folder, drive, or removable media disk. A preview area is provided but does not work with TIFF or PICT files.

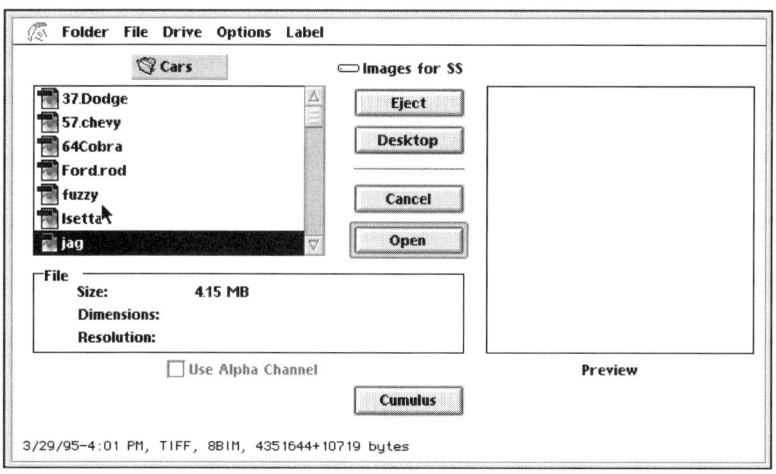

Figure 2.17 Selecting the Open command from the Converter menu is the first step in converting an image into an IVUE file.

Step 2. When the image is opened, it appears in a small window called the Converter Window.

Step 3. Once open, you choose the Save As command from the Converter menu. This brings up a dialog box that allows you to save the file in IVUE format. It's a good idea to append an ".IVUE" suffix to the file name to keep from confusing it with the original file. This dialog also gives you the option of using JPEG compression to compress the file. You can also select the Adapt Separations option if you know the final image will end up as a CMYK separation. (See Figure 2.18.)

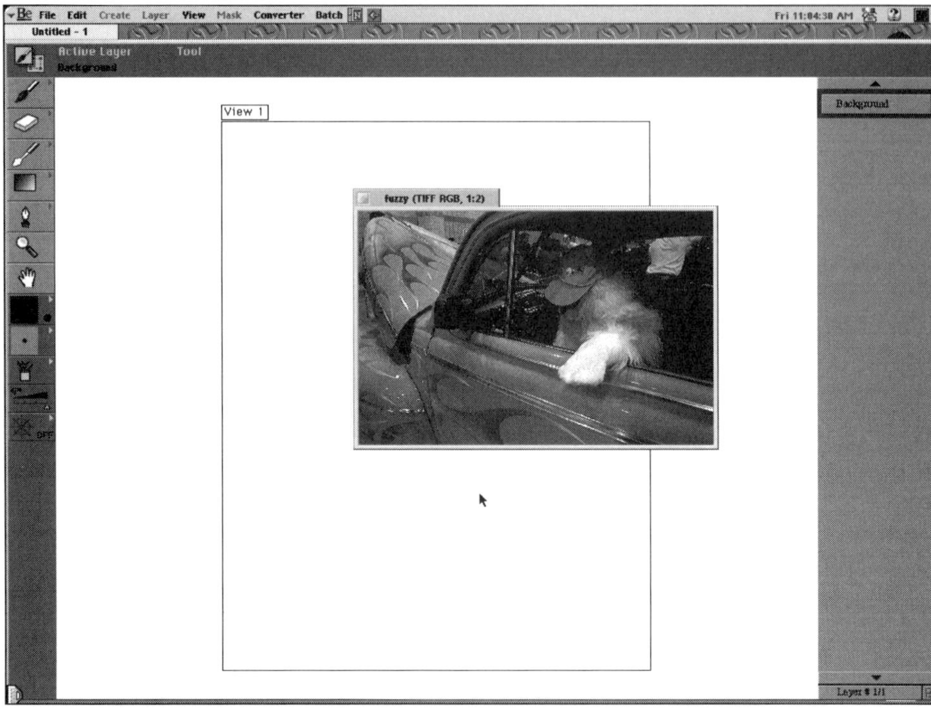

Figure 2.18 After opening, a TIFF format image appears in Live Picture's Converter window.

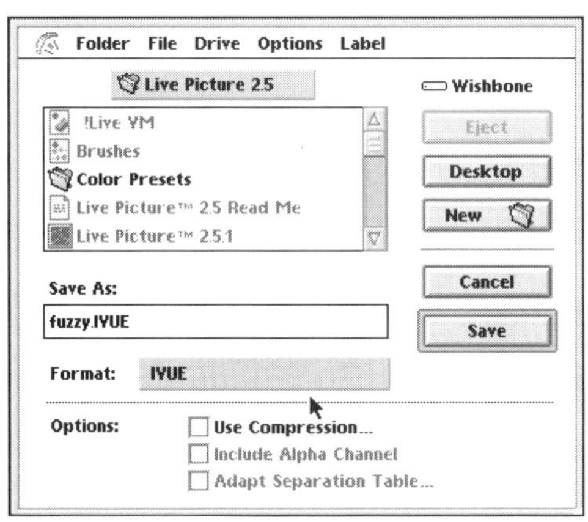

Figure 2.19 The Save As dialog box—from the Converter menu—is used to convert the file into IVUE format.

After conversion, IVUE images are placed on your document using the Image Inserting command. Unlike other programs, images being composited may be of different resolutions—a benefit of the resolution-independent FITS (Functional Interpolating Transformational System) technology used by Live

Picture. Other advantages include the ability to make multiple changes to color, brightness, and contrast on individual layers without affecting the entire composition. Live Picture does this with a dialog box that allows you to tweak an entire image or one of the three (RGB) layers to get it to look the way you want. The program's Image Silhouette feature lets you use objects as masks for other layers, and the silhouette can be used as a stencil to add color or texture.

Live Picture's speed and unlimited, nonlinear Undo functions lets users explore and generate alternative concepts quickly, and because the images are resolution independent, they can be scaled to any size while maintaining output quality. Users can take advantage of pressure-sensitive and unlimited-size brushes to create dramatic effects, and they can apply 49-bit brush strokes and gradients without banding or artifacts. In addition to Live Picture's real-time speed, Postscript-like resolution-independence, and true photographic quality output, the program is well-suited to working with other image editing programs, such as Adobe Photoshop. The latest version imports and exports EPS files and includes support for Apple's ColorSync 2.0, which helps users maintain color accuracy and consistency throughout the production process. With ColorSync enabled, users can preview Live Picture composites using Display Matching, Soft Proofing, and Gamut Warnings, and they can output using ColorSync's separation tables.

The current version of the program is compatible with Photoshop plug-in filters. Live Picture gives users the option of applying these filters to entire composites, or to single-image layers. In addition, the program supports Wacom Technology's Erasing UltraPen stylus, as well as the alpha channel—a separate channel tagged on to the traditional red, green, and blue channels that contains a value that indicates the amount of transparency for each pixel. (The alpha channel is where Adobe Photoshop files store transparency information.) Live Picture also lets users create alpha channels that can be exported to TIFF, Photoshop, and Live Picture's IVUE file formats for later use in other images. Live Picture also supports Canto Software's Cumulus image database manager, allowing users to insert images directly from Cumulus into Live Picture composites. They can also open Cumulus files in Live Picture, or merge Cumulus files with a Live Picture file.

Each subsequent version of Live Picture has reduced RAM requirements, and the current version runs in 18MB. Live Picture complements tools such as Photoshop and QuarkXPress, and users can import and export EPS files so that they can work on files created in QuarkXPress, Adobe PageMaker, or Illustrator, as well as other applications. Since some of Live Picture's most useful features have to do with layers and masks, they will be covered in more detail in Chapter 3.

System Requirements

Live Picture requires a Power Macintosh or Macintosh Quadra with a minimum of 18MB RAM. A pressure sensitive tablet, 48MB RAM, 25-bit graphics card, and large screen display are recommended for optimum performance.

LIVE PICTURE OVERDRIVE

Because Live Picture's list price might be a little expensive or intimidating for some users, the company introduced Live Picture Overdrive version 1.0. This is an image compositing program that offers fast, precise image editing and compositing tools to allow users to work on high resolution, multilayered files in real time. Based on Live Picture, Overdrive gives users the ability to scan images at maximum resolution without RAM constraints, as well as the ability to composite images in real-time, regardless of file size or the number of layers used. (See Figure 2.20 on CD-ROM.)

Using both Live Picture Overdrive and Adobe Photoshop, digital imagers will be able to leverage some of the best tools for high-resolution compositing as well as pixel editing. Registered users of Overdrive receive a free copy of FASTedit/IVUE, a Photoshop-compatible plug-in that allows users to work more efficiently on high resolution files by offering the ability to isolate specific areas of an image and avoid RAM and scratch disk overhead.

System Requirements

Live Picture Overdrive requires a Power Macintosh or Macintosh Quadra with a minimum of 20MB RAM, System 7.1 or higher, and a color monitor. Power Macintosh, System 7.1 or higher, a pressure sensitive tablet, 26MB application RAM, 25-bit video card, 1 GB hard drive, CD-ROM drive, and a large screen display are recommended for optimum performance.

MORE TOOLS FOR THE TOOLBOX

As TV's Tim Allen might say, "you never have too many tools." That same statement could be true for the pixographer. One of the most useful tools in your digital toolbox is file translation software. These programs allow you to move back and forth between platforms, or, as in the Photoshop example given earlier in the chapter, within the same platform. Here are two of the best programs available for file translation, and they do a lot more for the digital imager, too.

HiJaak Graphics Suite

It may sound like a cliché, but I consider Quarterdeck's HiJaak Graphics Suite 95 to be a graphics Swiss Army Knife for Windows. The package includes individual modules for file conversion, screen capture, and CAD-like drawing, as well as a HiJaak Paint module that will be of interest to digital imagers. The program's ability to add texture effects is a feature most photographers will enjoy using. Six different textures—the user's guide only tells you about four of them—can be applied from the Texture submenu of the Effects menu, and custom textures can be created by importing one of your own images. The software provides controls that lets you tweak the texture, but there is no preview window. HiJaak Paint includes a number of special effects and filters, including a Graham Filter that will enhance an image's background. The program has an impressive tool palette and toolbar, but the names of some menu items may be less than familiar. For example, the brighten/darken controls are labeled maximum/minimum. When you are finished with an image you can save it in the fifty different file formats that are an integral part of the HiJaak Graphics Suite design. If you are not sure which format to use, clicking Target Application lets you select the program you want to export to, and HiJaak Paint picks the most appropriate one.

DeBabelizer Toolkit and Pro

DeBabelizer 1.6.5 is the single most powerful and useful graphics application available for Mac OS users. I have never found a Mac or PC-based graphics file DeBabelizer would not open and convert. DeBabelizer Toolbox 1.6.5 opens over seventy different kinds of graphics files and displays them in a large preview window in the most impressive Open dialog found on any Mac OS graphics program. When you have stacks of files to convert, you can collect them into a batch and write a script to convert them as a group. If you are squeamish about scripting, don't be. The program includes a "Watch Me" command that lets you go through the step of converting a single file and automatically creates a script based on what you do. DeBabelizer Toolbox works with Photoshop-compatible plug-ins (see Chapter 6), and these plug-ins provide yet another way of bringing images into the Toolbox before retouching, enhancing, and saving in one of the many export formats.

Don't mistake DeBabelizer for Photoshop, however. The program's tool palette is much more limited, but when it's combined with available third-party filters, especially KPT Convolver, DeBabelizer can provide endless opportunities for manipulation and correction. The program was the first Mac application to support the PNG (Portable Network Graphic) format used on the Internet and World Wide Web. Webmeisters and surfers alike will appreciate a series of scripts, called ProScripts, that can be used to automatically process, filter, and color adjust Web-oriented graphics. Output can be delivered as GIF, JPEG, or thumbnail Web files that have an optimized color palette for speedier viewing. Four scripts are currently available, including WebSaveToAll, which saves your images as noninterlaced Thumbnail GIFs, interlaced GIFs, and JPEGs. DeBabelizer includes some built-in effects that Webmeisters might also find useful. A clever one is Background Removal, which allows you to remove the background, and a smart Shave Edges command to clean up the results. Accomplishing all this in DeBabelizer is much easier than using other graphics programs. DeBabelizer Toolbox 1.6.5 remains a must-have program for any Mac OS owner who works with graphics.

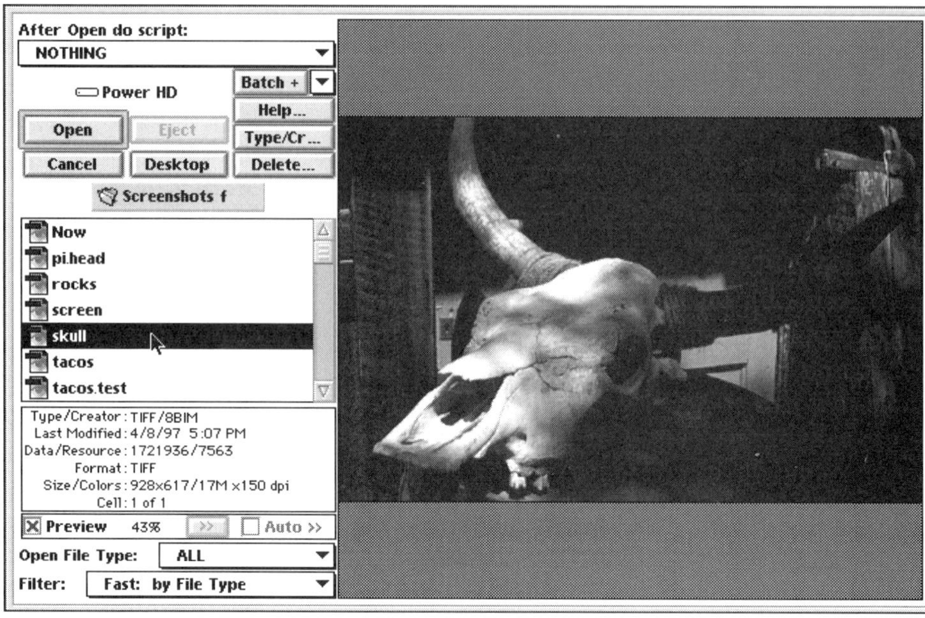

Figure 2.21 DeBabelizer Toolbox's Open dialog has such a large preview window that the program could easily be considered a file viewing program, too. Photo © Joe Farace.

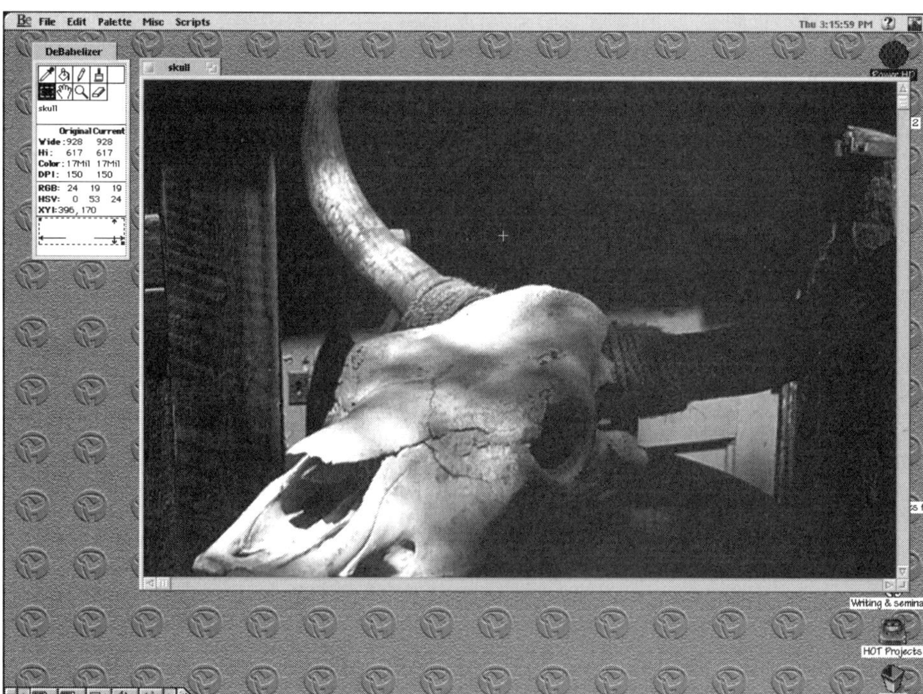

Figure 2.22 DeBabelizer's working window shows the image full size as well as its specification. Here, the image is shown at 928 × 617 pixels, with 17 million colors and a resolution of 150 dpi. Photo © Joe Farace.

Here's how easy it is to convert a file:

Step 1. After launching DeBabelizer Toolbox, I used the program's Open command to both view file names and see a preview of the image I was interested in. Clicking on the file name opens the image file.

Step 2. After the file is opened, you will see the image full size along with information about the file, including image width and height, number of colors, and resolution.

Step 3. After going to the Save As command in the File menu, you will see the Save dialog that provides more options to save the file in either a Mac OS or Windows file format than in any other graphics program available.

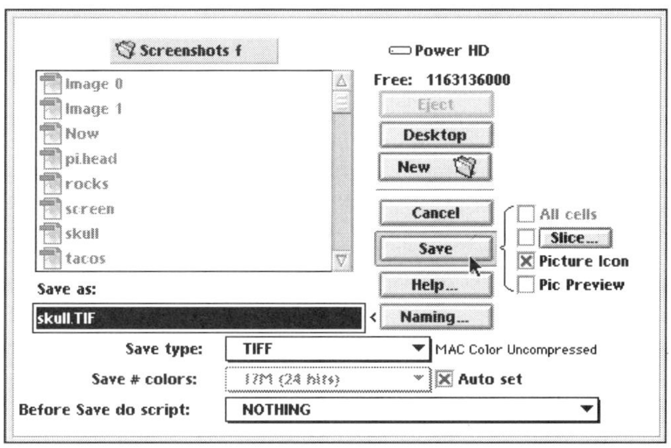

Figure 2.23 One of the strongest parts of DeBabelizer Toolbox is the Save dialog, which lets you save your image file in many Mac OS and Windows file formats.

At the beginning of 1997, Equilibrium Technologies introduced a Windows version called DeBabelizer Pro for Windows95 and WindowsNT 4.0. The premise behind DeBabelizer's automated graphics processing technology is that photographers and designers need to efficiently and automatically process content so that they can quickly deliver graphics across a range of platforms while maintaining the highest image quality. DeBabelizer Pro automatically prepares images, animations, and digital video through drag-and-drop scripting, batch processing, color palette reduction, image processing, and file-format conversion. DeBabelizer Pro for Windows offers a range of automated graphics processing capabilities, all in a single, integrated application. Some of the prominent features include: an easy-to-use, drag-and-drop, multiwindowed interface; batch processing with interactive scripting; hierarchical directory structures within batch lists; Equilibrium's proprietary SuperPalette technology for color palette optimization and reduction; bandwidth conservation tools for multimedia and World Wide Web graphics; translation support for over ninety file formats optimized for the Windows 95 and NT environments; and HTML Parsing, which allows users to create a batch list from all supported image types embedded in an HTML document by dragging the document into a batch list window.

CASE STUDY: JOHN BLAKE

John Blake is a commercial photographer located in Greeley, Colorado. Here, in his own words, he will show you how he used Adobe Photoshop and Live Picture to create a subtle, yet humorous digital image. All photographs and composites are © John Blake.

About the Photographer

John Blake is a native of Rockford, Illinois and a graduate of Bradley University in Peoria. He operates a commercial photography and digital imaging business in Greeley, Colorado. He also teaches advanced digital imaging at Aims Community College in Greeley. Blake, who has been involved with digital imaging since 1993, operates a pre-press service bureau for several graphic designers and employs his own photographs, as well as submitted photos, in the designer's layout. He created the digital composite "A Crowded Day at the Mall" as a self-promotion piece to demonstrate his ability to combine photography with his digital imaging skills. In the following section, he explains in his own words how he produced the composite image. (See Figure 2.24 on CD-ROM.)

A Crowded Day at the Mall

> Digital composites that are composed of one element out of context with the remainder of the image are the most appealing to me. I don't like composites that are a mish-mash of several unrelated elements. I try to stick to the old photographic saying that less is more.
>
> The main image is part of the Erechtheum, also know as the "Porch of Maidens," and is part of the Acropolis in Athens, Greece. I started with a photograph of a Grecian temple that was taken on a recent trip to Greece, because I liked the pattern of the similar figures. The image used was Fuji Velvia. (See Figure 2.25 on CD-ROM.)
>
> Deciding on the other photo or "out of context" element, on the other hand, was no easy task. After racking my brain for ideas with no luck, I decided to go through my stock slide collection. Finally, I came upon a slide of an elderly couple about to cross the street in the small town of Appenzell, Switzerland. She was carrying a large handbag in one hand and her husband had his right hand grasped around her left arm. The

image was photographed using Kodak Kodachrome 200 film. (See Figure 2.26 on CD-ROM.)

I figured that the image of the elderly woman would work for two reasons. From a subject standpoint, the elderly woman and her clothing were as different as could be from the Greek figures. From a technical standpoint, her body and head position were similar to the figures. That would make the woman fit in better with her newfound friends.

The two slides were scanned to Pro Photo CD six-resolution image pack files, and 72MB files were used. The Photo CD files were opened in Adobe Photoshop, using the Kodak Photo CD Acquire Module plug-in, and saved as TIFF files. The majority of the color and density corrections were performed using Photoshop's Levels and Curves controls. The rest of the work was accomplished in Live Picture. The reasons I used Live Picture to create the composite were threefold. First, there was the program's huge speed advantage compared to Photoshop in working on large image files.

The TIFF files were first converted to Live Picture's proprietary IVUE format. The next task was to drop out the background of the image of the elderly woman. This was accomplished in Live Picture's image silhouette layer, which is much more powerful than Photoshop's lasso and magic wand tools. The finished product was saved as a Live Picture FITS file. The FITS files was then saved as an IVUE file through the Build command in the File menu.

The statue IVUE file was then opened as a new document. The image of the woman was then added to the statue photo as an Image Insertion Layer. Using the Positioning toolbar, the woman's image was then scaled and rotated to match—as closely as possible, the size of the image she was replacing. Live Picture's cloning and colorize layers were the tools I used to create the stone texture for the woman's face and handbag. The opacity varied in the cloning brush as I cloned the stone texture primarily from parts of the faces of the other figures over the woman's face. My goal was to create an entirely new facial texture. I didn't want the "new" face to look like a copy of another. Live Picture's unlimited selective Undo feature was invaluable in the tedious trial-and-error procedure needed to accomplish the desired effect.

Originally, I decided to composite the photo of the woman pretty much as is. However, as I worked, I decided instead to modify the Greek figure to include the facial features of the woman, include the handbag, and build a new arm. Cloning and Colorize layers were used to create a full-length stone arm, fingers, and handbag. The new arm was built by first cloning the partial arm from another figure. The arm was extended by cloning smooth surfaces from other figures. The handbag's handle was created by cloning in part of the sky around the woman's arm. One problem area was left to be fixed. The handbag appears in front of the figure to the woman's left instead of behind it. To solve this, I duplicated the layer of the Greek figures and then erased everything on that layer but a small part over the handbag.

After the facial cloning was done, I fine-tuned the face by using the colorize layer. Using the colorize layer, I selectively darkened and lightened the face to various degrees by varying the opacity of the brush. There was a reflection of the sidewalk in the right lens of the woman's glasses. The reflection was eliminated by cloning part of the dark shadow behind the figures.

Using LP's Build command, the final composite was then converted to a single layer TIFF file and outputted on a FARGO Picture 310 dye-sublimation printer. (See Figure 2.27 on CD-ROM.)

3

Practical Digital Imaging

> *Would you like to squeeze a little extra mileage out of your computer—to be able to put it through its paces a little faster, reduce some of those annoying delays, and get your machine to do more things in less time?*
>
> ERNEST E. MAU

The late computer guru may have been talking about programming languages, but he could have just as easily been talking about a subject that is invaluable to all digital imagers: the use of removable media. In addition to software tools, the well-equipped pixographer needs to have a similar arsenal of hardware tools—in addition to a computer. For the digital imager working with the large file sizes, one of the most important tools is removable media. This chapter takes a look at how different kinds of removable media work and what their advantages and disadvantages are. This chapter also introduces tools that allow photographers to move graphics files back and forth between Mac OS and Windows-based computers.

DIGITAL FILM

Hard disks are wonderful devices. They come in an ever-growing number of sizes, and as capacities have increased, prices have decreased. But no matter how large a drive you purchase, all hard disks share a common fault: they are fixed drives. Some pundits think they are called "fixed" because they are permanently mounted to the computer chassis, but I prefer to think of them as "fixed" because their size is fixed and can never get any larger. Sure, there are any number of compression software packages available that will theoretically increase hard disk size by shrinking the size of the files that are stored on it, but I have never been a fan of these products. All that compression and decompression is asking for problems—especially for graphics professionals who really use their computers. Enter the hard disk that never fills up: the removable media drive. (See Figure 3.1 on CD-ROM.)

Magnetic vs. Optical

Removable media drives are computer peripherals that use data-storing cartridges that can be easily removed from the drive. These drives have many advantages for computer users—especially digital photographers. Sometimes called removable hard drives, they are more correctly called removable media, since the media being removed might just as well be optical as it is magnetic. People use removable media drives for many different things: they can make back-ups of the data on your hard disks and, next to a modem, they're the cheapest way of transporting graphic data from point A to point B. Without removable media, digital photographers and designers wouldn't have a way to take large image files back and forth to their service bureaus. Placing financial data on removable media and locking it in a safe-deposit box provides a level of security even the most ardent hackers cannot breach.

The performance of fixed or removable drives is measured by seek time or access time. Seek time is the amount of time required for the arm of a direct access storage device to be positioned over the appropriate track. Access time is the interval between a call for data and the time at which the completion of data delivery occurs. Some pundits are convinced that the only relevant measurement is sustained transfer rate, which measures the average number of bytes per unit of time passing between disk storage and processor storage. The truth is that a fast drive is usually just as fast, no matter how you measure performance.

Magnetic-based drives are typically based on the technology that IBM developed for the first hard disk that used two 30MB discs. Consequently, this kind of drive is often called "Winchester." This design, using off-the-shelf hard disk components and housed in a proprietary plastic shell, was the basis for the original and wildly popular SyQuest drives. Winchester is not the only hardware option for magnetic media. An interesting magnetic alternative is the Bernoulli box. It uses the read/write heads found in a traditional hard disk, but instead of a rigid disk, the Bernoulli disk is flexible (it's made of material similar to floppy disks); at high speeds, it bends to be close enough for the head to read it. During

Factoid: Who Is This Bernoulli Guy Anyway?

Daniel Bernoulli was a Swiss mathematician who lived in the eighteenth century. He is famous as the first person to express the principles of what became fluid dynamics. The use of the flexible disk, and the fact that the disk moves closer to or away from the read/write head depending on the speed of the disk, makes use of the so-called Bernoulli principle. Iomega paid homage to him when they designed one of the first removable media devices—the Bernoulli Box—in 1983.

a power failure, a hard disk must retract its head to prevent a crash, whereas the Bernoulli floppy naturally bends away.

Iomega vs. SyQuest

To me, the most important attributes a removable media drive should have are small cartridge size (for ease of storage) and low cost per cartridge. Access time, while important, is less so for most applications—especially for cold storage of graphic images. The current winner in the low-cost removable sweepstakes is Iomega's Zip drive. With a street price of around $150, Iomega's Zip drive's Bernoulli design produces an average seek time of 29ms. Pocketable, preformatted Zip cartridges, scarcely larger than a floppy disk, are less expensive than SyQuest's. As I write this, the street price for a 100MB cartridge is $19.95, compared to $60 for a 105MB SyQuest. Bundled software for Mac and Windows includes backup, file cataloging, disk duplication, and management utilities that feature read/write disk locking, formatting, diagnostics, and hard drive emulation. While the Zip is a new format, it has been widely embraced by service bureaus, printers, and the graphics industry. I have had two Zip drives (one for my IBM, the other for my Mac OS computer) in daily use for over a year. During that time the drives—and more importantly the cartridges—have performed flawlessly and have not been plagued with the kind of data error problems I encountered with early 44MB SyQuest cartridges.

Not to be outdone, SyQuest announced a similarly low-priced 135MB removable drive called EZ135 that has an average seek time of 13.5—twice as fast as Zip. The problem is that it was too little too late. Iomega countered by announcing the Jaz drive, an under $500 drive using 1GB cartridges. These high capacity cartridges will use all-Winchester technology and cost around $100. These new cartridges will not be compatible with SyQuest or Iomega's own Zip or Bernoulli drives. SyQuest's response—again a little late—is the 1.5GB SyJet drive.

Lest you think SyQuest is not a player in the removable media game, they are far from dead. They are still players because of an important fact: there are hundreds of thousands—maybe millions—of five-inch SyQuest cartridges and drives still in use. The original 44MB format was replaced by the 88MB drive, which in turn was supplanted by the 200MB drive. A 200MB drive will read both other cartridge formats, and while its design is a little long in the tooth compared to SyQuest's bullet-proof three-inch 270MB drive, it is nonetheless still quite popular because it can read all of the older five-inch cartridges floating around out there. (See Figure 3.2 on CD-ROM.)

The Nomai Alternative

Right now, the most popular removable media drive is Iomega's Zip. It's not that fast, and its capacity is not that large, but it's cheap. With the introduction of the Nomai 750.c, all that is about to change.

The Nomai 750.c removable media drive is as compact as a Zip drive, but instead of plastic, the drive is housed in no-nonsense black metal. Since comparisons with Zip and Jaz are inevitable, lets get them out of the way first. The 750.c is faster that Zip. Much faster. Its 10ms seek time is significantly faster than the Bernoulli-based Zip's 29ms. The Jaz, whose hard drive-type construction is similar to Nomai's, performs at 12ms—just a little slower. The cost per MB of storage is less than Jaz too: 12.5 cents versus 10.9 cents for Nomai. With a street price somewhere between a Zip and Jaz, Nomai delivers slightly better price performance.

Installation for Mac OS users is a snap. You connect a SCSI cable, load a driver off a floppy disk, and go to work. If Windows users don't already have one, they will need a SCSI card. Nomai offers an ISA card for $79 and a PCI card for $99. The Adaptec card I tried worked fine, and Nomai bundles Adaptec's EZ-SCSI 4.0 software to help you set it up. Unlike both Zip and Jaz, which provide SCSI in and SCSI out connectors on the back of the drive, the Nomai 750.c has only SCSI in. This means that the drive must be the last (or only) item in your SCSI chain. Like the Zip, there are only two possible SCSI addresses. In this case, you can use one or five.

Mac OS users may take a little longer to get used to the way the Nomai operates. To insert a cartridge, for example, you have to push a button located on the lower left-hand corner of the drive's face plate. When you do, a trap door drops, allowing you to insert the cartridge. The same steps are required if you eject a cartridge by placing it in the trash can on Mac OS computers. The disk is dismounted, but it is not ejected until you "push the button, Frank." Then you have to manually shut the front trap door. Windows users will not even notice these few additional steps, and Mac OS users will quickly get used to these idiosynchracies.

Other than the Phase Change Dual CD-ROM (so-called PD) drives developed by Panasonic and the SyQuest five-inch 200MB drive, few removable media drives can read and write cartridges in more than one format. Out here in the real world, people are used to interchanging floppies and some, that I have talked to, are frustrated by the lack of removable media compatibility. Well, the Nomai 750.c is compatible! The Nomai 750.c accepts its own 750 and 540MB cartridges, and two 750MB carts are included in the package. The 750.c also works with 135MB cartridges designed for the SyQuest EZ135 drives. Wait, there's more. The Nomai drive also reads and writes SyQuest 270MB cartridges. While SyQuest has discontinued this drive, it is well known around service bureau circles as the most bullet-proof cartridge SyQuest ever made. What this compatibility means is that you can use the 750MB cartridges for data back-up and off-line storage, and save the inexpensive SyQuest 135 cartridges for sharing images with clients or delivery to service bureaus.

Real world performance matched the specs. Access is accompanied by high-speed whirs and R2D2-like clicks that let you know the drive is working but are not annoyingly loud. I tried both SyQuest 135EZ and Nomai 750 cartridges, which are similar in shape but different in profile. Both cartridges seem less substantial than the more expensive media used by Zip and Jaz. For a short-term test like this, durability is harder to test, but Nomai provides a five-year guarantee on their disks. When a cartridge is in the drive, a green LED lights up informing you of that fact. A pretty cool feature, until I realized that because of the trap door, it is a necessity.

The 750MB capacity makes Nomai an ideal solution for temporary (or permanent) storage of data you will be writing to CD-ROM, and many people will think of many more uses for the additional storage, including back-ups. If you have been naughty, not nice, and have not being doing those back-ups the way the good doctor has recommended, now's the time to take care of that problem and purchase a Nomai 750.c.

Optical Drives

Optical removable media drives are more properly called magneto-optical (MO). They use a laser to heat a plastic disc to change its reflectivity, which creates media that can be erased and reused. One of the negatives of optical drives is that writing data to optical media typically requires three spins. The first erases existing data, the second writes new data, and the third verifies that the data is there. When compared to magnetic drives, all this spinning tends to reduce performance. Typical performance specifications for magneto optical drives (based on the Fujitsu 230MB unit) are seek times of 30ms, access time of 40ms, and an average write transfer rate of .44MB per second. On top of that, the drives are more expensive that magnetic drives—although the media is less so. Unlike their magnetic competitors, manufacturers have agreed upon standardized 230MB and 640MB formats. (See Figure 3.3 on CD-ROM.)

Until now, the only multiformat removable drive was the ill-fated 20MB "floptical" drive that read its own special MO discs and conventional floppy discs. All that's changed with the Phase-change Dual CD-ROM (so-called PD) drives developed by Panasonic. The Clark Kent exterior of these drives hides the fact that they are a combination rewritable optical disc and quad speed CD-ROM drive. The CD-ROM aspect of the drive differentiates between Audio CD, CD-R (read only), CD-ROM XA, and multisession Kodak Photo CD discs. The capacity of the disc is not 230MB but a solid 650MB. The writable optical disc uses phase-change dual technology instead of the magneto-optical technique. Under PD, disc writing is accomplished without the use of a bias magnet. Unlike traditional MO, Phase-change technology is usually limited to about 100,000 write cycles—about one-tenth as many as magneto-optical. Panasonic's new media overcomes this liability by using a new alloy on the disc's recording layer and has been tested at 500,000 cycles. Improvements are expected to raise that to 1 million cycles. By combining two different functions in a single unit, Panasonic hopes users will not notice an average seek time of 165ms for optical disc and 195ms for CD-ROM.

With street prices running between $500 and $600, depending on manufacturer (they all use the same Panasonic mechanism), and $59 per cartridge, the drives are competitively priced.

Another Optical Drive

The sleeper in the removable media sweepstakes is Compact Disc Recordable (CD-R). Drives and media keep getting less expensive and software keeps getting better. CD-R drives can be purchased for around $500, and media can be as low as eight bucks—for 650MB. WORM (Write Once Read Many Times) media does not behave like the other media covered in this chapter. Even magnetic tape can be erased, but not CD-R. With plunging drive costs and an interest in moderately priced, high-capacity media, CD-R drives are poised to become the next big thing. What's standing in the way? Ease of use, for one thing. With most software, you can't simply drag a file from your hard disk to the CD-R disc as you would with other media, but the software is getting better. CD writing programs, like Adaptec's Toast Pro and, to a lesser extent, Corel's CD Creator 2.0 are making writing CD-R discs easier, and I expect it will get even better. (See Figure 3.4 on CD-ROM.)

CD-RW (rewritable) drives are expected to be the next big thing. Because CD-RW drives use a new directory structure, as well as lasers that have a different reflectivity, discs created on them will not be compatible with the current generation of CD-ROM drives. The next generation of multiread CD-ROM drives will be able to read CD-RW discs. Prices for CD-RW drives are expected to be competitive with CD-R drives, but they will have to overcome the reality that CD-R drives produce discs that can be read by the many millions of computers that were originally delivered with CD-ROM drives built-in. How successful CD-RW will be depends on what happens with DVD (Digital Video Disc). Some pundits are predicting that DVD will replace the CD-ROM format. There is much there to like in the new format—a 4.7GB (that's GIGAbytes) capacity, for one.

The success of CD-ROM was built on the runaway hit of CD audio. DVD has been slower to roll out. While home entertainment DVD units are beginning to trickle out from Toshiba, Sony, and Pioneer—among others—the software has been slower to appear. Some major players in the movie game have yet to release titles for DVD, and without wide acceptance of the movie format, I don't expect DVD-ROM to catch fire with computer users. Nevertheless, a DVD-RAM (a rewritable DVD format) is under development, but compatibility problems immediately rear their head. The first generation of DVD-ROM drives will not be able to read DVD-RAM discs.

For some reason, magnetic tape is more popular with Windows and DOS users than with Mac heads, but that is changing as multi-GB drives become less expensive and the thought of backing up these huge drives sinks in. The cartridges come in many different designations: there is QIC (Quarter Inch Cassette),

XL (long), and QW (wide-long) models, and variations on these names. The variety of tape formats may not help acceptance, which is further aggravated by the fact that data is stored in a serial format, rather than the random method used by other removable media. When coupled with the inherently slower access time, magnetic tape has never gotten the respect it deserves. Tape has one major feature that will endear it to thrifty computer users—it is cheap and provides the lowest cost per MB storage of any removable media. This makes tape the ideal media for people who use their removable media drives for back-up or archival purposes. Mag (magnetic) tape drives are slow. That's why DAT (Digital Audio Tape) drives are becoming popular for both Mac and Windows users. DAT tapes transfer data at rates up to 9.2MB per minute and have reliability rates in excess of even the best hard drives. (See Figure 3.5 on CD-ROM.)

USING DISKS ON "OTHER" COMPUTERS

One of the most ubiquitous forms of removable media is one that was not mentioned at all in the above analysis—the floppy disk. Yet the lowly floppy disk remains the single lingua franca of computing; no matter what kind of computer you have—Mac OS or Windows—you have a floppy disk drive. Yet reading floppy disks from other computers can be a challenge. Recently, a photographer called me asking how he could convert some of his Mac OS-based photographic files into a form that could be used by his client, who needed them in a Windows-based format. Here's what I told him.

Cross-Platform Blues

When converting files between Mac OS and Windows computers, it helps if you have software that allows your computer to read (or mount) disks that were formatted on the "other" machine. Apple's Macintosh PC Exchange (that is part of the system software) lets Mac OS computers read and write disks formatted on IBM-PC and compatible machines, as well as disks created on Apple II computers. The latest version of PC Exchange also recognizes DOS SCSI hard disk and removable media drives, such as Bernoulli and SyQuest. This was helpful for my friend, since he had to deliver his converted files on a DOS-formatted SyQuest cartridge. In addition to allowing your Mac OS computer to read and format DOS disks, Macintosh PC Exchange provides file conversion directly from the desktop. For example, a .PCX file can be preset to open as a Mac OS PICT file and can be opened just by double clicking the file's icon.

One of the most useful tools you can have is something that lets you read disks formatted on that "other" computer system. By using DataViz's MacOpener software, Windows95 users can have the same flexibility that users of Macintosh PC Exchange have. In addition to allowing Windows users to read and write Mac

OS-formatted floppy disks from within the standard Windows Open dialogs, MacOpener supports SyQuest, Iomega Zip and Bernoulli, CD-ROM, Magneto-Optical, and even Mac OS hard drives. MacOpener gives PC-compatible users easy access to most of the Mac OS-formatted digital stock photo discs available. The main limitation will then not be the system software but whether or not your program will read the Mac OS-formatted file.

From One Platform to Another

DataViz's MacLinkPlus supports 550 file translation combinations and the company's implementation of Apple's Easy Open concept makes file conversion as easy as double-clicking a file. The MacLinkPlus package includes a utility called Document Converter that transforms a PC file into Mac OS readable form by dragging the file—or folder (directory, for PC users)—on top of Document Converter. When you do, Document Converter automatically converts the files into a previously defined Mac OS format. You can set it once, then forget it. The latest version includes a handy utility called FileView that lets Mac OS users quickly view the contents of a file without actually opening it. FileView also provides information on using that file with different Mac OS, DOS, or Windows applications and even provides a few tips on how to convert the file you just opened. If you're a (World Wide) Web head, you will appreciate the inclusion of the Internet Translation Kit. The HTML (HyperText Markup Language) format used on World Wide Pages can be converted into any Mac OS, Windows, or DOS format that's currently supported by MacLink Plus; any GIF (Graphics Interchange Format) or JPEG (Joint Photographic Experts Group) graphics files referenced by the HTML code are automatically converted in Mac OS PICT or Windows WPG or WMF files. (See Figure 3.6 on CD-ROM.)

If you need a Windows utility that will convert Mac OS files in PC readable form, take a look at DataViz's Conversion Plus. It lets you exchange files between Mac OS and PCs, or even different PC programs, while retaining all of your file formatting—something important for text or database applications. The latest version includes a file preview feature that lets users preview a file before converting it.

CASE STUDY: DIGITAL SELL SHEET

Marketing is an important part of any professional photographer's business. I constantly and consistently have to keep in touch with existing clients and new stock photo buyers. One of the ways I do this is by creating and mailing an 8 1/2″ × 11″ promo sheet that features five to ten stock photographs, along with text reminding potential clients that when they need this kind of image—please give me a call.

The format for my sell sheets is simple. The top of the page has my name and the bottom carries another line with my name, address, phone, e-mail, and website information. In between this minimum of text are stock photographs. In the past, I created these promo pieces photographically, and they were expensive to set up and produce. It also took a lot of time. Recently, I started designing them with my computer using desktop publishing software and printing them on a FARGO dye-sublimation printer. Since there is no darkroom or lab expenses associated with placing the photographs used for the sell sheet, I can afford to create more and different promo pieces. The only direct outside cost is having the images scanned. If you have a film or flatbed scanner, that cost can be eliminated. To create an all-new marketing piece, I use an old sell sheet document as a template and simply replace its images with new ones.

You can use Corel WordPerfect or even Microsoft Word to create any desktop published document, but I use Adobe PageMaker because of its ease of use in working with image and text elements. Other photographers may prefer QuarkXPress, and the methods I will describe will be only slightly different in that program. The examples of the two programs used—Adobe Photoshop and PageMaker—are Mac OS versions, but the same software is available in Windows version and the commands and menu structure area are almost identical. Where there is a variation between platforms, I have noted it. Here is the creation of a new sell sheet from a blank piece of (digital) paper.

Making a Digital Sell Sheet

Step 1. I started by opening Adobe PageMaker 6.5 and creating a blank 8 1/2 × 11-inch page.

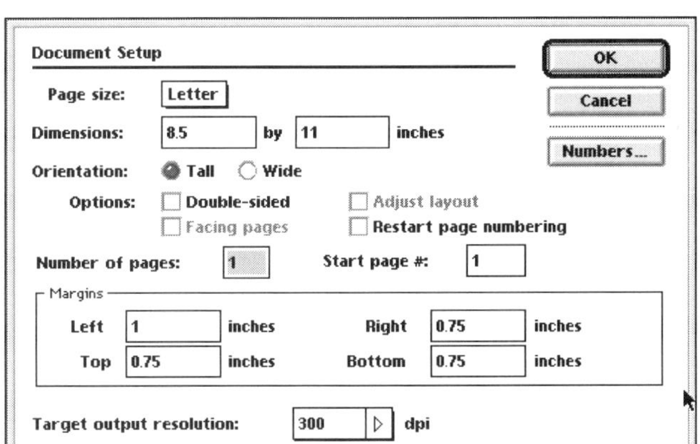

Figure 3.7 PageMaker's Document Setup dialog box lets you specify how big the page will be and what the margins are like. Since I plan to print on a 300 dpi printer, the resolution was set at that number.

Step 2. Using PageMaker's text tool, I typed my name on the sell sheet using a distinctive type face. Initially, I chose Adobe Skia to represent how my name would appear in my promotional materials. If you are not already doing it, choose a different-looking typeface—or logo—and use it in all of your materials from mailing labels to business cards. Later on I used Adobe Photoshop along with KPT Actions (see Chapter 1) with the same font to create something that looks more three-dimensional. I saved the new "name" as a TIFF file for later use in promotional material and on my Website. In this example, I used PageMaker's Place command to place the new text where I wanted it.

This is also the time to place the rest of the text that will appear on your sell sheet. In addition to showing the typical mailing address and phone number, be sure to list your fax number and e-mail address. If you have a site on the World Wide Web, be sure to include this information, too. The sell sheet is a marketing tool, and you want to make it possible for potential clients to contact you via telephone, fax, or e-mail. If your website does not include your e-mail address, it should, along with a link that when clicked will take anyone visiting the site to the e-mail portion of their Internet browser.

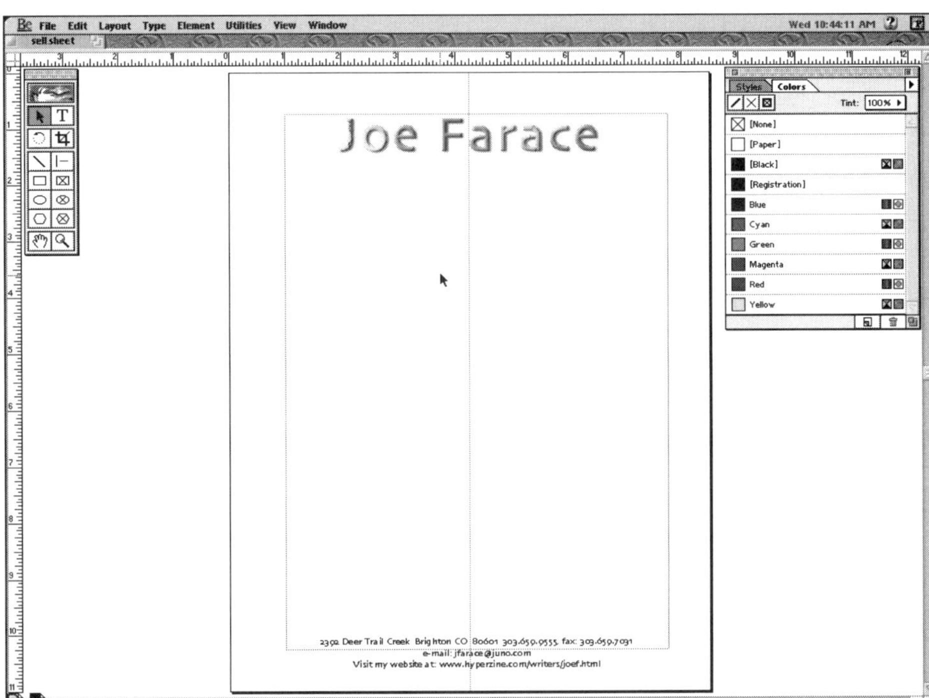

Figure 3.8 Using Adobe PageMaker's Place command, I placed the text of my name that had been enhanced using Adobe Photoshop and KPT Actions from MetaCreations.

Step 3. As in all printed pieces, some preplanning was called for. Since this one was going to highlight my travel photography, I selected a group of images showing both foreign and American locales and had them transferred to Photo CD. Once I had the images on disc, I launched Adobe Photoshop and selected the first image that I was going to place on my sell sheet. Since all Photo CD images need some sharpening I used Photoshop's Unsharp Mask command to tweak the photograph's sharpness. Then I saved the image onto an Iomega Zip cartridge as a TIFF file. Windows users might want to use a .BMP format, but TIFF is just as good for placement in the Windows version of PageMaker.

While in Photoshop, you should take the time to add additional enhancements to the images. This can be as simple as cropping off the black edges that inevitably appear when 35mm slides are transferred to Photo CD—this never happens when negatives are digitized—or the stronger cropping that I did of a Japanese woman in period costume to minimize background distractions. Photo CD scans are also almost always somewhat flat, and adding some contrast with Photoshop's Brightness and Contrast controls usually helps enhance the color—if that is the effect you are trying to achieve and it fits your style.

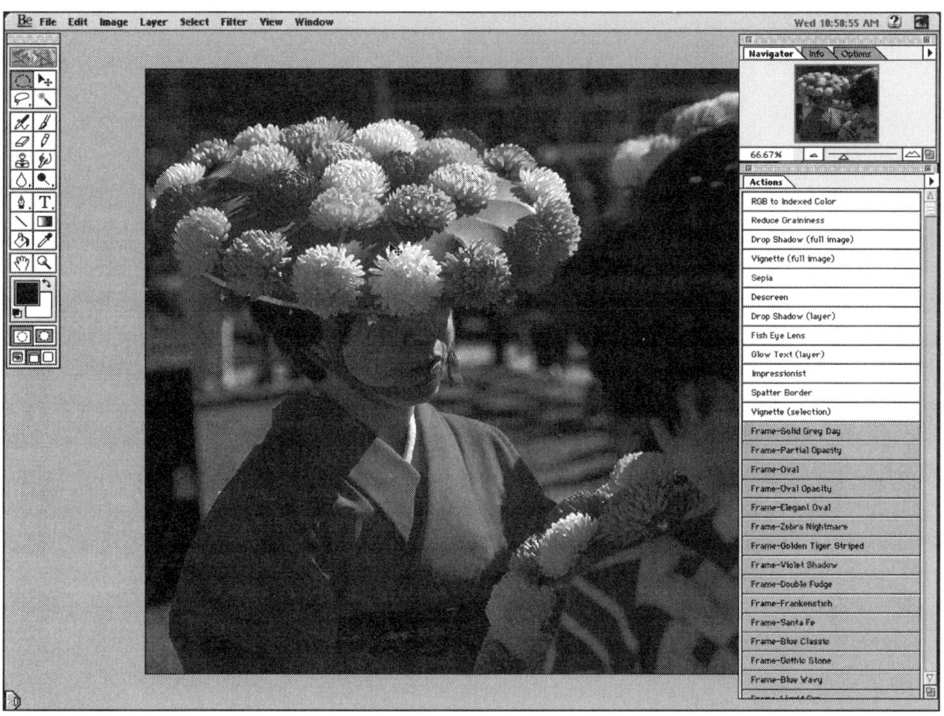

Figure 3.9 Adobe Photoshop is used first to tweak the sharpness of images to be used on the final sell sheet. Photo © Joe Farace.

Step 4. If you have enough RAM, you should keep both Adobe Photoshop and PageMaker open at the same time. This makes it easier to move back and forth between the two programs. If you don't, the best approach is to prepare all of your images first, save them to a removable media cartridge, them place them into the sell sheet.

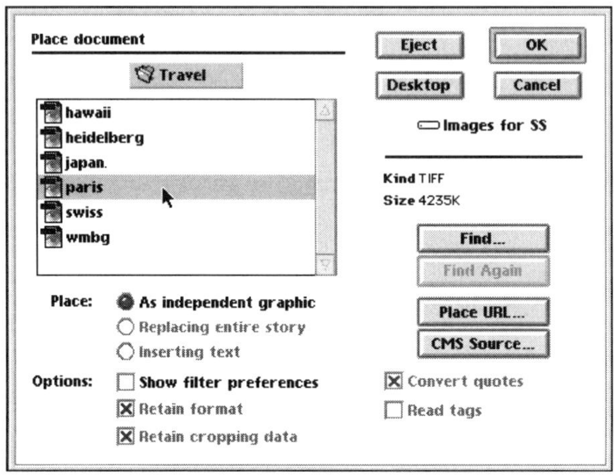

Figure 3.10 PageMaker's Place Document command is used to select the image and place it in the sell sheet.

The next step is to use PageMaker's Place command to place the images—one at a time—into your document. Be sure to click on the As Independent Graphic button. This will give you more control over the image when it's finally in place, and you will be able to move and resize the photograph more easily.

Step 5. After selecting the image you want, PageMaker displays an Importing File dialog showing the file being loaded. You then have a choice of including the full image in the document or just a reference to the original. Choosing the first option (YES) makes the full 902K (or whatever) image part of the PageMaker file, but after placing several images this way, the sell sheet file size can get huge. The choice is yours, but I prefer to only place a reference to the original image stored elsewhere on your hard disk. This makes the PageMaker file smaller, but it also reduces the on-screen (only) resolution of the photograph.

Step 6. Next, I use the Place command to place two or three other photographs on the page. These are usually resized either before they are placed, or sometimes after they are placed. Having photographs of different sizes on the page helps give it some visual interest. Resizing is a matter of choosing the "Pointer" tool and

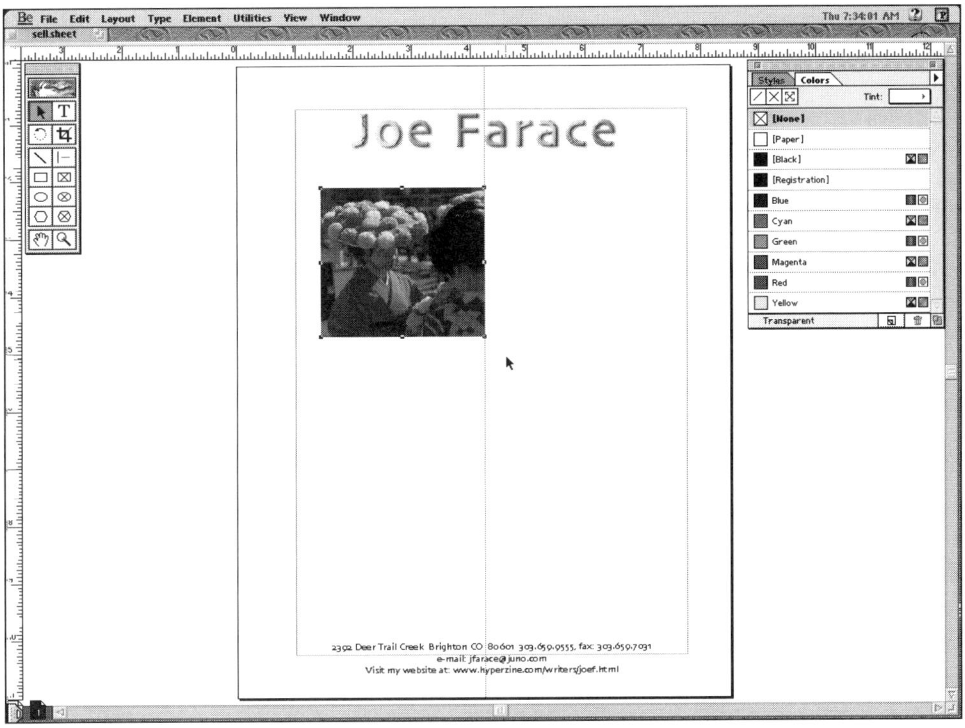

Figure 3.11 The stock image is now part of the desktop publishing document. Photo © Joe Farace.

selecting the image. This step brings up handles that allow the image to be resized. Holding the Shift key while resizing an image allows that image to retain its original ratio while it's being resized. For this example, I created seven images, but only placed six.

For some photographs, I use PageMaker's line tools to draw a box in a contrasting color, usually red, around them, but I don't do it to the larger images. Why? Because I don't think it looks good that way. But there are few, if any, rules in design, and the best thing to do is to try different effects to come up with what you think might look good. If it does not, use the Undo tool to remove it.

Step 7. When I printed my first promo piece, I pasted the photographs onto a plain white background, and although it looked nice, something was obviously missing. I thought about adding color, but I did not want to use a color so that it would compete with the colors in the photographs, so I decided to use a grayscale photograph as the background. Since the photographs on this new piece were travel related, I selected an image that was a photograph of clouds. While I could have gone outside and photographed the clouds in the Colorado skies, I instead used a disk of textures produced by Letraset called Background and Borders, which contains grayscale

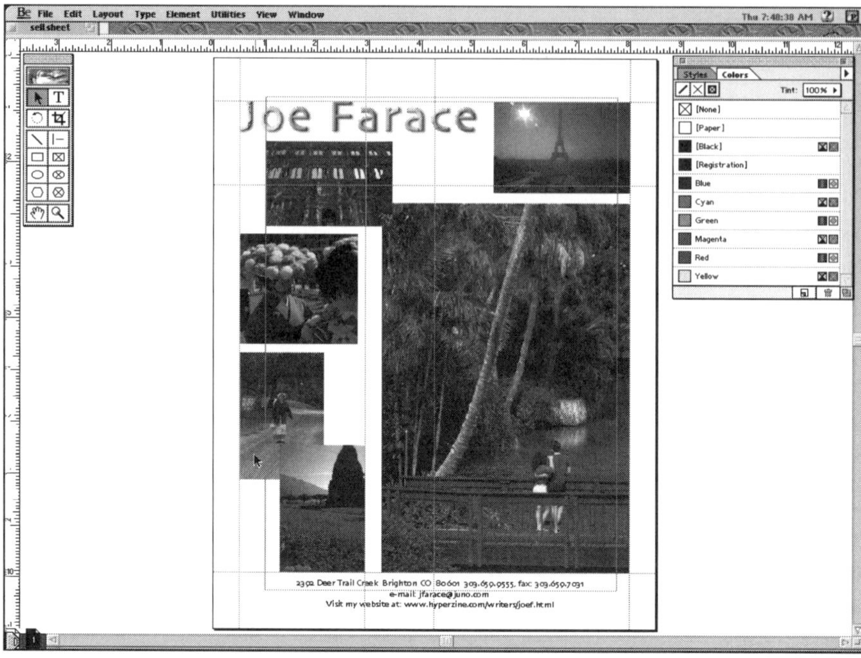

Figure 3.12 There are no rules for placing images on sell sheets. Place them and resize them according to the overall design of the piece, or the importance of certain topics to your target market. Photos © Joe Farace.

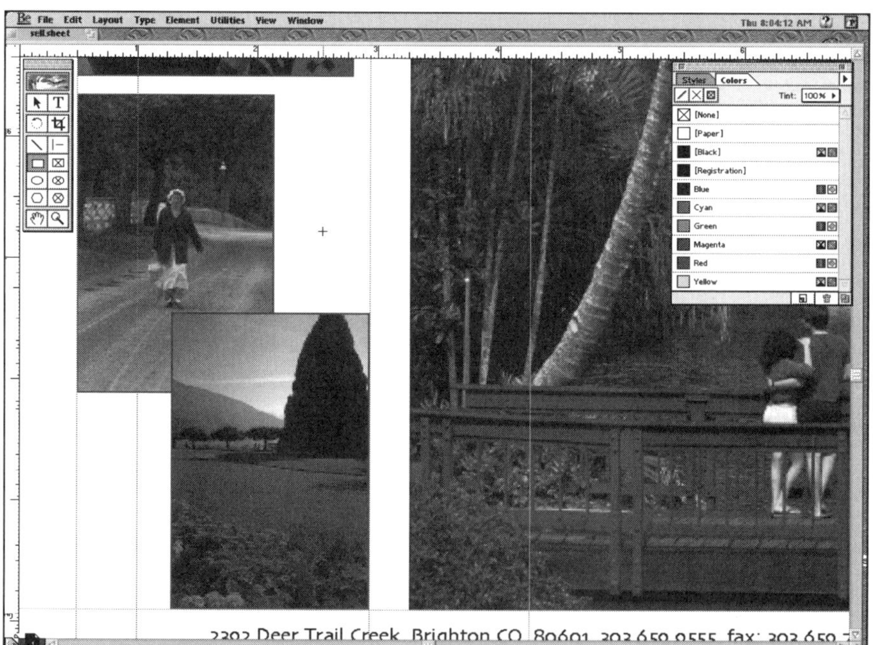

Figure 3.13 The best way to draw borders around photographs is to view the images at 2X and 4X the normal screen view. This will make it possible to see the real edges of the images so that no gaps appear. Photos © Joe Farace.

TIP: Making Photographs into Backgrounds

All of the rules that apply to good photographs work exactly the opposite when you want to turn an image into a background. In the above example, I wanted the focus to stay on the colorful photographs. After opening a color stock digital photograph of white clouds against a blue sky background with Adobe Photoshop, I used the Mode command to turn the photograph into a black-and-white. I reduced the sharpness of the photograph by repeatedly applying both Photoshop's Blur then the Blur More commands to soften the image even more. In the final step, I used Photoshop's Brightness and Contrast controls the opposite way that I normally use them. I gradually added more brightness while simultaneously lowering the image's contrast to create a soft, flat look—exactly the opposite of the kind of brightly colored photographs that would be placed on top of the background.

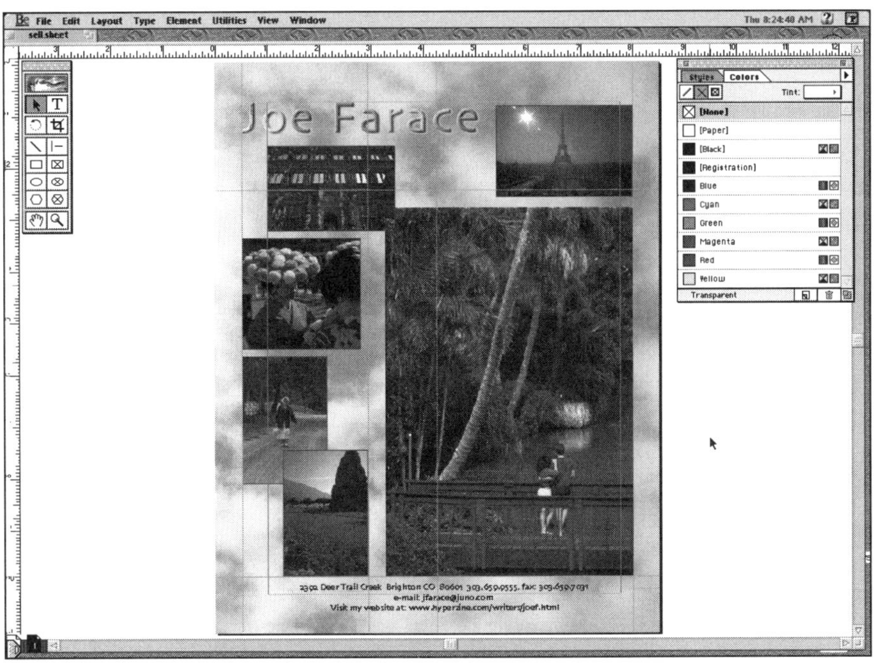

Figure 3.14 With the cloud background pasted in, the sell sheet is ready to be printed. Total time to create it from start to finish—less than two hours.
Photos © Joe Farace.

TIFF and JPEG images of many different textures. I pasted the "Clouds" TIFF image on top of my promo piece, and used PageMaker's Send to Back command to place it on the background. Now, the brightly colored photographs popped off the background and the colors seemed more intense than when they were displayed on a plain background. (See Figure 3.14.)

4

Working with Layers, Floaters, and Channels

> *While there may be some doubt as to where the computer revolution may be heading, one thing is for certain. Whenever we get there, we won't have enough RAM.*
>
> DAVE BARRY

If all you create are single, traditional images, you do not really need to know how the Layers function of image editing programs work. If, on the other hand, you want to create images that combines graphics, text, and other photographs, a knowledge of using Layers is indispensable.

UNDERSTANDING LAYERS

Images in Adobe Photoshop, and other image editing programs, can be composed of many parts. The base of a Photoshop document is its background, which you can think of as the paper used in a conventional "wet" darkroom technology. Layers are like additional emulsions on the surface of that paper that allow you to create effects without interfering with what is on the other coatings. Layers are a powerful tool that let you create dramatic dimensional images and can be found on other professional editing programs as well.

One of the easiest ways to understand the layers function is to imagine an image that has sheets of clear acetate stacked on top one another. Any kind of image—text, graphics, or photograph—can be placed on a layer. Where there is no image on a layer, you can see through it to the layers below the clear areas. At the bottom of the stack of layers is the background. In Photoshop, there are restrictions in what aspects that layers must share. (Later, when looking at how Live Picture creates composite images, you will see that this product has overcome some of these limitations.)

The advantages of using any program's layers function is that you can manipulate part of the completed image without affecting any of the other parts. This can be as simple as adjusting color, or it can include manipulation, such as the addition of a drop shadow. Version 4.0 of Photoshop added a new kind of layer, called an adjustment layer, which allows you to apply tonal and color corrections to all of the layers underneath it. This will let you try different combinations of how layers react with one another, and when you achieve the desired result on-screen, you can merge the adjusted layers.

The Layers Palette

In Adobe Photoshop, one of the tools that helps you work with—and navigate through—layers is the Layers Palette. It features a visible display of all of the layers in an image starting from the topmost to the background. The Layers Palette is used to create, hide, display, copy, merge, and delete layers from a document. Photoshop allows you to create up to 100 layers for each image, but the actual number of layers you can create is limited to how much memory is installed in your computer. You can create new layers by using the New Layer button that is at the bottom of the Layers palette, or simply by dragging and pasting a selection into your image. If you have a problem, such as a difference in resolution, Photoshop will prompt you as to what the problem is and how to fix it. You can also copy layers between two open Photoshop images. Layers can be added by using the New Layer button at the bottom of the palette or the New Layer command, which can be found by clicking on the black triangle in the upper right-hand corner of the palette. (See Figure 4.1 on CD-ROM.)

Adjustment Layers

Photoshop's Adjustment Layers allows users to have the ability to perform color adjustments without affecting the original image's data. This allows you to experiment with different adjustments, such as hue and saturation, brightness and contrast, and overall color balance, and gives you the option to undo or refine adjustments later. Adjustment Layers allows for color correction via a mask (more on masking later in the book) through which an image adjustment can be applied. An adjustment layer does not make permanent changes to the underlying image pixels and can be modified any number of times without degrading image quality. Adjustment Layers can be hidden or discarded at any time, or moved up and down in the Layers palette. (Layers is another powerful tool that will be covered later.) They can also be applied with the same opacity and blending mode controls used for image layers. The following image commands can be applied with an adjustment layer: Levels, Curves, Color Balance, Brightness/Contrast, Hue/Saturation, Selective Color, Invert, Threshold, and Posterize.

Adjustment Layers can be a powerful tool because they let you experiment with color or tonal adjustments to an image without permanently modifying that image. All of your changes or adjustments are made to the layer that acts as an overlay through which the underlying image will appear. Here, let me show how to create an adjustment layer.

Step 1. As in all Photoshop operations, this one starts with opening an image. This is a Photo CD scan that was opened with Kodak's Photo CD Acquire Module. If you want to edit a selection of the image, make a selection using any of Photoshop's selection tools.

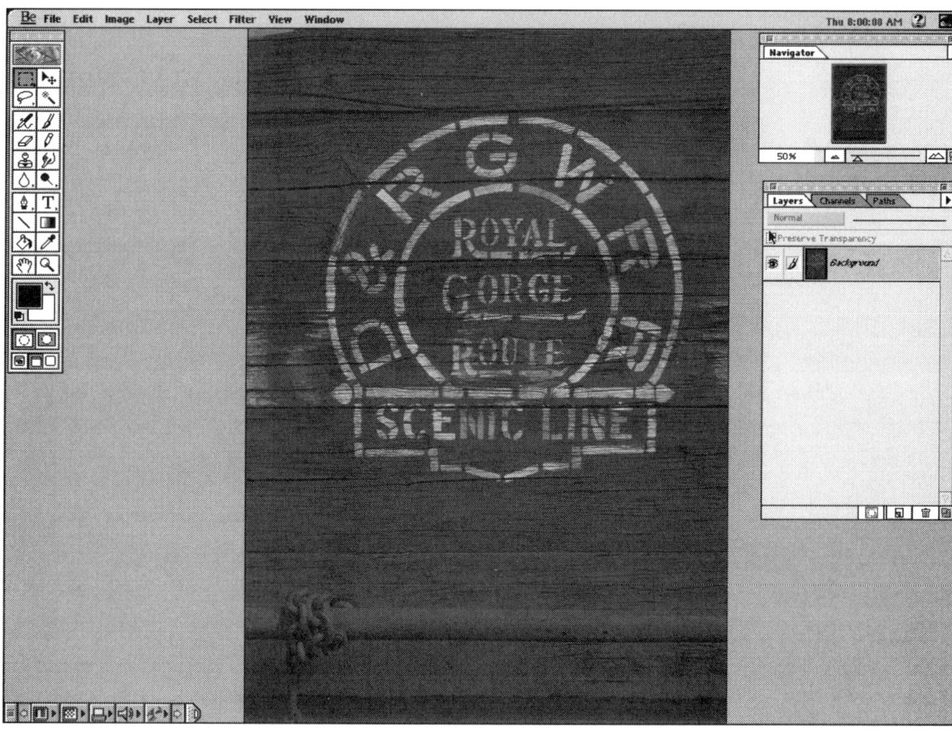

Figure 4.2 The process starts with opening an image. This Photo CD scan was opened using Kodak's Photo CD Acquire Module plug-in. Photo © Joe Farace.

Step 2. Creating an Adjustment Layer is as simple as going to Photoshop's Layers palette, clicking on the pop-up menu, and choosing New Adjustment Layer. (See Figure 4.3.)

Step 3. When you choose New Adjustment Layer, an Adjustment Layer dialog box opens giving you the option of naming this particular layer. Since names are so much easier to remember than "Layer 1," I called this layer "boxcar." (See Figure 4.4.)

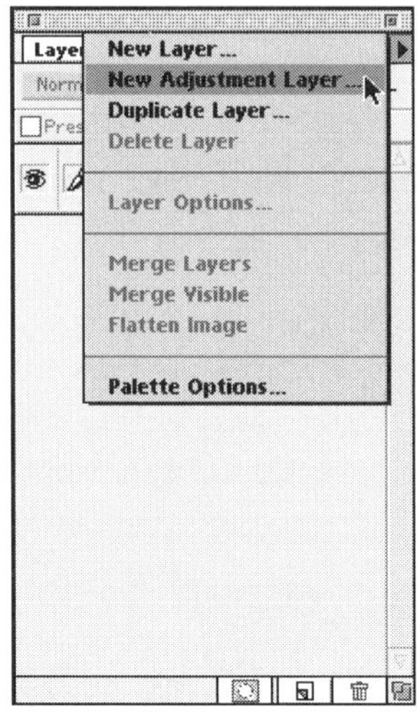

Figure 4.3 The New Adjustment Layer is found in Photoshop's Layers pop-up menu.

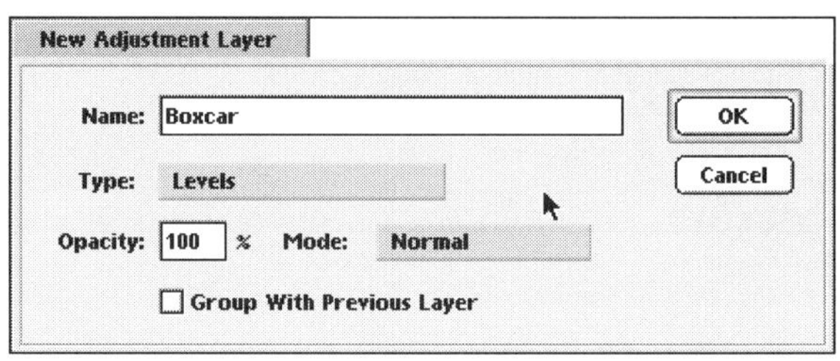

Figure 4.4 The Adjustment Layer dialog box lets you name the layer and choose what kind of adjustment you want to make.

Step 4. The next dialog that you see is one that might remind photographers of an H&D Curve. This dialog allows you to adjust the brightness and contrast of an image using Layers—and since only the layer is affected, the original image is untouched. The Input sliders are under the curve and there are three controls: Shadows (the black triangle), Midtones (the gray triangle), and Highlights (the white triangle). To add sparkle to the highlights—and increase overall contrast—move the Highlights slider to the left. When you do, the Midtones come along. To darken shadows, move the Shadow slider control to the right. To tweak the overall photograph, use the Midtones slider. (See Figure 4.5.)

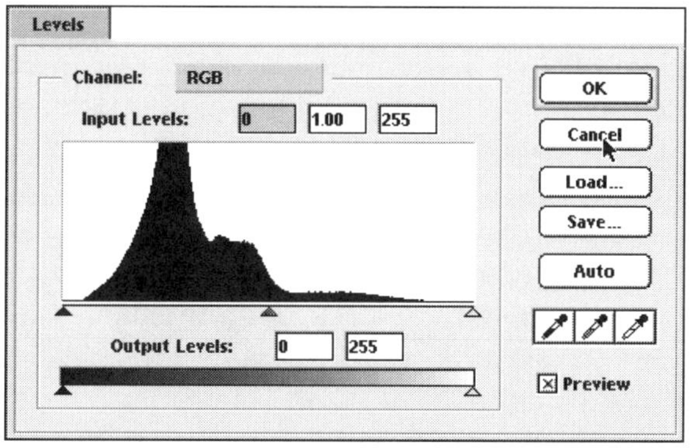

Figure 4.5 The last dialog you see after creating an Adjustment Layer is the Levels dialog, which allows you to adjust an images' brightness and contrast by manipulating the newly created layer.

METACREATIONS' PAINTER

One look at the Painter combination of tools, palettes, and the subpalettes that MetaCreations calls "drawers," and you will know you are in for something different. Painter has some of the features of Adobe Photoshop, including layers as well as selection and correction tools, but the program also lets users work with brush strokes resembling those created with traditional media.

The current version includes several new technologies including Shapes, which permits seamless blending of raster and vector imagery. Shapes creates vector objects that can be modified using the kind of Bezier editing tools that are found in drawing and illustration programs, like Adobe Illustrator and Macromedia Freehand. Unlike traditional illustration software, the vector objects in Painter are anti-aliased, and they can be made semitransparent or given bitmap compositing. These objects can easily be converted to bitmap "floaters" (Fractal's term for layers) and painted on.

Painter 5.0's expandable Plug-in Brushes and Dynamic Plug-in Floaters provide an extensible architecture. Dynamic Plug-in Floaters create layers with outrageous special effects. Unlike traditional image layers that let you collage static image elements, Dynamic Plug-in Floaters perform image-processing effects (like burning and tearing) that update automatically. They can also create new objects like a liquid metal painting layer. Painter's Dynamic Floaters can be moved, changed, and reapplied without altering the original source material. The Liquid Metal Dynamic Plug-in Floater lets you work with metallic paint that shines and reflects the environment. Turn off the reflection mapping, and the layer looks like pools of water that refract the canvas image. Each drop is an object so it can be moved independently. And each drop flows and clings to each other, with surface tension, like real liquid. Imagine painting with Mercury.

Glass Distortion and Kaleidoscope create floating lenses that distort underlying layers. When you move the lens to a new area of the canvas, it updates automatically—just like moving a piece of glass over your painting. Burn and Tear let you singe or tear the edge of a floater. Just dial in the amount you want and Painter calculates the effect. It never destroys the original. At any time you can redial the value to change the look. There is even a collection of Dynamic Floaters that perform the functions of Photoshop 4.0's Adjustment Layers.

Painter 5.0 has more than 100 new Plug-in brushes. The Scratch Remover Brush makes your dirty scans look great. The Hue Brush lets you recolor and tint your photographs. The Gooey Brushes turn images into liquid pools, allowing you to stretch, pinch, pull, twist, and bulge. The Super-Cloners let you transform an image into a hand-rendered painting, as well as let you scale, twist, skew, and mirror at the same time. The Super F/X brushes paint with fire and neon, adding glow to your canvas. The new Layer Brushes let you create and paint on transparent layers, just like painting on a sheet of glass that overlays your canvas.

Painter also has something you have never seen in any image editing program: the Image Hose, which allows computer artists to paint with sets of objects. Instead of color, a "hose" lets you spray elements in a random or structured fashion to create beautiful, complex imagery. MetaCreations even created an optional CD-ROM called "Garden Hose" that includes "hoses" full of flowers and plants. Painter 4 ships on a CD-ROM that includes more than 200 new patterns, more than 60 Image Hose nozzles, more than 100 paper textures, and dozens of selection paths, color sets, interface sets, and technical notes.

No two artists work in the same way. Painter 5.0 lets you customize your palettes to suit your personal style. Brushes, Art Materials, and menu items can be torn-off and placed on custom palettes. Build palettes that hold just the tools you use most frequently, or create custom palettes for a particular project. A new Crop tool, redesigned Magic Wand, and improved Paint Bucket makes editing easier. Customizable function keys, keyboard entry of slider values, and the ability to save and restore palette locations, all make working with Painter easier, faster, and more accurate. Painter supports your favorite plug-in effects like MetaTools KPT, but includes a few of their own.

Painter users can also import artwork created in Illustrator 5.0 format—which is written by both Macromedia Freehand and Adobe Illustrator—and add texture and transparency using Shapes. The Shapes feature lets users combine raster and vector imagery in unique ways, using floating selections created in Photoshop and Painter with vector-based artwork created in Illustrator and Freehand, to develop object-oriented artwork that does not look like it was created on a computer. Painter 5.0 reads and writes Photoshop 4.0 files, preserving layers, channels, and paths, which makes the work flow more efficient than ever.

Painter may have a slightly steeper learning curve than some of the other programs in this book, but in the hands of a photographic artist, it can be used to create stunning photographic images.

System Requirements

The system requirements for MetaCreations' Painter are Mac OS: PowerPC only, Macintosh (68K not supported), System 7.5 or later, 12MB of application RAM (20+ MB recommended), Color Display (25-bit recommended), and CD-ROM drive.

Windows: 486DX, Pentium or Pentium Pro-compatible PC, Windows 95 or Windows NT 4.0 (Windows 3.1 not supported), 16MB System RAM (32MB for Windows NT), SVGA Video (25-bit recommended) and CD-ROM drive are also required.

MAKING A MOSAIC

One of Painter's most interesting tools is the Mosaic brush, which lets you create realistic mosaic effects by painting with "tiles" on a blank canvas or over a scanned photograph. Each tile is an independent object that "knows" about every other tile and modifies its shape so it fits perfectly with already existing tiles. Both tiles and grouting can be erased and reshaped to create the perfect mosaic design. Painter also permits the use of multiple floating selections that saves users from having to save different versions of their work when producing complex effects.

Here's how to use the program to turn one of your own photographs into "tiles." In this example, I used a color slide of a picnic table umbrella taken in Vail, Colorado that was digitized onto a Kodak Photo CD. My reason for selecting this image is that I thought its abstract colors would create a "stained glass" look. Although this example works with an abstract subject matter, John Blake has used it with realistic subjects as well.

Step 1. Since Painter accepts Photoshop-compatible plug-ins, I used the Acquire menu to open the Photo CD image. (See Figure 4.6.)

Step 2. Next, I cropped the image using Painter's Crop Tool, which works much like Photoshop's used to—before version 4.0. I cropped off the black border that is inevitable in Photo CD scans

Mosaic Tip #1

Painter lets you set preferences that specify where the program looks for plug-ins. This saves you from having to duplicate or copy all of your plug-ins, thereby saving hard disk space. After Installing Painter, I specified the "Plug-in" folder inside my Adobe Photoshop folder (directory), giving the program access to all of the import, export, and filter effects that I use in Photoshop.

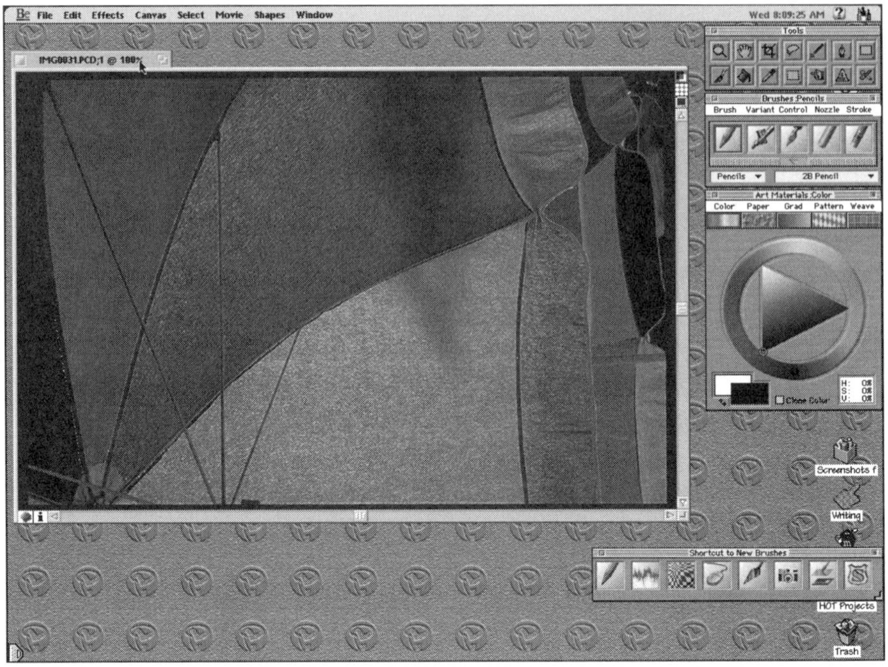

Figure 4.6 The first step to creating a Mosaic is opening up the image. As you can see, the Painter interface is dramatically different from other image editing programs. Photo © Joe Farace.

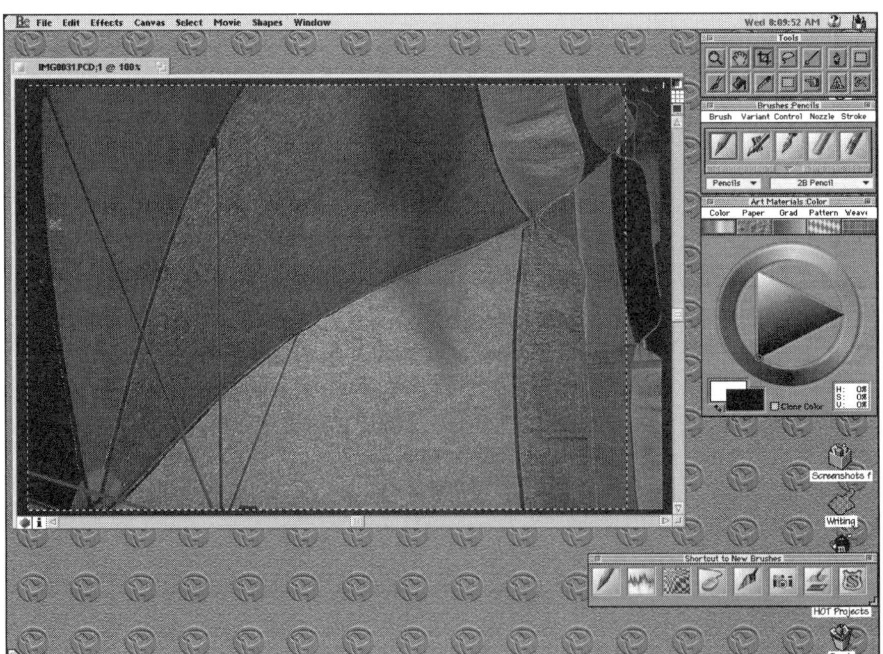

Figure 4.7 Painter's Crop tool was used to crop the black border and simplify the image's composition. Photo © Joe Farace.

Mosaic Tip #2

For your first mosaic effect, you can leave the defaults where they are, or you might try setting the Width and the Height at 11, the setting at "Randomness," and the "Cut" to 36. Leave the Make Mosaic dialog box open so that you can toggle the tracing paper option off and on. I also suggest you wait until you are almost finished making the mosaic to choose the actual grout color you will use.

of slides. To keep the image simpler and help achieve the "stained glass" look I wanted, I cropped some of the excess detail on the right-hand side of the image. (See Figure 4.7.)

Step 3. Next, chose Clone from the File menu. This creates a duplicate (clone) file of the original image with the title "Clone of IMG031."

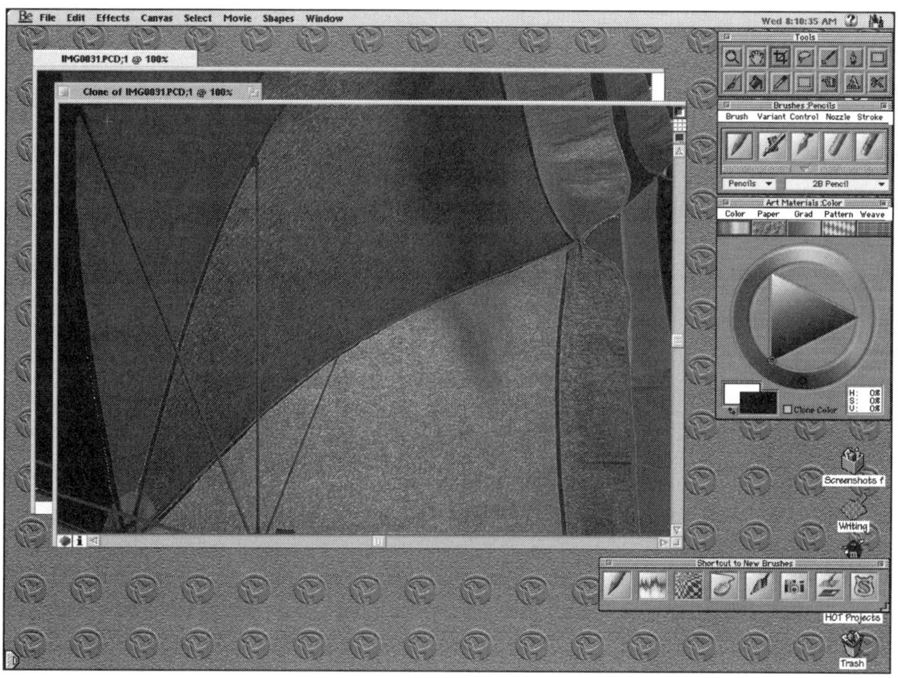

Figure 4.8 Choosing Clone from the file menu created a duplicate copy of the original image. Photo © Joe Farace.

Step 4. Then I chose Make Mosaic from the Canvas menu. This brings up the Make Mosaic dialog, which allows you to set grout color as well as its width and length. Leave the defaults where they are, for now, but be sure to check the "Use Tracing Paper" box. When you do, you will see a ghost image of your original (or source) file showing through the "tracing paper." (See Figure 4.9.)

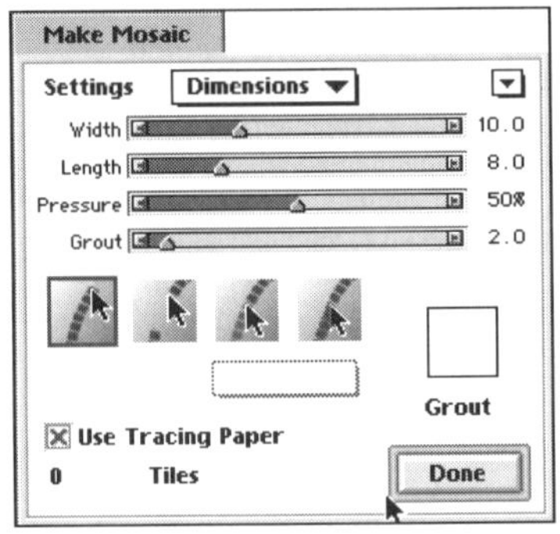

Figure 4.9 The Make Mosaic dialog box controls all of the aspects from tile shape to grout in the mosaic process.

Step 5. Click Use Clone Color in Color Palette. This allows the Mosaic tool to use the colors that are in the cloned image.

Step 6. The best place to start making tiles is by creating an outline of the major shapes in the image. If you are the kind of person, who used to outline the pictures in their coloring books, this will come

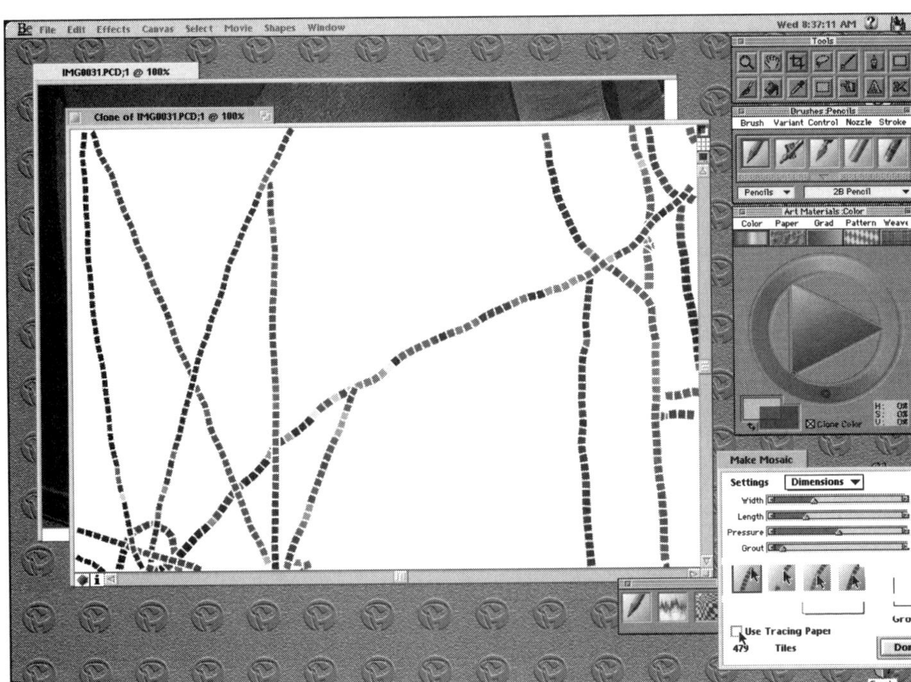

Figure 4.10 To check your progress, turn the Use Tracing Paper off and on during the process. Photo © Joe Farace.

Mosaic Tip #3

You may have to click the "grow box" in the upper right-hand corner to see another set of color controls that includes the Use Clone Color checkbox.

naturally to you. Carefully outline the outside of all the major shapes in the photograph. This can be done with a mouse, but using a drawing tablet and stylus (see Chapter 7 for more information) will be more comfortable for most people. To see how you are doing with your tile laying, toggle between the Use Tracing Paper checkbox on the Make Mosaic dialog.

Step 7. Fill in the outlines. When filling in the outlines, think about how the rows of tiles fit together. As you lay in a new course of tiles, try to overlap the previous course just a little. This will ensure that there are no gaps between courses. If you accidentally leave too much space, go back and create a new course to cover the gap. When you are finished, experiment with different grout colors. I tried everything from white to black—Painter allows you to make these changes without affecting anything that you have

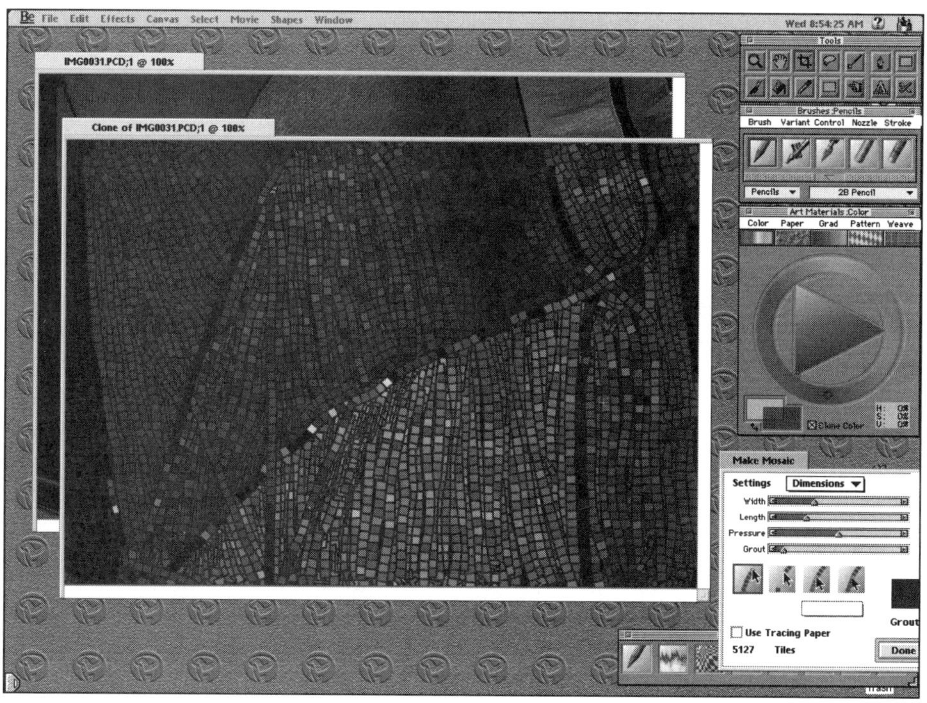

Figure 4.11 Experimenting with the grout color allowed the author to find the look he wanted for the final image. Photo © Joe Faracc.

done up to that point. I settled on a dark gray—almost black—because it gave the stained glass look I was after.

Step 8. When you have finished, you might want to render the image at a higher resolution to improve on-page image quality. Start by choosing Resize from the Canvas menu and select Re-render Mosaic. This allows you to resize the image by doubling the pixel values you see in the dialog. When you have finished, click OK. (See Figure 4.12 on CD-ROM.)

FLOATERS

MetaCreations' Painter uses a layer-like concept called "floaters." They define a floater as an image—or portion of an image—that floats above the canvas (background) that you are working on. You can copy and move floaters around the document to create the composition that you want. A floater is actually a separate image, so every floater added to a document introduces another layer of information. Because they are independent, you can also work on the background image without affecting the floaters.

Painter uses three different kinds of floaters. Each type has some characteristics in common with the others, but differs in how you create it and what you can use it to accomplish.

Shapes. These floaters are vector-based objects, which makes them the ideal tool to create text. Therefore, Shapes do not contain any pixel information. Shapes have controls for adjusting their outline's paths; you can create shape paths, then convert them to your selection.

Image. This kind of floater is a discrete image that can float above the background image. Unlike Shaper, these floaters are stored as pixel information and have a mask (more on masking in Chapter 5) to define the shape and opacity. You can paint and apply effects to image floaters.

Reference. These floaters are temporary, low-resolution versions of image floaters. You convert an image floater into a reference type when you want to transform it by dragging its handles. After you have finished making the changes you can covert it back into an image floater.

When using the RIFF (Resource Interchange File Format) format that Painter prefers, floaters stay floating even after a file has been saved, which allows you to make changes later on if you want. If you save in another format, all of the floaters in the document are composited onto it; further changes to floating elements are not be possible if you save in Adobe Photoshop 3.0 format.

Floater Tip

You can change a floater's name by double-clicking it in the F.List palette. When you do, you will see an Attributes dialog. All you have to do is type a descriptive name, then click OK.

However, floaters will be assigned to appropriate image layers, making it easy to coordinate work with both programs in your toolkit.

The Floater List

Since you need a place to keep track of your floaters, Painter's interface provides a list that also has features to control them. To open the Floater List palette, click the F.List icon on the Objects Palette. It lists all of the floaters in the current document, with any selected floater highlighted and shown in bold type. If there are no floaters selected, everything on the list appears in plain type. The floater list is arranged according to the layers, with the higher layers on the top. Painter even assigns different icons to each floater type. (See Figure 4.13 on CD-ROM.)

Drop Shadows Using Floaters

One of Painter's many advantages is that it can create an effect in a few steps what in other image editing programs needs many steps. Take adding a drop shadow, for example. In the last chapter, I showed one way to create a drop shadow in Adobe Photoshop. Here's a way to create a similar effect in Painter.

Step 1. I opened a file containing a photograph of a flower. The image was from MetaCreations Power Photos IV stock photo disc. Then I converted it to a floater by selecting the flower (not the background) and choosing Float from the Edit menu. This makes the flower appear as an item on the F.List palette. (See Figure 4.14.)

Step 2. The next—and last step—is to choose Create Drop Shadow from the Effects/Objects menu. This causes the Drop Shadow Dialog box to appear. The menu lets you control the offset of the shadow, its opacity, and its softness. In most cases, soft shadows look better than hard-edged ones. The way Painter accomplishes the softness is by applying a Motion Blur filter to the edges, but this all happens at once. (See Figure 4.15.)

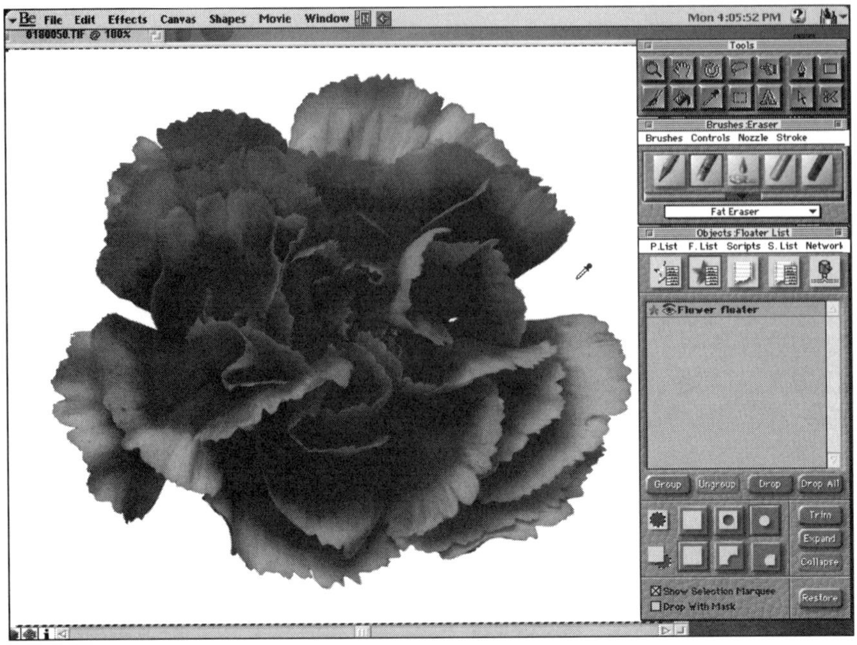

Figure 4.14 This flower from MetaCreations Power Photos IV stock photo disc was opened and converted into a floater using the Float command. Photo courtesy MetaCreations.

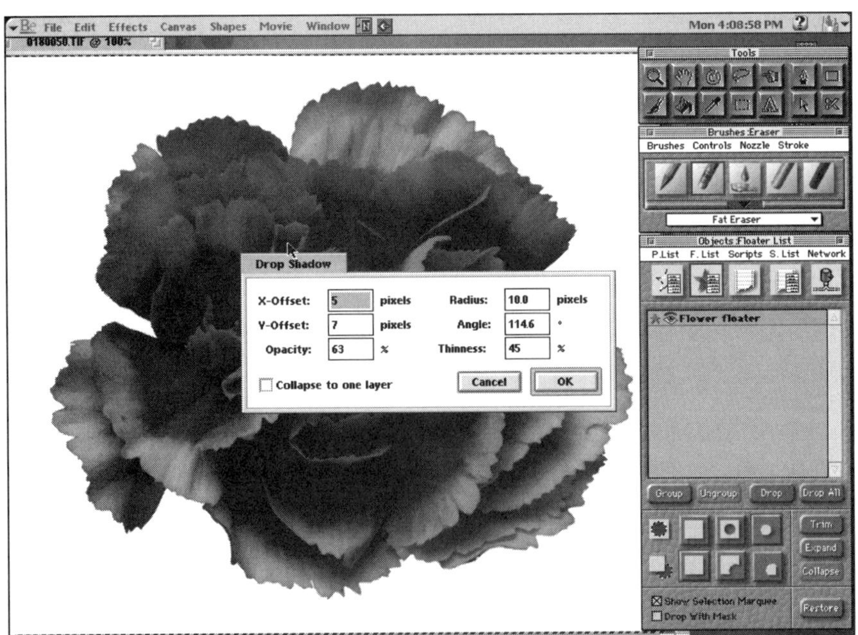

Figure 4.15 Painter's Drop Shadow dialog lets you control the offset and distance the shadow is from a floater, along with its opacity.

TIP: CIELAB Color

This color system was created by the Committee Internationale d'Eclairage to produce a color space that consists of all visible colors. The CIELAB system, sometimes shortened to just LAB, forms the basis for most contemporary color-matching systems. It lets you convert, for example, RGB images to LAB to CMYK to produce accurate color matching, because it offers the largest possible color gamut and is the only format delivering device independent color.

Step 3. You're done! That's all there is to creating a drop shadow effect with Painter using floaters. Notice that the description of the floater in the F.List palette is automatically appended to read "and shadow."

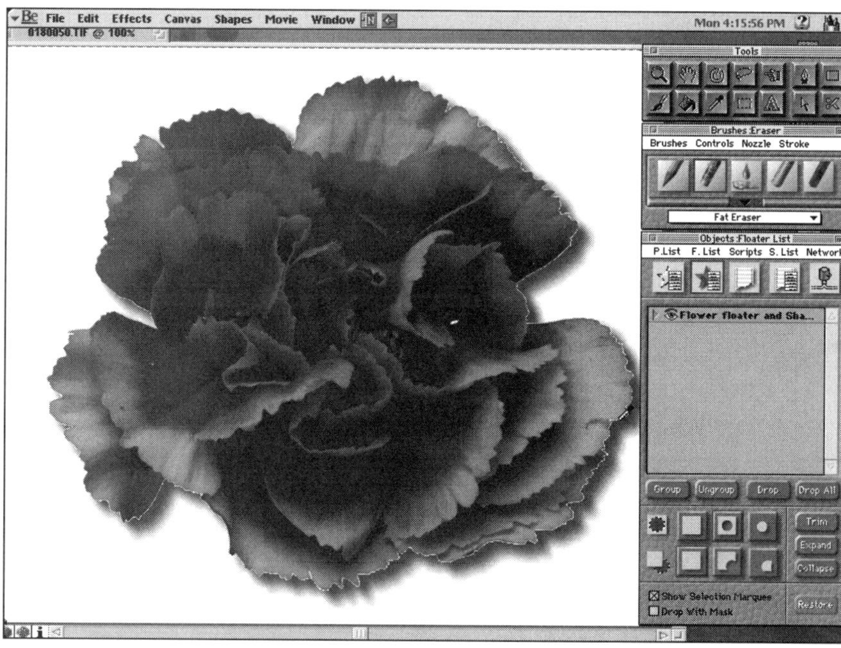

Figure 4.16 Creating a drop shadow with a floater, as you will discover, takes less time to do than it does to read about it—and the effect is attractive.
Photo courtesy of MetaCreations.

CHANGING CHANNELS

Every Photoshop image contains one or more channels, which contain information about all of the color elements in the image. A CMYK image, for example, has at least four channels, one each for cyan, magenta, yellow, and black. One way of thinking about Photoshop channels is to think of each one as a separate plate used in the four-color printing process—in that each color is applied by a different plate. As we will see in the next chapter, channels may be added for storing and editing masks. These extra channels are sometimes called alpha channels.

Theoretically, an image can have up to twenty-four channels. Bitmap, grayscale, duotone, and indexed color (like GIF) images have only one color. RGB and LAB mode images contain three channels—one each for red, blue, and green. CMYK images have four. You can add channels to all of these image types with the exception of bitmap images.

One of the fun effects you can create with channels is a colored mezzotint feature. While experienced Photoshoppers may want to try the program's built-in Mezzotint filter, the creative possibilities are wider using techniques like this.

Step 1. Using Adobe Photoshop, I opened a stock photo from PhotoSphere using the Photo CD Acquire module. The Channels palette shows the RGB channel plus the red, blue, green components of the image as grayscale photographs.

Step 2. In the nest step, split the image into separate documents using the Split Channels command that is found in Adobe Photoshop's Channels palette. (See Figure 4.18.)

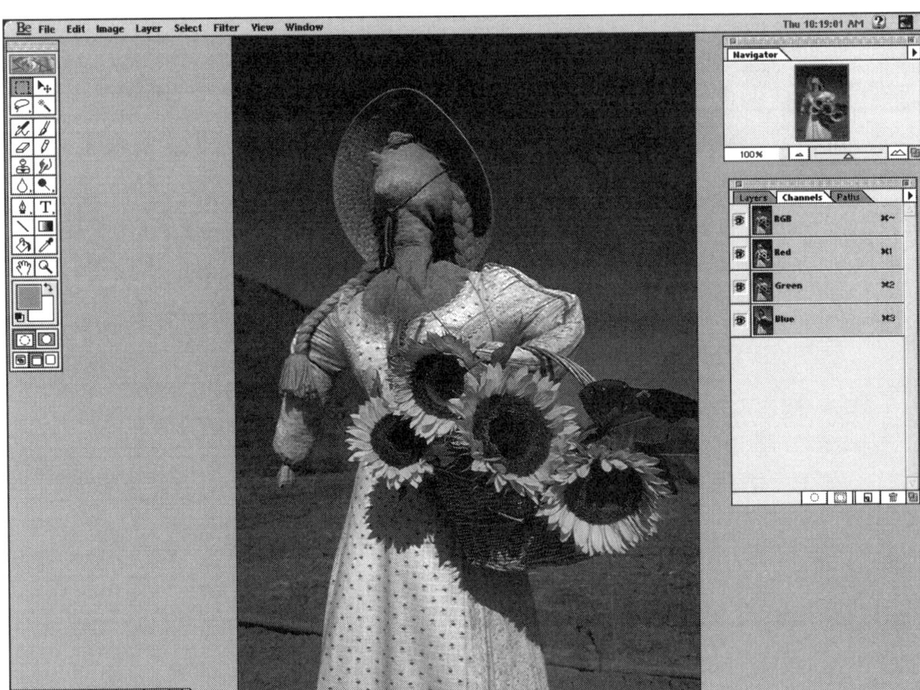

Figure 4.17 The starting image is shown alongside Adobe Photoshop's Channels palette. Photograph © PhotoSphere Images Ltd.

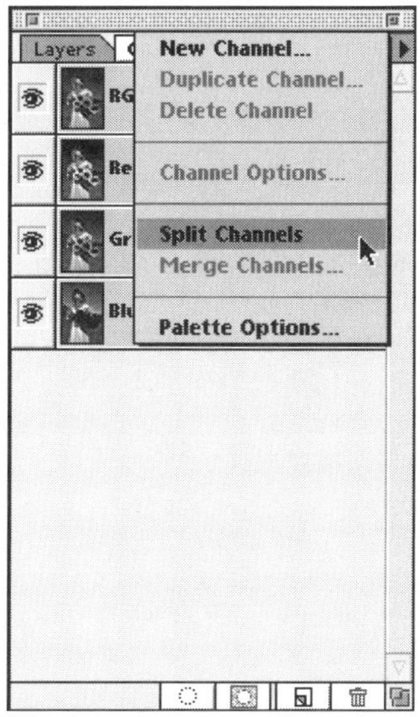

Figure 4.18 Split the image into separate documents using the Split Channels command in Adobe Photoshop's Channels palette.

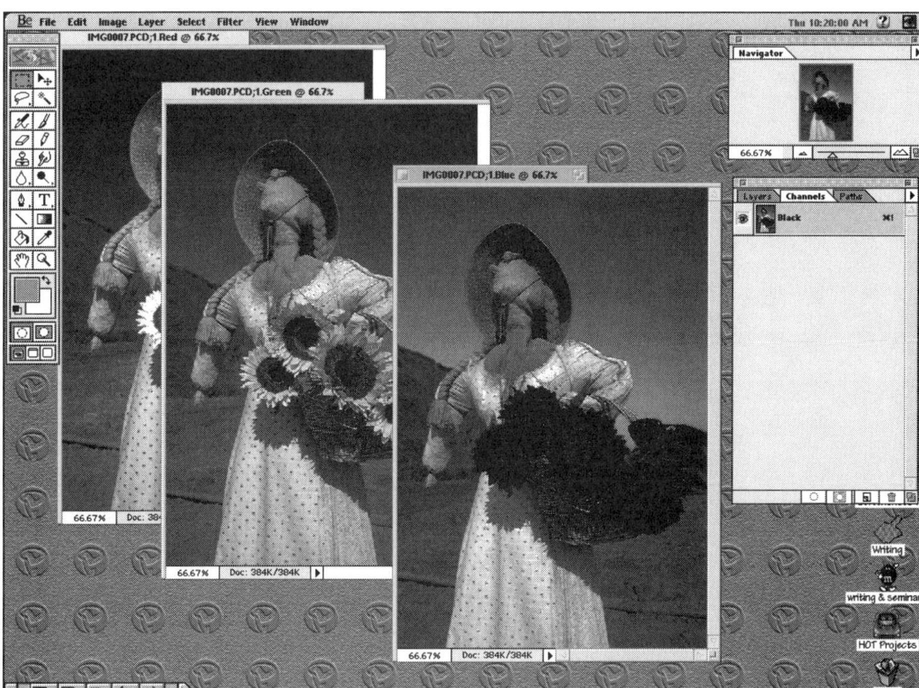

Figure 4.19 After splitting the documents into three parts, your workspace will look like this. Photograph © PhotoSphere Images Ltd.

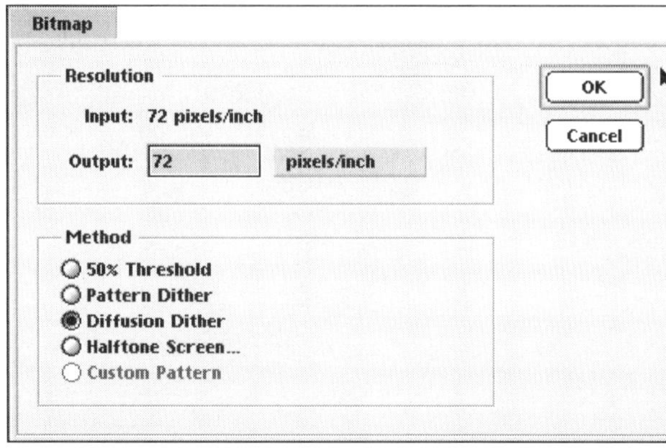

Figure 4.20 When converting the split files into Bitmap images, you will see this dialog that allows you to specify the method of dithering that the image will use.

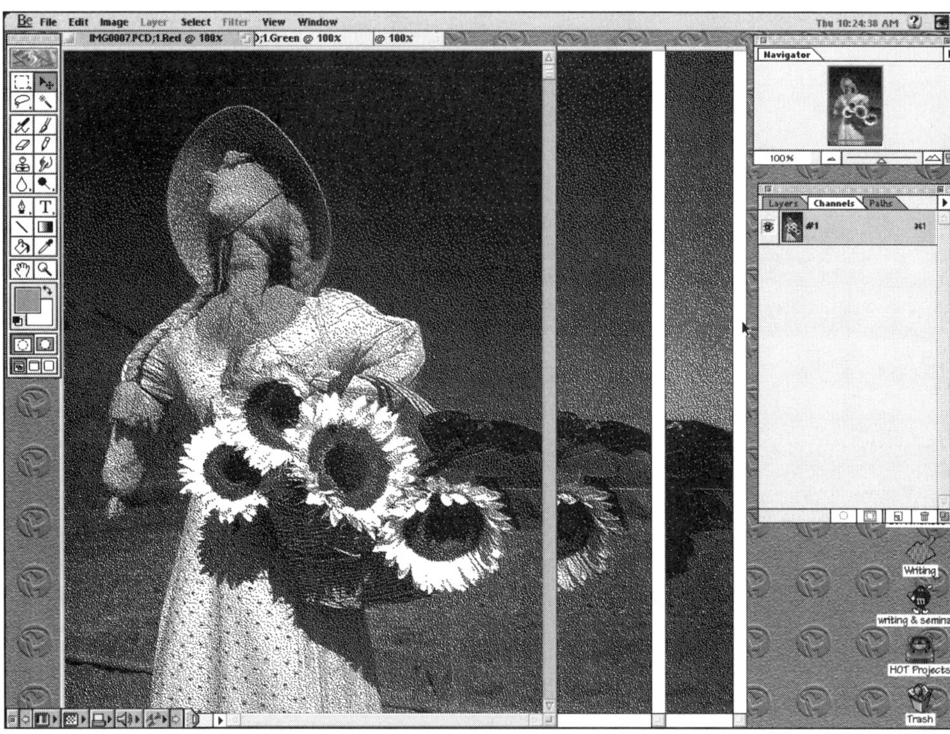

Figure 4.21 After converting the images into Bitmap, this is what they will look like.
Photograph © PhotoSphere Images Ltd.

Step 3. Next, convert the split images into Bitmap files by using the Mode Menu. The Bitmap dialog box gives you a choice of several different dithering methods. For this example, I used "Diffusion Dither," but feel free to experiment with the method used.

Step 4. Using the Mode menu again, convert each split image into a grayscale file. Then, use the Merge Channels command in the Channels palette to produce the final result. (See Figure 4.22 on CD-ROM.)

There is much more to channels than this. In the next chapter, you will see how channels can be used to store and edit selections, which can be used as masks.

CASE STUDY: DIGITAL BROMOIL

One of the favorite darkroom techniques of Pictorialists, like the late Edward L. Bafford, was the bromoil print. This conventional process starts with the creation of a black-and-white print using traditional darkroom methods, with the image typically printed on a textured paper like Kodak's Portrait Proof Mural paper. The print was then treated with a "tanning" solution that bleached the image almost to the point of invisibility and hardened the gelatin on the print in proportion to the depth of silver that was deposited. Every bromoil practitioner seemed to have their own proprietary formula for their home-brew tanning chemistry. After fixing and drying, the tanned print was hand-brushed with a boar's-hair paint brush using oil-based ink. During this process, the hardened portions of the emulsion accept more ink, while the other softer areas accepted less ink. This feature allowed the bromoil maker to eliminate distracting elements, and even add compositional elements, while stroking with their ink-filled brushes. The finished print exhibited artist-like brush strokes, and some photographers, like Bill Mortensen, even toned their bromoil prints to give them a cooler or warmer appearances.

I had an idea of trying to create a similar effect using only the standard digital tools found in Adobe Photoshop 4.0.

The Hunchback of Notre Dame

Like most of the images you will see in this book, "The Hunchback" had a practical purpose. During 1996, I produced a series of quarterly client mailings that featured black-and-white images made in various world capitols. The first mailing was Washington, D.C., and the focus of the second was to be Paris. For this mailing, I selected an image that I had photographed outside the Cathedral of Notre Dame featuring street players in costumes related to Victor Hugo's tale of the hunchback. The original image was photographed with a Nikon FM2 and 44-86mm lens using Kodak Ektachrome film and was digitized using Kodak's Photo CD process. The image of the hunchback seemed like the kind of classic story-telling photograph that Bill Mortensen would have made, and it inspired me to digitally try to apply some of his darkroom techniques. It's at this point we pick up the story.

Step 1. Using Adobe Photoshop 4.0 and Kodak's Photo CD Acquire Module plug-in, I opened the color image as a black-and-white photograph. Since I was going to convert it to black-and-white anyway, opening the image that way automatically cut the image size by one-third and made the Open process go faster.

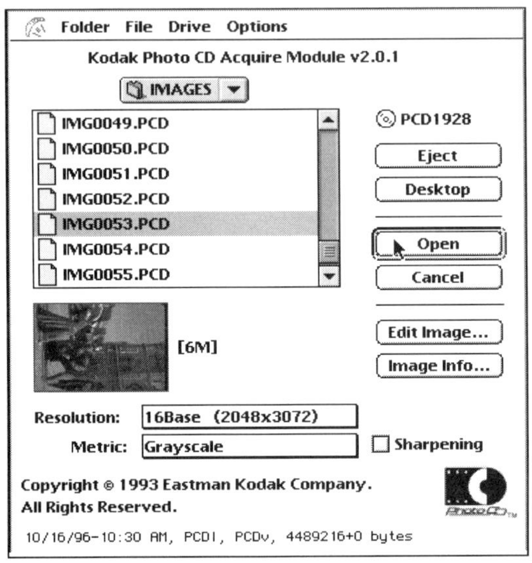

Figure 4.23 Kodak's Photo CD Acquire plug-in was used to import the 2,048 × 3,072 pixel image and automatically converted the image into grayscale. Photo © Joe Farace.

Step 2. Since vertical (portrait) Photo CD photographs are typically imported as horizontal images, I used Photoshop's Rotate command to properly orient the image from horizontal (landscape). (See Figure 4.24.)

Step 3. Photo CD images, especially from 35mm slides, tend to have some black areas surrounding the image, so I used Photoshop's Crop tool to remove most of this extraneous data. Since I ultimately planned to modify the edges of the print, this is an optional step. In this example, I did not have to crop all of the black area out. You'll see why, when I get to the final steps. (See Figure 4.25.)

Step 4. All Photo CD scans need to be sharpened, so the next thing I typically do is sharpen the images—something not possible with conventional darkroom techniques. Photoshop provides a Sharpen menu and Sharpen command, but I suggest you use Unsharp Mask instead. This command includes a preview window that allows

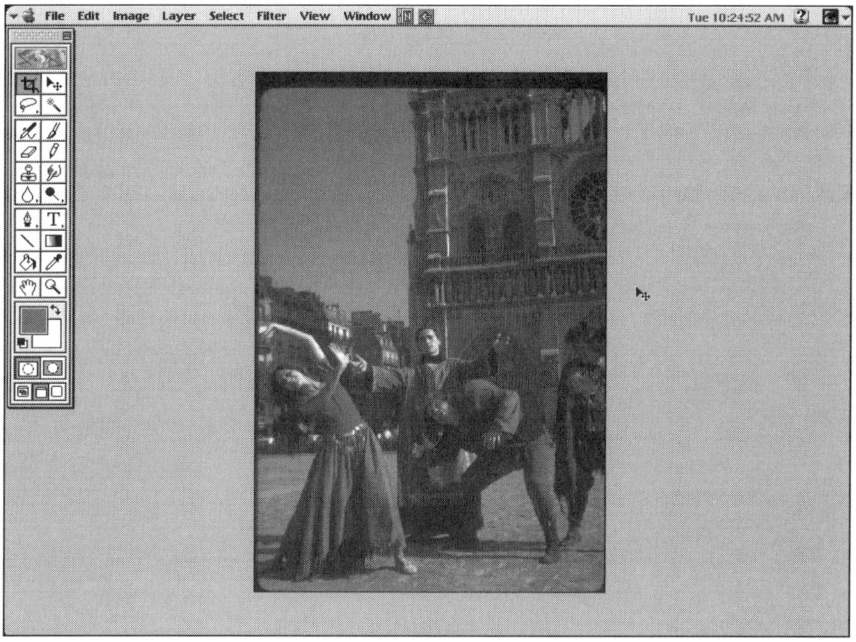

Figure 4.24 In the Image menu, I used the Rotate Canvas command to turn the image 90 degrees counter-clockwise. Photo © Joe Farace.

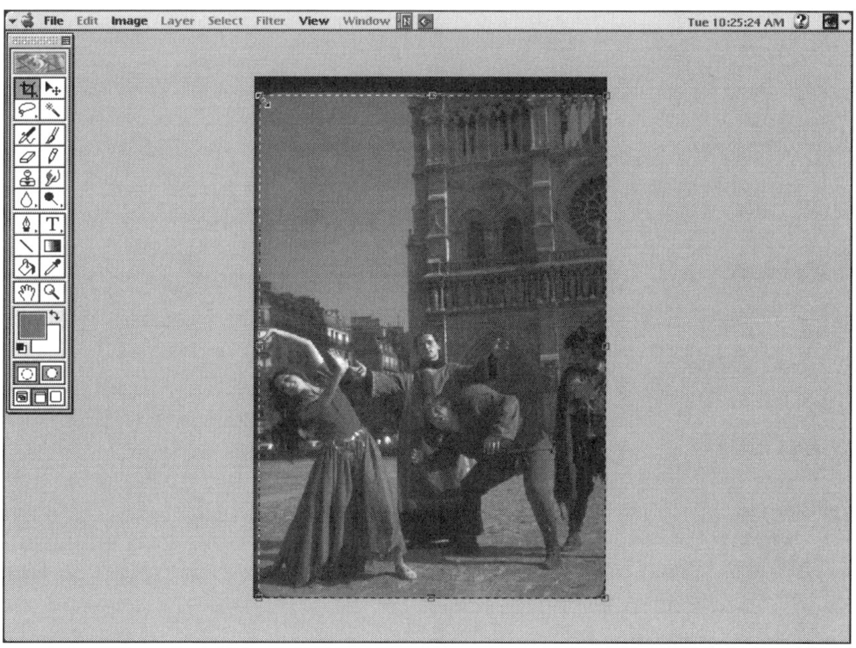

Figure 4.25 The black edges surrounding the slide mount were removed using Photoshop's Crop tool. Photo © Joe Farace.

TIP: Unsharp Masking

One rule of thumb when applying Unsharp Mask to an image is that the higher the resolution, the higher the percentage may be that is applied. Smaller sized (and lower resolution) images fall apart if only 50% Unsharp Mask is applied, but don't be afraid to apply more than 100% to a full-resolution Photo CD digital photograph.

you to preview the sharpness of the finished image before it's sharpened. Controls include Plus and Minus Zoom buttons underneath the preview window. There are also three sliders that let you control sharpness and unsharpness, but I recommend that you ignore all but the topmost one until you gain more experience. Sliding the Amount slider displays the actual percentage of sharpening that will be applied to your photograph. The preview window continuously updates the effect of sharpening on the image, so keep moving the slider until the preview looks as sharp as you want it to. (See Figure 4.26.)

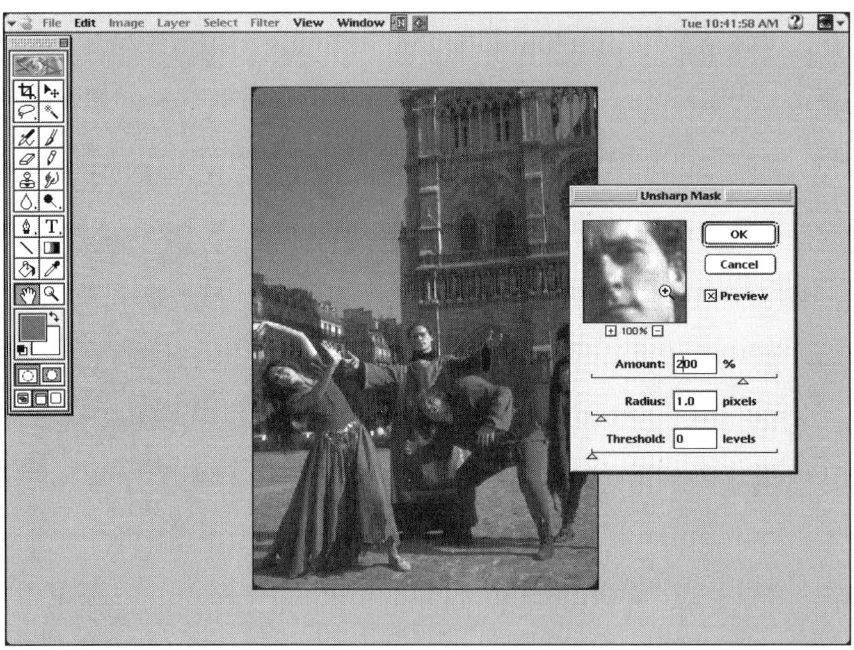

Figure 4.26 All Photo CD images need to be sharpened, especially this one that was not too sharp to begin with. Using a 200% factor with Photoshop's Unsharp Mask command made the image as sharp as it was ever going to be.
Photo © Joe Farace.

TIP: Magic Wand

If an area is not selected with a single click, it is usually because the "tolerance" number is set too low. Since increasing the tolerance sometimes makes the selection too big, I prefer to just use the Shift-Select technique. Here's how it works: if your sky — or whatever — is not selected the first time you click the Magic Wand, hold the Shift key and click the Magic Wand as many times as you have to in order to select the area you are interested in.

Step 5. Not all color images translate well into grayscale, and inevitably some tweaking will be required. Here, I wanted to adjust brightness and contrast to produce more separation between the people in the photograph. You can always use Photoshop's Brightness and Contrast controls, but I always try Auto Levels first. Found in the Image/Adjust menu, Auto Levels works just as many times as it doesn't, but if it turns ugly, I simply select Undo. In this case, it worked great.

Step 6. Since Bromoil artists always enhanced the sky in their photographs, I decided to use Photoshop's Clouds command (found in the Render submenu under Filters) to do the same in the bland sky area occupying the upper left-hand quadrant of the photograph. Since Clouds creates an effect using the differences between Photoshop's Foreground and Background colors, I used the Eyedropper to select a color from the existing sky for the foreground and left white as the background. Using the Magic Wand, I clicked on the sky area to select the entire sky area.

Then I chose Render/Clouds and the program applied "clouds" to the selected area. In previous versions of Adobe Photoshop, this was the sky you were stuck with, but version 4.0 (and later) provides a Fade command every time you apply any effect. Selecting Fade Clouds from the Filer menu brings up a dialog box that lets you vary the effect from zero to 100%. I used 75% to tone the effect down and create just a hint of clouds. (See Figure 4.27.)

Step 7. The next step involves the application of the brush lines that appear in bromoil prints. Since the tool I chose for this will use the selected foreground color, I changed it from the gray sky to black. Next, I selected Filters/Sketch/Graphic Pen. This brings up a dialog box that lets you control stroke length, light/dark balance, as well as the direction of the stroke. There is a preview window to see what changes in the settings accomplish, but since

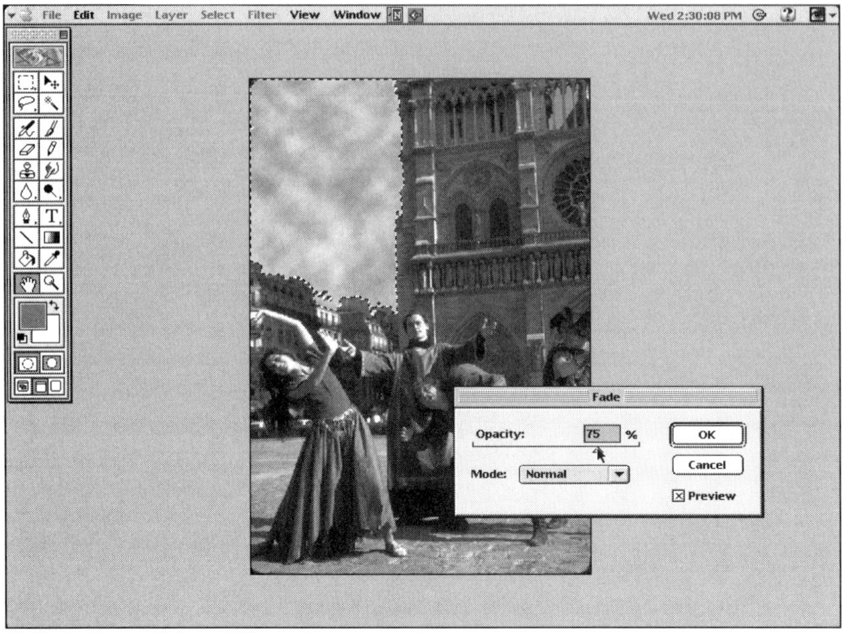

Figure 4.27 Using Photoshop 4.0's new Fade command, the Render/Clouds effect can be varied to suit your own tastes. Photo © Joe Farace.

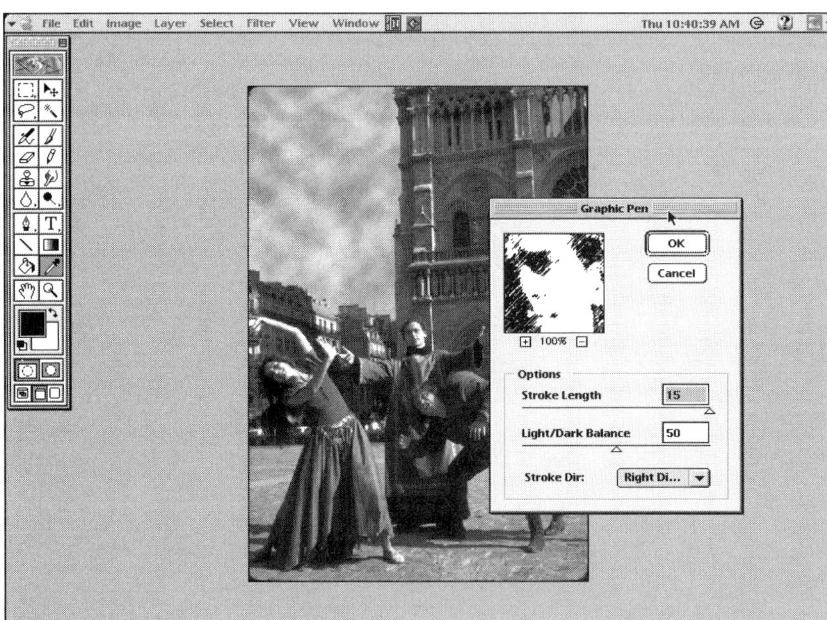

Figure 4.28 The Graphic Pen filter was formerly part of the Adobe Gallery Effects package but is now integrated into Photoshop 4.0. Here it was used with black selected as a foreground color to apply bromoil-like brush strokes. Photo © Joe Farace.

I believe in keeping it simple, I accepted the default settings and applied the filter. One of the reasons I was unconcerned about the general effect is explained next. (See Figure 4.28.)

Step 8. The results of applying the Graphic Pen filter looked more like a sketch than a photo, so I used the Fade Graphic Pen command to blend the strokes into the image. The Fade command is dynamic, so you can see the effect on your entire image as you move the slider. For this example, I used a 50% fade factor, but let your own taste be your guide.

Step 9. Since many bromoil printers toned their prints, I decided to apply a sepia tint to the finished image. As you will see this effect is quite easy to accomplish in Photoshop; the hard part is cutting through the layers of folder/directories to find the sepia presets. Start the toning process by converting the grayscale image into a duotone. This is done by selecting Duotone from the Image/Mode menus.

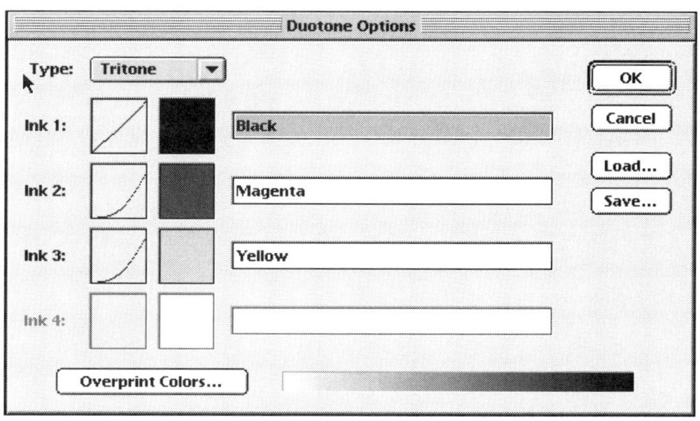

Figure 4.29 Selecting Duotone from the Image/Mode menus causes the Duotone Options dialog box to be displayed. This is your gateway to the sepia presets.

To get through the nested folders containing the sepia presets, click the Load button in the Duotone Options dialog. This will begin a series of steps working through various Open dialogs as you burrow through the folders/directories to find what you are looking for. Mac OS users should start by opening the Goodies folder; Windows users can skip this step. Then, you should open the Duotone Presets (duotone in Windows) folder, and select the Tritones folder (tritone on Windows). Inside the Tritones folder, open the Process Tritones (process on the Windows version) and you will find four different sepia files named: BMY Sepia 1, BMY Sepia 2, BMY Sepia 2, and BMY Sepia 2. When you double click on any one of these files, the settings are loaded into the Duotone Options dialog box.

Clicking OK applies the affect to the image. You might want to experiment with the different Sepia options, but my experience is that the first one approximates what most photographers think of as "sepia." (See Figure 4.30 on CD-ROM.)

If you plan on simply printing the image, you can save it and be finished, but be aware that layered images—and that's what a duotone or tritone image is—can only be saved in Photoshop's native format. If you plan on importing into a desktop publishing program, like I did, you should convert the image into RGB. This is done by going to the Image/Mode menu and selecting RGB. At this point you could be finished, but I always like to add one more flourish to this kind of vintage-looking image—creative edges.

Feeling Edgy?

Who says photographs have to have square edges? The hottest trend in photographic print competitions is prints with irregular, ragged, and artistic edges. Even National Geographic magazine, long a bastion of photographic conservatism, used soft-edged photographs in their story about cartographer David Thompson. I decided to add artistic edges to the image of "the hunchback." While there are many ways to accomplish this effect, here's the easiest way to produce interesting results.

I felt that Auto F/X's Photographic Edges Photoshop-compatible plug-in would add the finishing touch to the digital bromoil. There are two types of effects possible with Photo/Graphic Edges: Outset and Inset. An outset effect is one in which the entire image is fused into the shape of the effect and seamlessly blends into the edge of the effect. An Inset effect leaves a border around the image. Since Photographic Edges is a plug-in, it will work with any image editing program that accepts Photoshop-compatible plug-ins.

Photographic Edges is available in three volumes. Volume I contains traditional edges, including deckled, ripped and torn, semi-transparent, and darkroom-style effects. Volume II features geometric, abstract, impressionistic, and digital edges, as well as circles, ovals, triangles, diamonds, polygons, hexagons, and stars. Volume III contains hand-painted, hand-crafted brush stroke effects originally created using painted and mixed medium techniques, such as watercolor, oils, acrylics, charcoals, airbrush, and scratchboard.

Step 1. To get started with the edging process, I opened the hunchback image using Adobe Photo at the point where I left off. (See Figure 4.31.)

Step 2. From the Auto F/X submenu of the Filters menu, I selected Photo/Graphic Edges. This brings up a dialog box that contains all of the controls needed to add artistic edges to a photograph along with a preview window. (See Figure 4.32.)

Step 3. The first—maybe only—button you need to click is the Select Outset Effect button. When you click this button, the plug-in

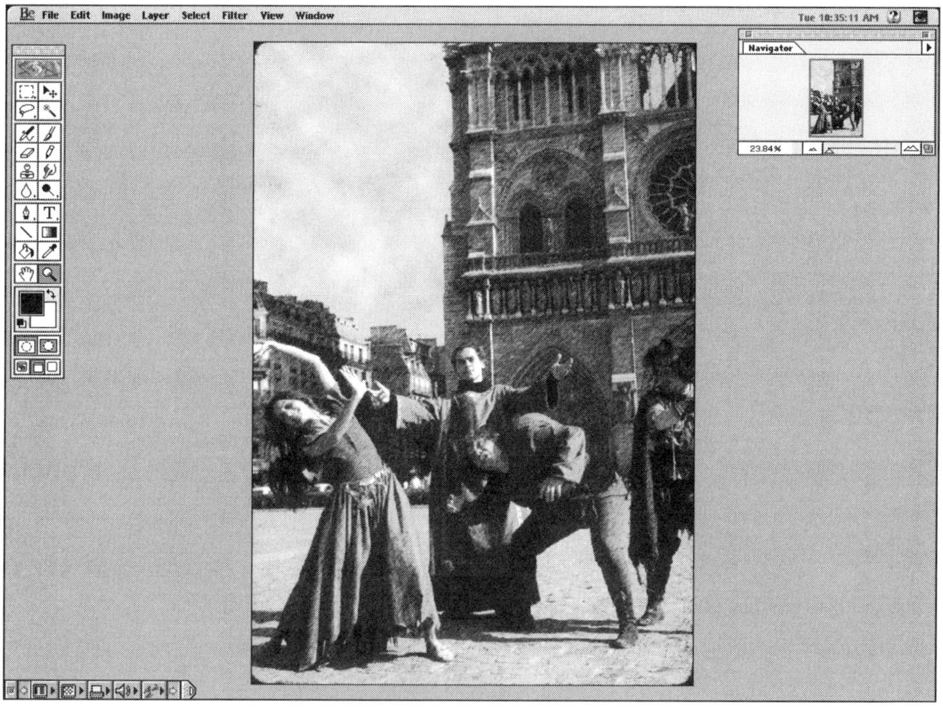

Figure 4.31 The starting point for the creative edges process was the last step in the digital bromoil process. Photo © Joe Farace.

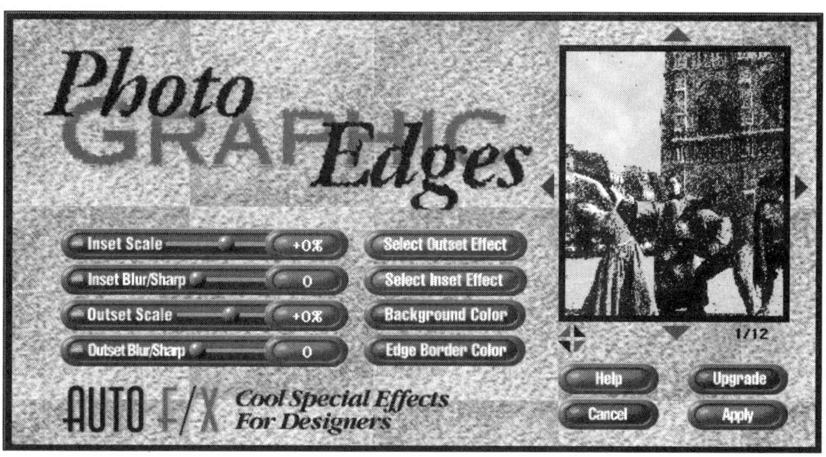

Figure 4.32 The Photo/Graphic Edges dialog box contains all the controls needed to add inset or outset creative edges to your photographs.

directs you to specify where the actual edge files are located. To select which edge you want to use, browse through Auto F/X's documentation, which contains large thumbnails of all of the edge files contained on the CD-ROM.

Tips: Edges

The original edge I selected for this photograph covered too much of the image, so I used the Outset Scale Slider to increase the amount of image showing through. When I got it close, I held down the Option key (on Mac OS; on the PC use Alt) and used the slider to scale the opening in the vertical direction. Then I held the Command (Mac OS; Ctrl on the PC) to increase the horizontal size.

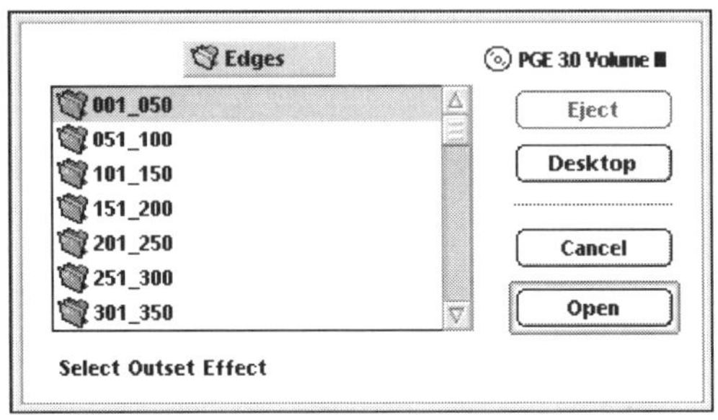

Figure 4.33 A standard Open dialog is used to locate and access the selected edge file.

Step 4. After selecting an edge, the preview window will be updated to show how it looks with your photograph. One of the first things you should do is decide if you want sharp or soft edges. The Outset Blur/Sharp slider in the dialog box lets you tweak sharpness or softness to suit your taste. You can rotate the edge effects using the black and red triangles that rest under the lower left-hand corner of the preview window. You can also flip or mirror an edge, using the red and green triangles located on each edge of the preview. Depending on where you are going to use your image, you can also select a background color (the default is white) by clicking the Background Color button and using the standard color picker. Or, you can skip most of Step 4 completely, click the Apply button, and you are finished. (See Figure 4.34 on CD-ROM.)

5

Masking Techniques

One of the most powerful image editing tools available is the mask. Many image enhancement programs have the ability to create masks—or stencils—that are placed over the original image to protect parts of it and allow other sections to be edited or enhanced. Cutouts or openings in the mask make the unmasked portions of the image accessible for manipulation while the mask protects the rest. Graphic artists who previously used Rubylith material to create masks will be glad to find that digital masks are part of their repertoire too. There are many tools that can be used to create masks. In this chapter you will find that each image editing program has different ways to create selections and—ultimately—masks.

MASKING MODES

Many image enhancement programs have the ability to create masks—or stencils—that are placed over the original image to protect parts of it and allow other sections to be edited or enhanced. Cutouts or openings in the mask make the unmasked portions of the image accessible for manipulation while the mask protects the rest.

Quick Mask

There are three ways to create masks in Adobe Photoshop. The first is Quick Mask Mode, which lets you create and view a temporary mask. In case you are wondering why you want a temporary mask, temporary masks are useful when you don't want to save the mask to use later. This prevents you from adding unnecessary file overhead and keeps the image file as small as it can be. It also saves storage space and speeds opening the file. Another advantage of Quick Mask is that it lets you view a mask and the image simultaneously. Quick Mask uses a Rubylith-like overlay to show what area is being masked, and you can add or subtract from the mask area using tools from Photoshop's palette. Here's how to create a Quick Mask.

Step 1. Using Adobe Photoshop and the Photo CD Acquire Module, I opened an image of an antique streetcar originally photographed on color negative film and digitized with Kodak's Photo CD process.

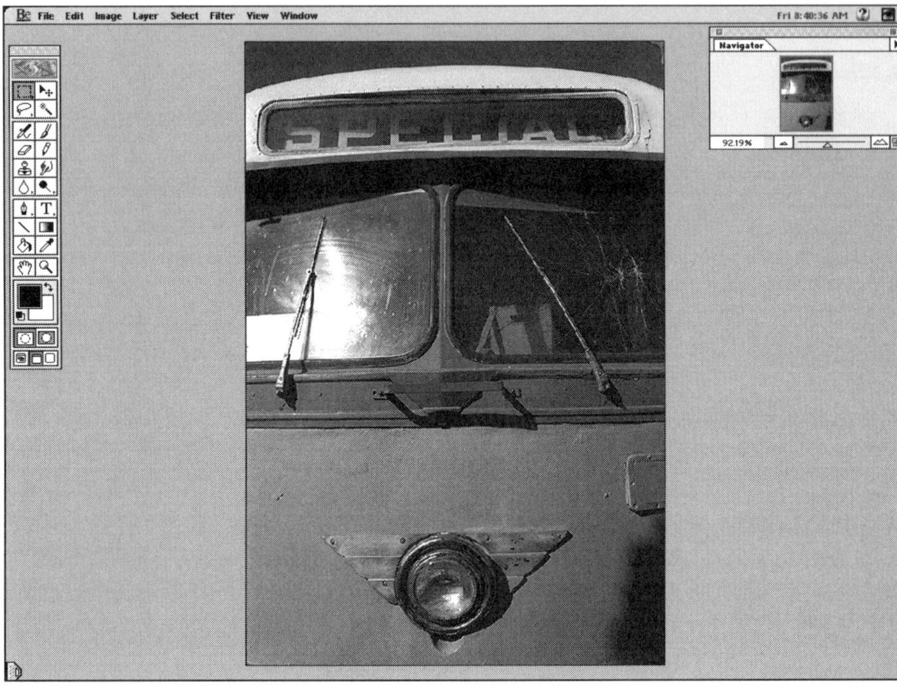

Figure 5.1 This Photo CD image of the front of an old streetcar was opened in Adobe Photoshop. Photo © Joe Farace.

Step 2. Use any selection tool to select part of the photograph you want to alter. In this case I used the Magic Wand tool to select part of the area of the image of a vintage streetcar. While the Magic Wand is usually a pretty good selection tool, it works best when the area selected is more homogenous than this one. You will notice that some smaller, light areas were not selected, nor was the shadowed area in the lower right-hand corner. Not to worry. That's why Quick Mask was used. (See Figure 5.2.)

Step 3. Click on the Quick Mask button that is located just under the foreground and background color boxes near the bottom of Photoshop's tool palette. When you do, those sections that are not selected will be covered with a color overlay (reminiscent of Rubylith) that covers the unprotected area.

Step 4. Now we get to the real power of masking. This mask area can be expanded—by using any of the painting tools—or contracted

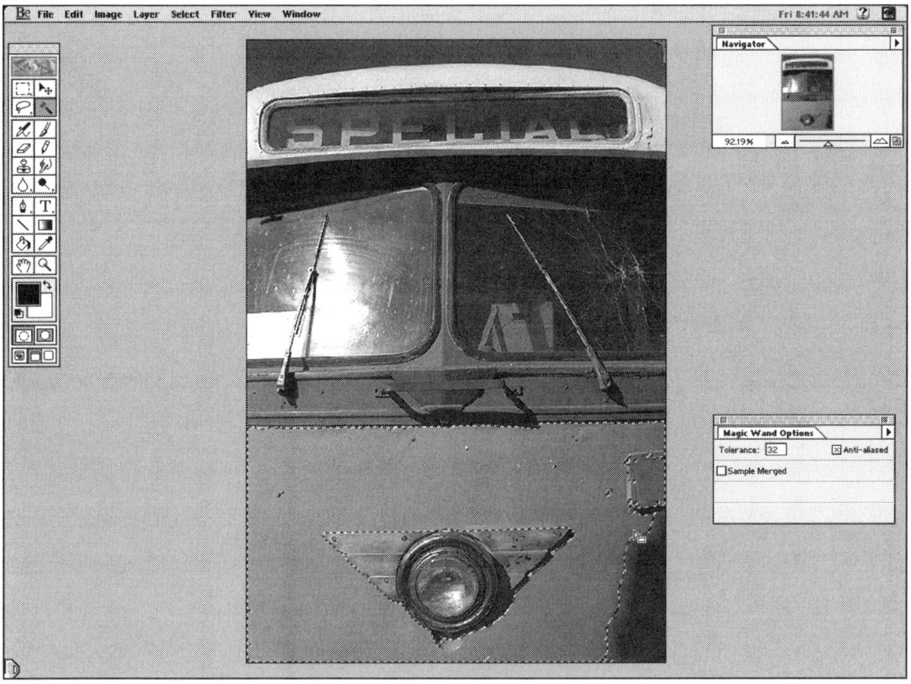

Figure 5.2 The Magic Wand, with Tolerance set at 32, was used to Click-Select as much of the yellow area as possible. Photo © Joe Farace.

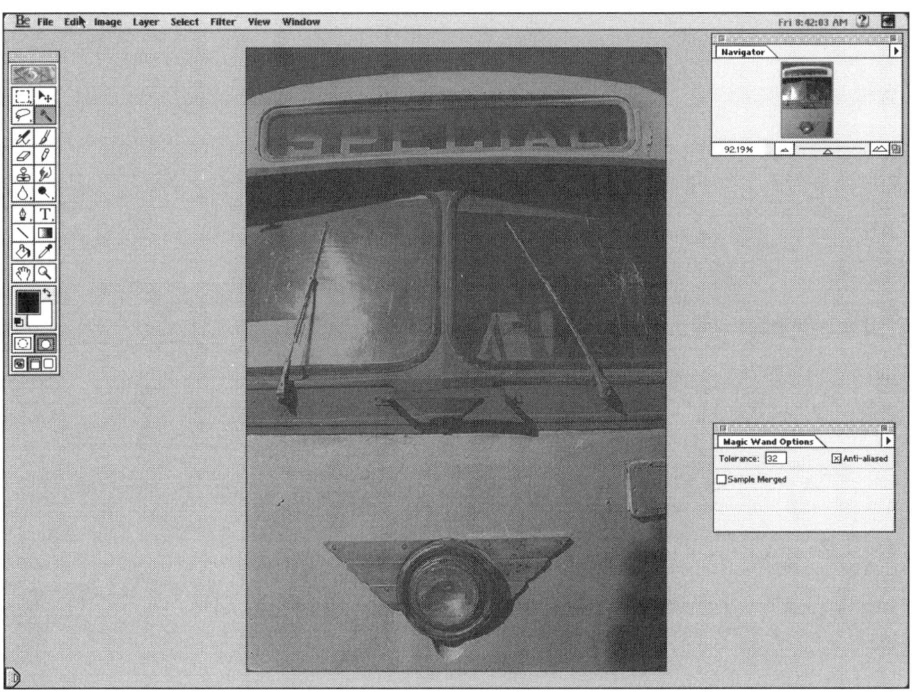

Figure 5.3 After clicking the Quick Mask button, the nonprotected (nonselected) area of your image is covered in a Rubylith-like mask. Photo © Joe Farace.

by using the eraser. When you create a Quick Mask, Photoshop creates a temporary Quick Mask channel in the Channels Palette to indicate that you are working in Quick Mask mode, but the joy of Quick Masking is that you do all mask editing in the standard image-working window.

To edit this mask, I chose the eraser tool and used it to remove portions of the mask I wanted uncovered. I started with the shadow area in the lower right-hand corner, then used the eraser to remove small bits of mask that covered the front of the street car. For the really small parts, I increased magnification (with the Magnifying Glass tool), so that I could get into all of the nooks and crannies. (See Figure 5.3.)

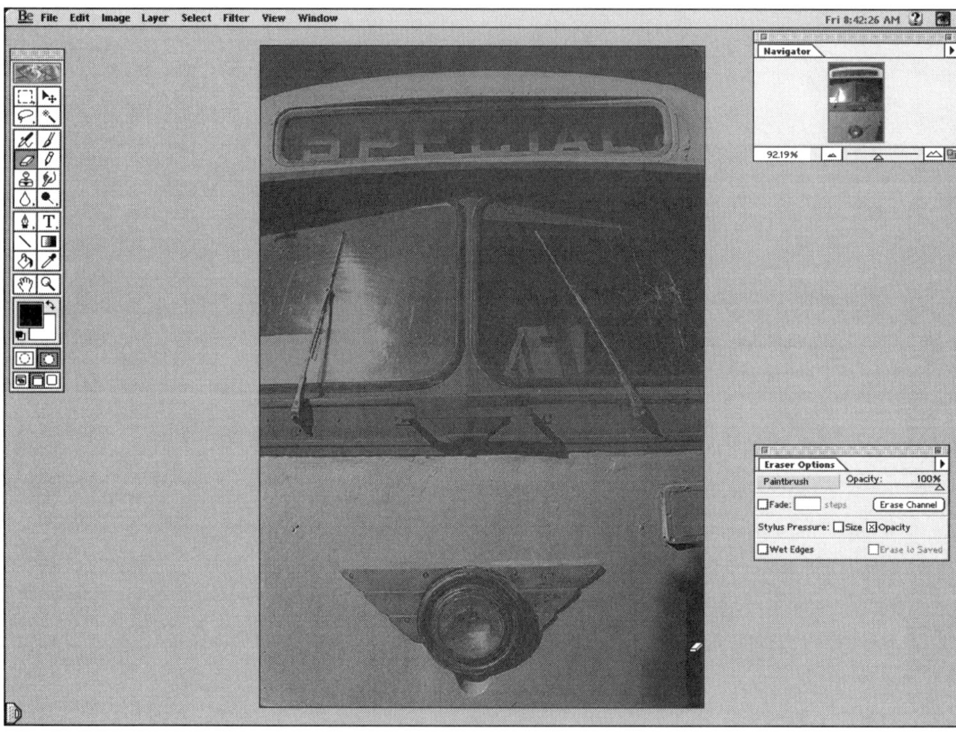

Figure 5.4 Using the eraser, the author removed portions on the Quick Mask that he wanted to expose. Photo © Joe Farace.

Step 5. When the mask covered just the areas that I wanted, I clicked the Standard Mode button (next to the Quick Mask button) to turn of the Quick Mask. When you do that, the unprotected area of the Quick Mask is now surrounded by the standard selection border—"marching ants."

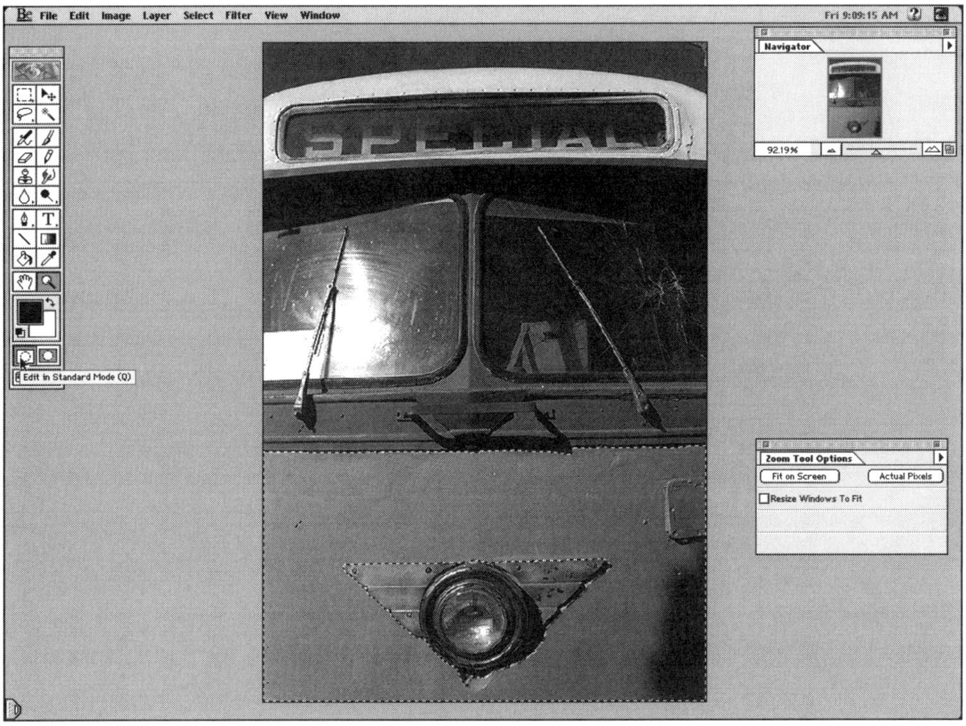

Figure 5.5 After cleaning up the mask, the author clicked the Standard Mode button, converting the mask into a selection. Photo © Joe Farace.

Step 6. At this point, you can apply any changes that you want to the selected area. Using the Selective Color dialog box (found under Image/Adjust/Selective Color), I tweaked the primary yellow color to produce a golden yellow of the type used by the streetcars of Baltimore Transit Company in their heyday.

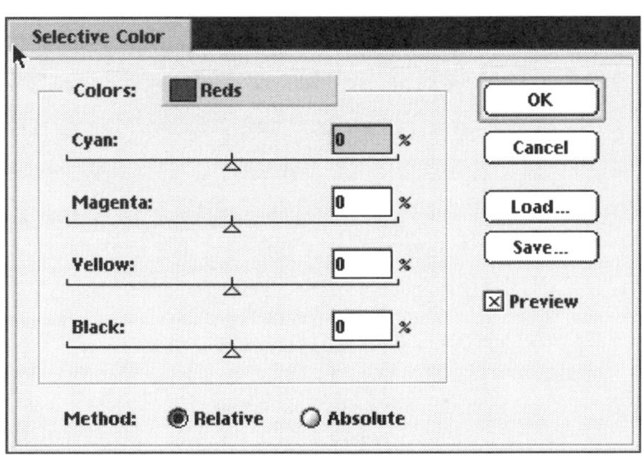

Figure 5.6 Using the Selective Color command, the author manipulated the original color of the streetcar.

TIP: Selective Color

It's easy to get lost when manipulating colors — especially if you are working with a color similar to the original. Checking the Preview box lets you see the changes in colors when working with this dialog box, but it's a good idea to, every now and then, unclick it so that you can see the original color.

Step 7. When the colors were how I wanted them, I clicked OK to finish the Quick Masking and color adjustment process. While only subtle changes were made using this technique, an effect—or plug-in—could be applied to any Quick Masked area. (See Figure 5.7 on CD-ROM.)

Alpha Channels

In addition to working with the temporary mask that the Quick Mask technique can produce, you can create new channels called alpha channels. Each image can contain up to twenty-four channels, including all color and alpha channels. All new channels have the same size and resolution as the original channel. You can add and delete alpha channels, and you can specify a name, color, and opacity for each channel. You can edit a mask in an alpha channel using the normal painting and editing tools. One difference between masking with alpha channel and Quick Mask is that selections stored in alpha channels are permanent and can be used again in the same image or even in another image. You can save a selection to either a new or existing alpha channel. You can then store that selection permanently and use it as a mask for your image.

Let's create a new alpha channel for a mask:

Step 1. I opened a Photo CD image of the same streetcar as the previous example, but this one focuses on the headlight. I used the Magic Wand tool to select the yellow area around the headlight. Then I used the Inverse command to reverse the area to select the headlight and chrome trim. (See Figure 5.8.)

Step 2. Choose New Channel from the Channels Palette menu. If you like keyboard commands, you can Option-click (Mac OS) or Alt-click the New Channel button at the bottom of the palette. This brings up a dialog box that provides several options. Channels are automatically assigned a default number according to the order in which they are selected. You can accept the number scheme or name the channel so that you can more easily keep track of its function. At this point, you should also choose the display options. Alpha channels have the same options that Quick Mask provides. (See Figure 5.9.)

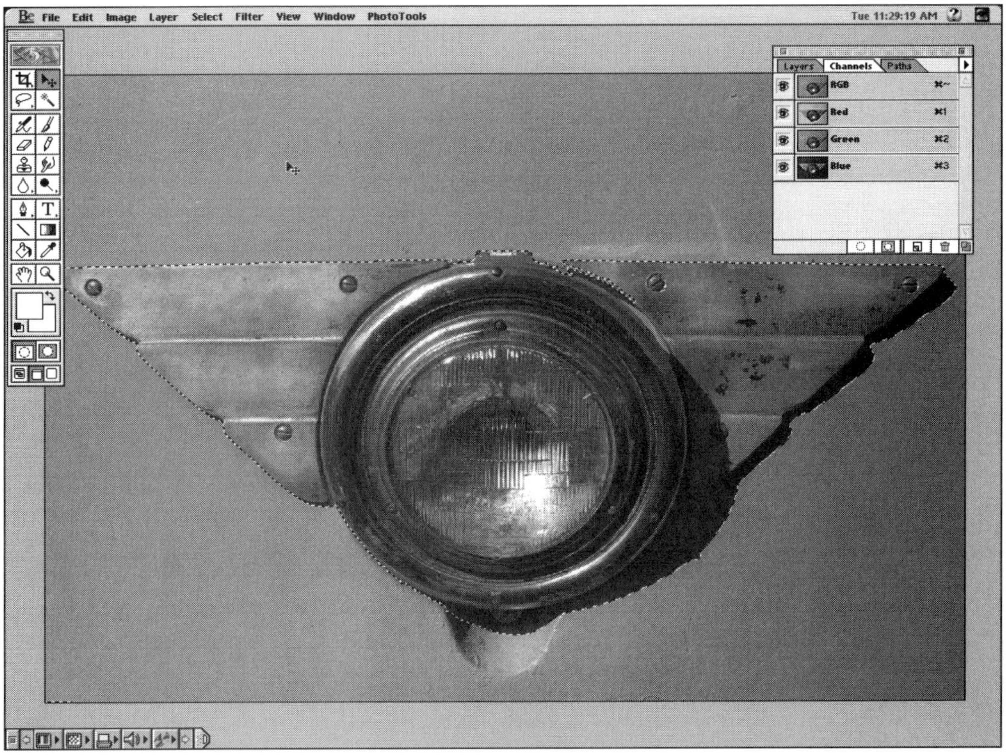

Figure 5.8 The photograph of a streetcar was opened in Adobe Photoshop. The Channels Palette is also open, showing the RGB plus individual color layers of the image. Photo © Joe Farace.

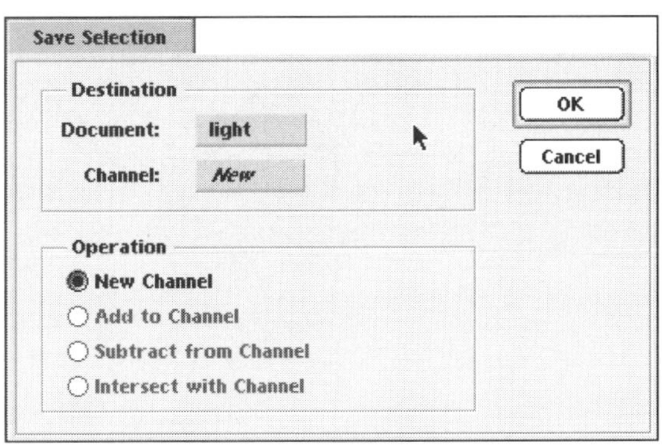

Figure 5.9 To create a new alpha channel, simply choose New Channel from the Channels Palette.

Step 3. When you click OK, a new 9-bit grayscale channel appears at the bottom of the Channels Palette and is the only image displayed in the working window. (See Figure 5.10.)

TIP: Surfing Channels

It's a good idea to keep Photoshop's Channel Palette open when you are creating or editing any channels, so you can see all of the elements associated with an image — at the same time. For the same reason, you should keep the Layers Palette visible, too. The command to open this and other working palettes may be found under the Windows menu item in the menu bar.

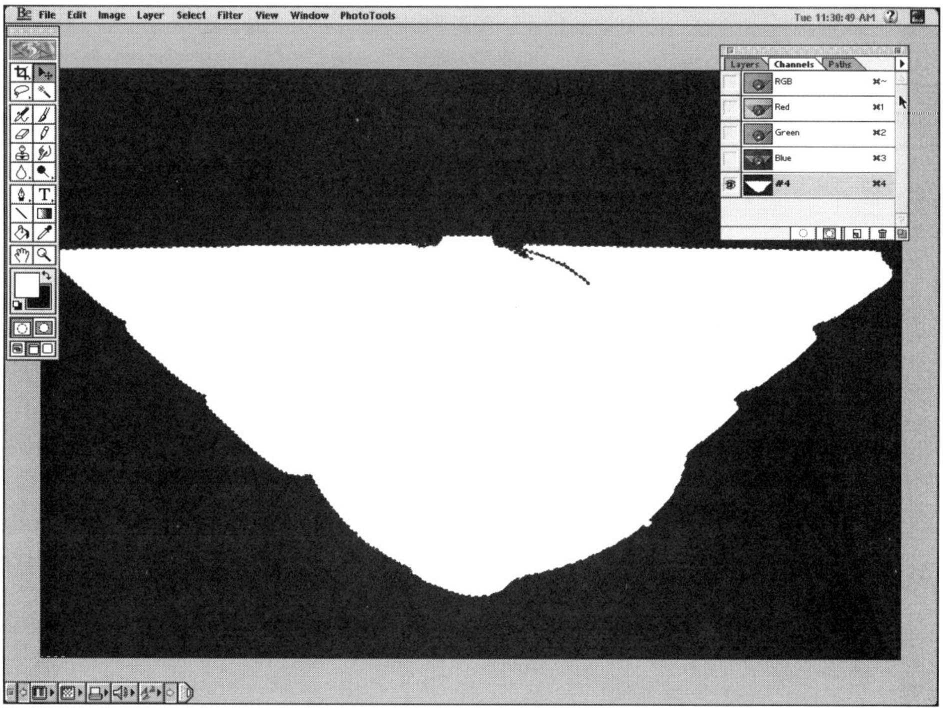

Figure 5.10 The mask channel looks similar to the Quick Mask, only it is part of the original image.

Layer Masks

A layer mask lets you control how different parts of a layer are hidden or made visible. By making changes to the layer mask, you can apply effects to that layer without affecting any of the pixels in the original image. You can apply the mask and make the changes permanent, or remove the mask without making changes, or save the mask as part of a layered document.

A layer mask is a 9-bit grayscale channel that uses black or white as its background color. Whatever is white is seen as clear and allows the image below it to come through. The black areas block images.

A layer mask can be accessed from both the Layers or Channels palette. It appears as an additional thumbnail to the right of the layer's thumbnail in the Layer's palette. In the thumbnail, black indicates the portions of the layer that are hidden and white indicates the portions of the layer that are revealed. Gray is used to indicate the portions of the layer that are partially visible. Here's a brief look at making and modifying a layer mask.

Step 1. Using Adobe Photoshop, I opened a photograph of the side of a railroad tender made on Kodak color negative film and digitized using Kodak's Photo CD process. Since I knew the Layers palette would get a workout in this example, I opened it, too.

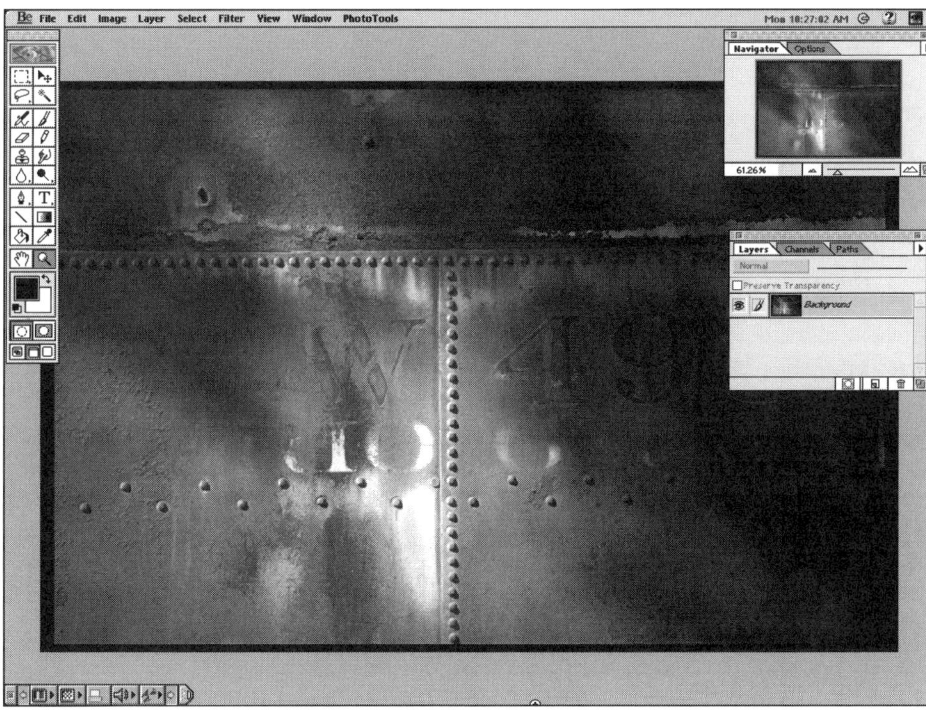

Figure 5.11 A Photo CD image of a tender, made at the Colorado railroad museum. Photo © Joe Farace.

Step 2. Since I planned on adding another image layer, I had to first create one. The Layers palette has a New Layer command, which brings up a dialog that allows you to name your example. The default is a number, but naming layers will make it easier to keep track of layers—even if you only have two. In this example, I named the second, now empty, layer "train." (See Figure 5.12.)

Step 3. I opened another Photo CD railroad image to blend with the background. It was copied onto the Clipboard with the Copy

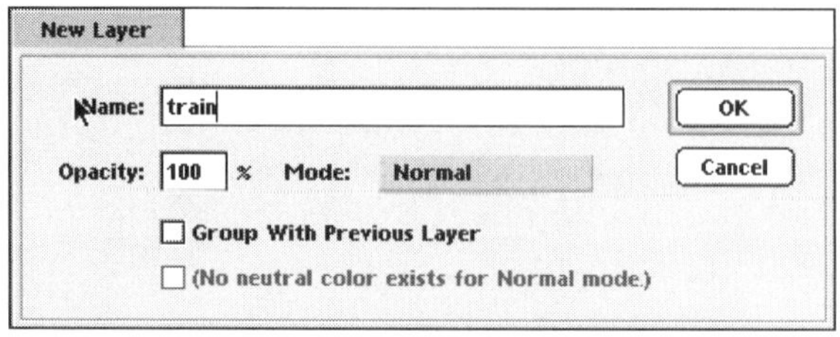

Figure 5.12 The New Layer dialog lets you name and control the function of layers that are added to your background image.

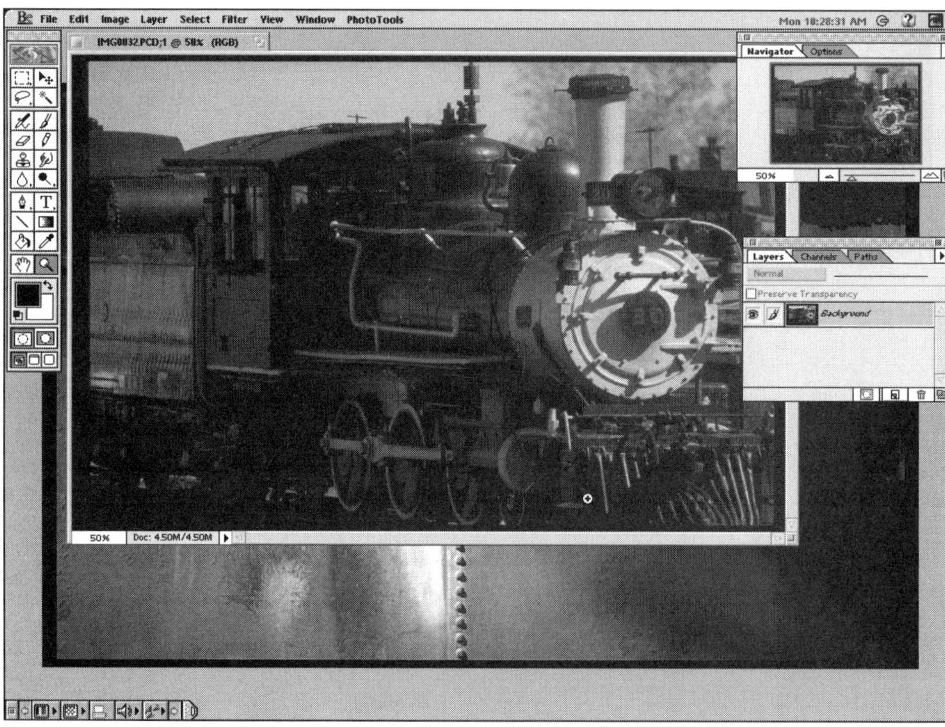

Figure 5.13 A second Photo CD image was opened, copied onto the Clipboard, and pasted into the new Layer. Photo © Joe Farace.

command. The Paste command was used—after selecting the new Train layer—to paste it into the new layer.

Step 4. Using the Layers menu, I chose the Add Layer Mask/Hide All command. This produced a black mask covering the Train layer that is visible in the Layers palette. I chose a big, soft-edged brush from the Brushes palette and brushed white (clear) color over the mask in the area of the front of the locomotive. While I was making the opening larger, Photoshop's Navigator window showed

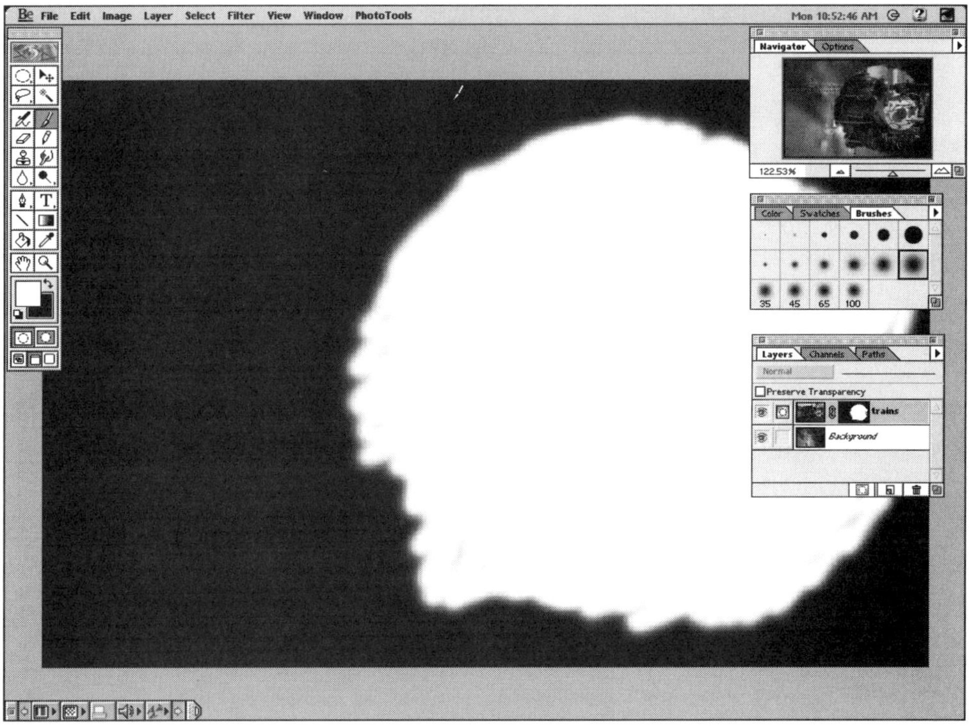

Figure 5.14 You can select the Layer Mask for modification by Option-clicking (Mac OS) or Alt-clicking (Windows) on its icon in the Layers palette.

me the programs I was making by showing what the finished image looked like.

(See Figure 5.15 on CD-ROM.)

PLUGGING INTO MASKS

If you have ever tried to use a digital imaging program to create a mask in order to composite one image onto a different background, you know how challenging it can be. One of the easiest ways to create a composite image is to use Photron's Primatte S-100, a Photoshop-compatible plug-in distributed by Photoflex.

Primatte

For this example, I will use Adobe Photoshop, but Primatte works with any graphics program that supports Photoshop-compatible plug-ins. (See the next chapter for more information about plug-ins.)

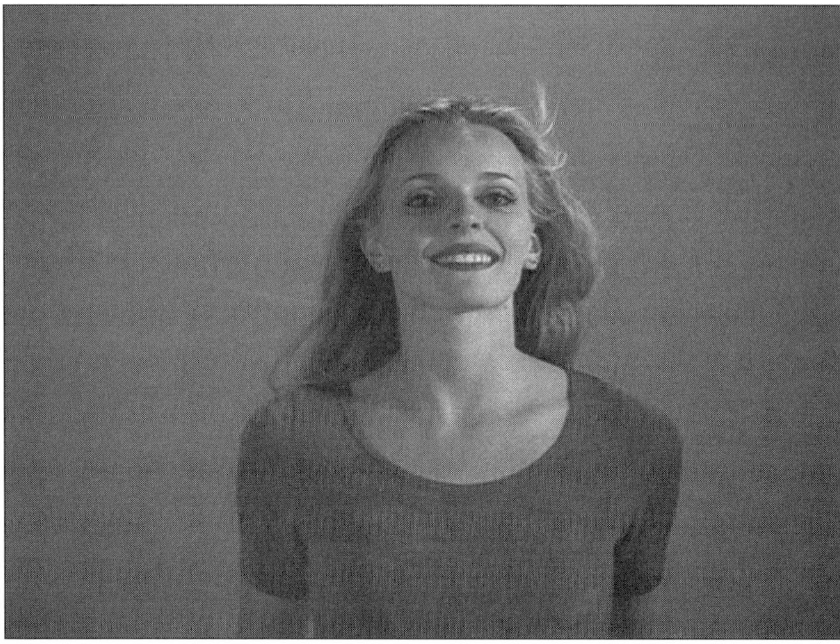

Figure 5.16 This portrait was used as the foreground image in the composite. Photograph ©1997 Ralph Portillo.

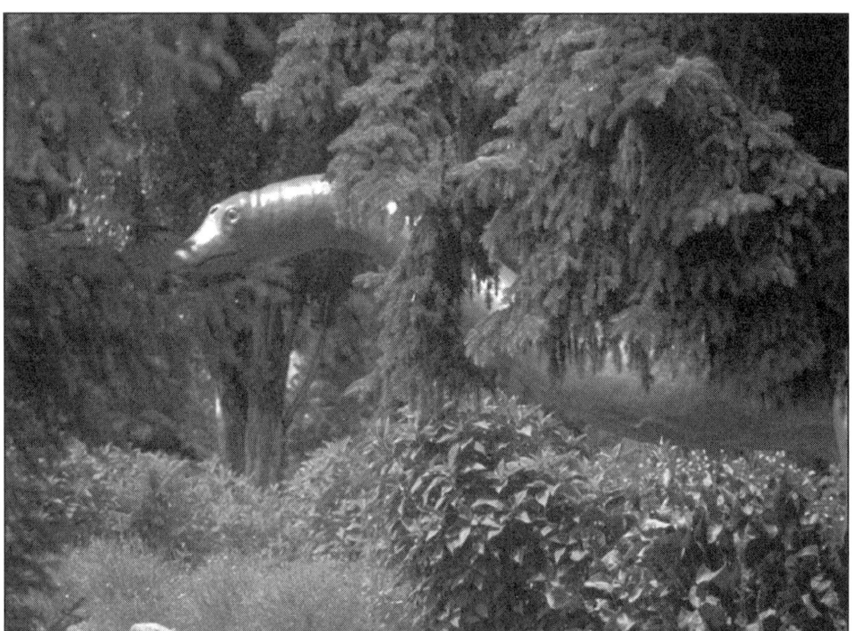

Figure 5.17 The background was the author's photograph of a Brachiasaurus made at the Utah Field House in Vernal, Utah. Photo © 1995 Joe Farace.

Step 1. I opened two images—one for the foreground and one for the background—in Adobe Photoshop. The foreground portrait was created by Ralph Portillo, the background was an image that I photographed at the Utah Field House in Vernal, Utah.

Step 2. The next thing I did was make sure that both images were of identical size. Most compositing programs and plug-ins, like Primatte, require that the foreground and background images be exactly the same size before they can work. The best way to do this is to use your image editing program's Image Size command to resize and change the resolutions of both images so that they match exactly. You may notice that some minor amount of cropping may be required—it was in the example that follows—to get the pixel sizes of the images to be the same. If you take these few steps before you do anything else, the rest of the process will go smoothly.

Step 3. Before you can do anything with the images, you need to launch Primatte from Photoshop's Filters menu. When you do, a two-step dialog box asks you to assign which image is to be the foreground. Always assign the background image first—this is the way Primatte expects it to happen. Then I selected the foreground image and chose Primatte from Photoshop's Filters menu. The same dialog box appears, asking what will be the foreground.

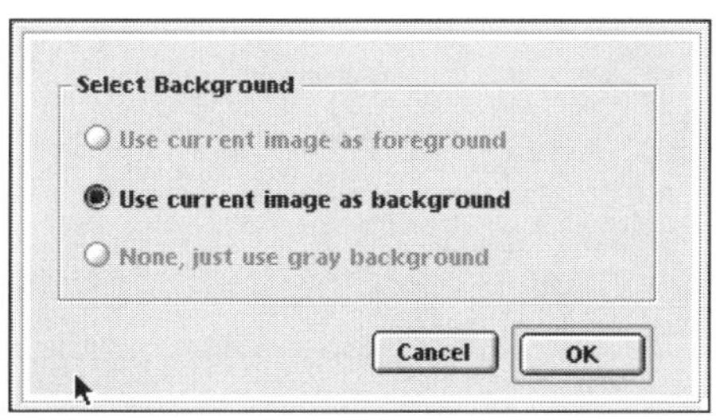

Figure 5.18 The first Primatte dialog asks you to assign foreground and background images. Always assign the background image first.

Step 4. After you assign the foreground image, Primatte's working window automatically opens and you will see the foreground image—only—inside a large preview window. Your workspace in Primatte includes all the tools you need—including Undo and Redo—to create composite images.

Step 5. To select the background, I dragged my mouse across the blue background. This process selects the colors that will be dropped out of the composite, but the initial swipe will rarely be perfect. At this point, Primatte will have created both a foreground and a background mask, which will be used to drop the foreground image onto the background image. You can view the mask by clicking on the BG (background) button. At that point, you will see what needs to be done to improve the mask. To clean up the mask and to make black areas blacker or white areas clearer, you drag the mouse over any leftover spots or noise that might be left. If you click on the FG (foreground) button, you will see the foreground mask that will be preserving your foreground image. You can use the same kind of click-and-drag techniques on the foreground mask to eliminate any elements that you do not want to appear.

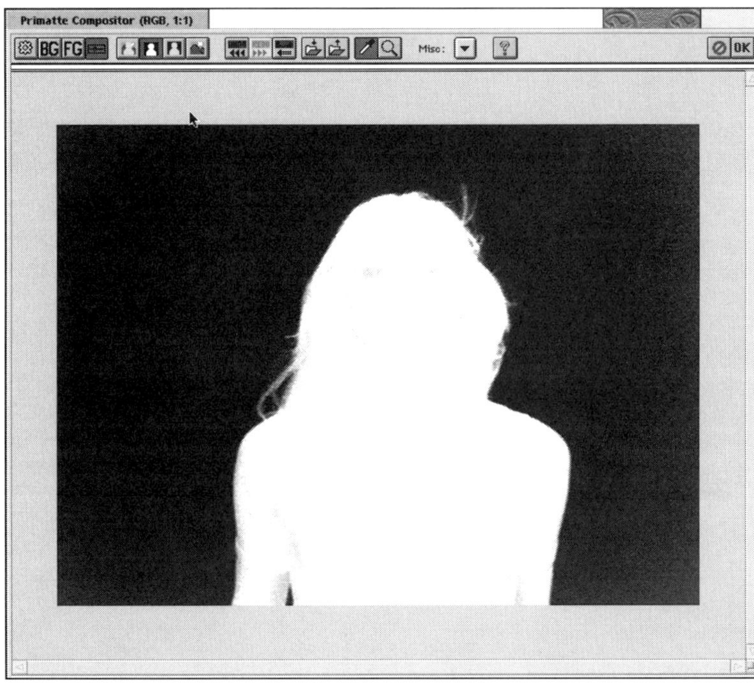

Figure 5.19 The simple act of dragging the mouse across the background created this mask, but a little more work needed to be done to make the black areas blacker and the clear areas clearer.

Step 6. After the initial application and tweaking of the masks that Primatte created, the composite will be nearly perfect, but one final step is required. The weak link of most compositing software is the incomplete way they handle wispy objects, like hair or smoke. Primatte's Tune Colors button lets you zoom into these tricky areas around the foreground image's edges and remove residual color. You can change the color of any pixels left of the original image's background color by selecting the offending color with the Eye Dropper, then tweaking three sliders in the Tune Colors dialog box.

Other dialog box settings allow you to control the mask's softness of the color closest to the background or foreground.

Step 7. All of the above steps actually take less time to do than to read about. The composite that you see here was completed in less than five minutes. After you are finished, you can save or export the finished mask as a Photoshop channel. To do that, you should create an extra channel for your foreground image before making the composite. (See Figure 5.21 on CD-ROM.)

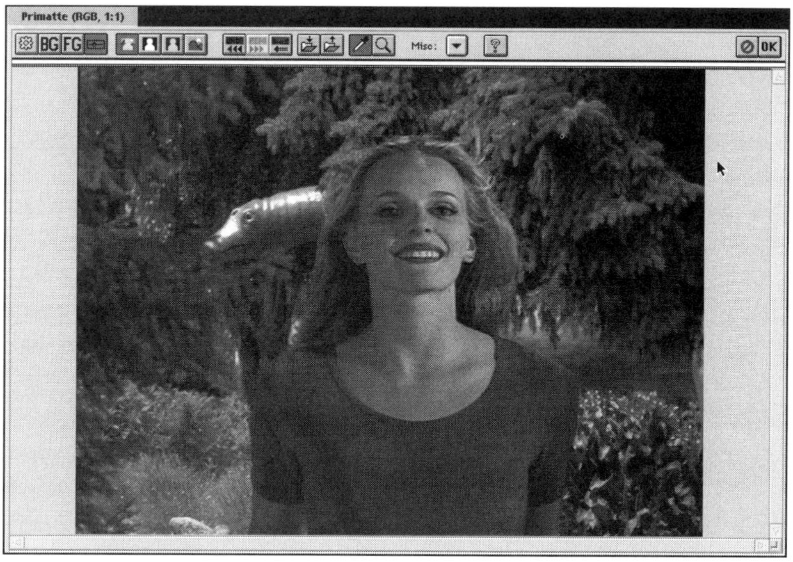

Figure 5.20 At this point you are almost done. Photos © Ralph Portillo and Joe Farace.

Primatte Tips

In addition to making sure that your foreground and background images are the same size, here are a few tips and a workaround to help you when creating composite images with the Primatte plug-in. The compositing process works best if you have an image that was planned to be composited and was photographed against a plain or "blue screen" background. To get you started, Photoflex includes a small, collapsible blue screen background called a Flexdrop. The Flexdrop is useful for close-up details or small products; larger blue screen backgrounds are available from the usual sources, including Photoflex. When it's not possible to use a foreground image that was photographed in this manner, you can use Photoshop's Irregular Selection tool to draw an area around a foreground object or person and fill it with a blue screen-like color before using Primatte. Then, you can use the Primatte plug-in to tweak the mask just as you would in the steps shown above. This workaround takes more time and somewhat more skill than using the plug-in the way it was designed, but it works.

Mask Pro

Extensis Mask Pro makes creating professional quality digital masks and cutouts easy and efficient. The plug-in speeds up and simplifies the process of creating digital masks by providing users with precise control over the retention or elimination of image areas. By adding or subtracting colors from Mask Pro's palette, users can brush along the edge of an image and create a mask in a fraction of the time it takes with traditional tools. (See Figure 5.22 on CD-ROM.)

CASE STUDY: CREATING A T-SHIRT DESIGN

The T-shirt design produced in this example was created on a Power Macintosh 8100, but all the software featured in this section is available for IBM-compatible computers as well. The images used are KPT Power Photos from MetaCreations. The software used to create the T-shirt design is Adobe Photoshop. I tested several different graphics packaged for this project, looking for one that would be the easiest to use, but I ultimately came back to Photoshop. Part of the reason is the simplicity of the interface, that is, its ability to work on multiple layers. All images are © MetaCreations.

Junkyard Art

The concept was to create an original-looking design using techniques that readers could use to create their own artwork. The design would consist of several items: background, foreground, and type. Here's how it went.

Step 1. The background chosen was from KPT Power Photos III, volume 13, "Junkyards." I was so impressed with the images on this disc that I decided to create the entire design using elements from it. To serve as the background, I opened the file containing a photograph of stack of crushed cars. (See Figure 5.23.)

Step 2. I decided to make some changes to the photograph so that it would not look so literal. I started by changing the edges of the image to make them look ragged. (Techniques for creating the edges are the same used in the Digital Bromoil project in Chapter 2. Take a look at that section for specific details.) The edge effect here is more subtle and that's intentional. All I wanted to do was roughen the edges—not radically change them. (See Figure 5.24.)

Step 3. I accessed Acetone from Photoshop's Filters menu and used it to posterize the background. This creative plug-in tool, from Second Glance Software, allows you to convert an image into a limited number of colors. I started with six colors but gradually

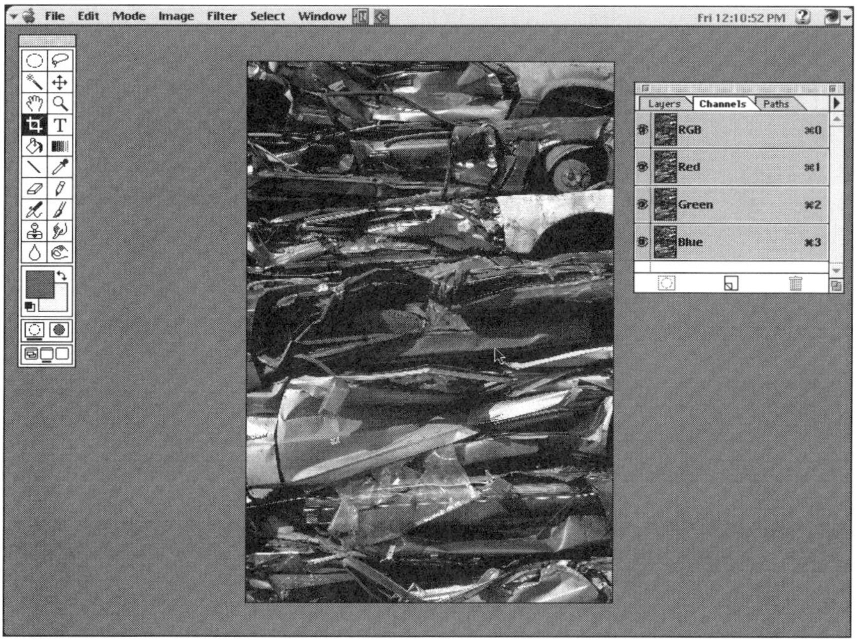

Figure 5.23 Nothing says junkyard like a stack of crushed cars. This image was taken from MetaCreations, KPT Power Photos III, volume 13, and it was opened in Adobe Photoshop. Image © MetaCreations.

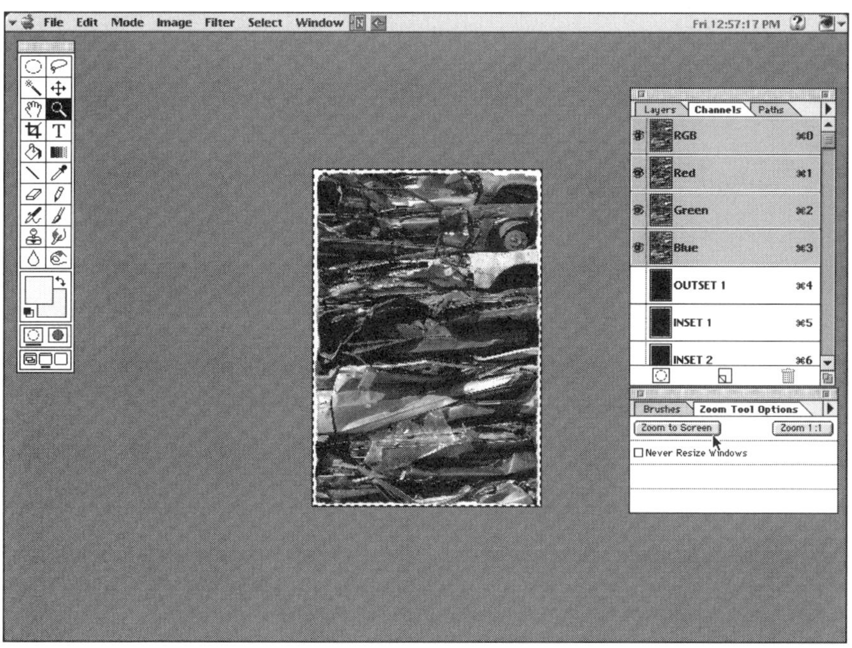

Figure 5.24 Using an "edge" file from Auto F/X's Photo/Graphic Edges CD-ROM, I changed the rectangular edges of the stock photograph to something more irregular and, I hope, more interesting.

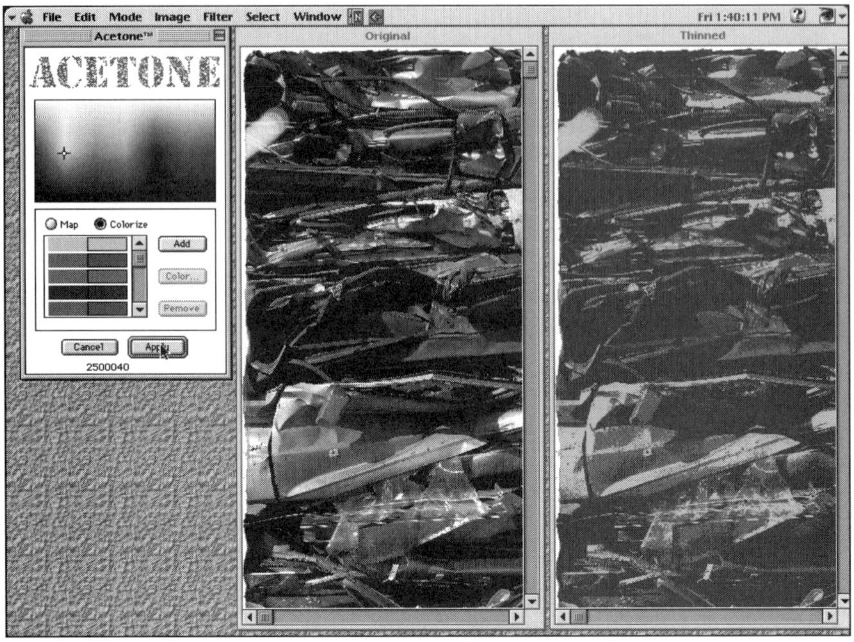

Figure 5.25 Using a plug-in called Acetone, I posterized the crushed car's image. Acetone is part of the Second Glance Software package that was designed for screen printers—the kinds of people who would create actual T-shirt designs.

added and subtracted colors to get the image to look the way I wanted it. Acetone's interface lets you see before-and-after images so that you know exactly what you are doing.

Step 4. With edges added and the image posterized, the background looked exactly as I wanted it. Next it came time to add the foreground. All junkyards need a dog, so I opened a "dog" file on the CD-ROM disc. Like most KPT Power Photos, this one has no—or a glaring white—background that allowed me to manipulate the photograph as an object. I used the Free Rotate command in the Image menu to rotate the dog slightly, then used the Magic Wand to select the white background. I went to the Select menu and chose Inverse to reverse the selection to select the dog, then copied it onto the Clipboard. (See Figure 5.26.)

Step 5. I pasted the dog into the lower left-hand corner of the image using Photoshop's Paste command. Now, I had foreground, but something was missing. To balance the dog, I found a humorous warning sign on the Junkyard CD-ROM, which could be pasted into the upper right-hand corner. I used the same techniques to place it as the dog, but before placing it I used Photoshop's Skew and Perspectives commands to give the sign a less squared-off look. (See Figure 5.27.)

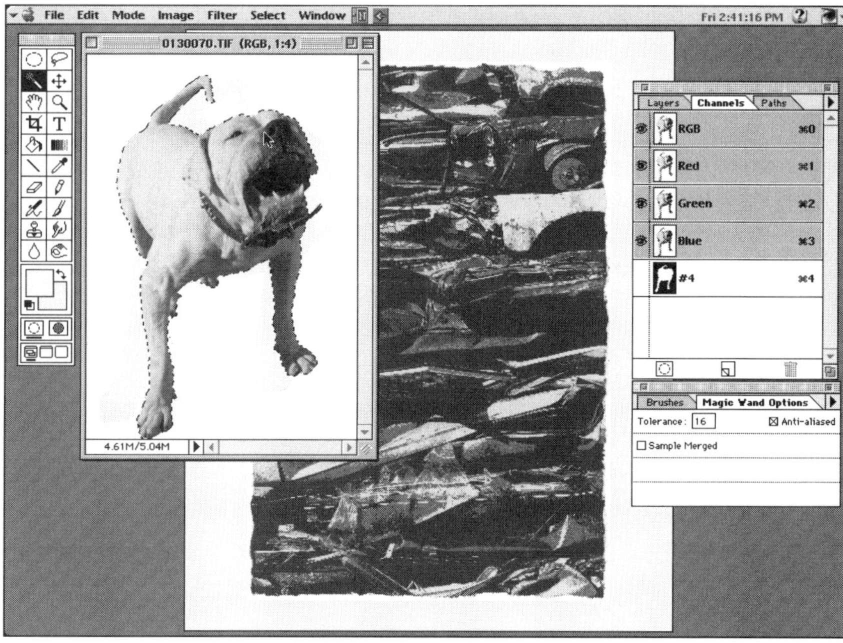

Figure 5.26 A junkyard dog was selected from the disc and was reduced in size using Photoshop's Image Size dialog. This put the dog in scale with the background. Then the dog's image was selected and rotated. Image © MetaCreations.

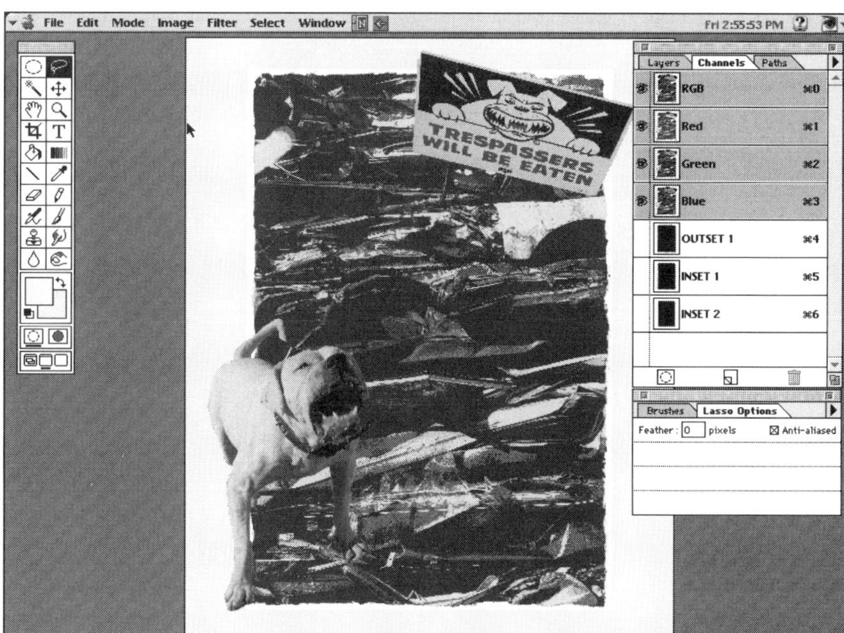

Figure 5.27 Using Photoshop's Skew and Perspective controls, I rotated a junkyard warning sign and placed it in the upper right-hand corner to balance the dog in the opposite corner. Image © MetaCreations.

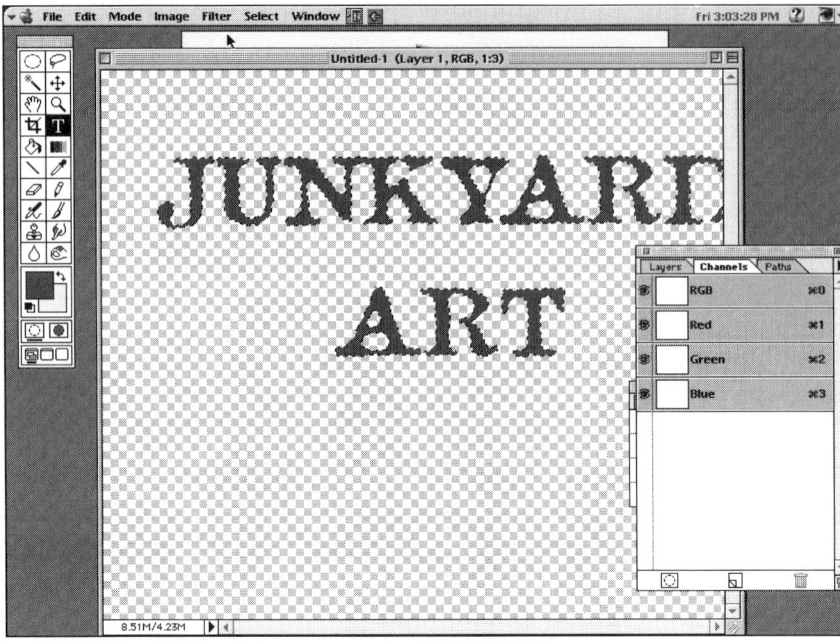

Figure 5.28 Every T-shirt design needs some kind of type. The Typeface used for this design is just a large Times Roman font, colored a bright red to stand out against the complex photographs making up the design.

Step 6. The last step was adding text, so I opened a New window in Photoshop and used the text tool to type the words "Junkyard Art" in 65-point type. Type is already selected, so I used the paste command to place the type where I wanted on my almost-finished design. The text looked flat, so I decided to add a drop shadow by using Alien Skin Software's Drop Shadow filter. Before I could apply it, the text had to be converted into a layer by using the Convert to Layer command. Then I opened the Drop Shadow filter to let me control the amount of shadow along with its softness and color.

The final design is ready to be turned into a T-shirt. If you like the drop shadow effect, you could have converted both the dog and sign into layers and added a drop shadow to them. What is left after all this work is a unique T-shirt design that is possible for anyone to create using these basic software and hardware tools and a little patience. (See Figure 5.29 on CD-ROM.)

6

Plug-in Power

In 1986, a new Mac OS application from Silicon Beach Software called Digital Darkroom began a trend in software design: the use of plug-ins. When Photoshop was introduced in 1990, Adobe expanded the plug-in concept, making it a key part of the program's design. Digital Darkroom may just be a footnote in software design, but its legacy lives on.

PLUGGED IN

Plug-ins are little software applications that increase the functionality of image enhancement and graphics programs. One of the best features of Adobe Photoshop is that it was designed with an open architecture. This open-ended design accommodates small software applications called "plug-ins" to extend the program's features. The judicious use of plug-ins can increase the functionality of off-the-shelf graphics programs and allow users to customize them to fit the projects they work on. Plug-ins are typically stored in a single folder or directory that your image editing program checks each time the software loads. That's why, when you launch the program, you typically see the names of the plug-ins displayed on the "welcome screen." Any plug-ins that your program finds during this process are available for immediate use.

When you install one in a program's "Plug-in" directory or folder, it appears as a menu item and is, in effect, plugged into the software, becoming an integral part of it. While the most popular cross-platform standard was created by Adobe Systems for Photoshop, compatible plug-ins can be used with other image manipulation programs including Ulead Systems' PhotoImpact, MetaCreations' Painter and Dabbler, Apple Computer's PhotoFlash, Pixel Resource's PixelPaint Professional, Macromedia's xRes, MicroFrontier's Color-It!, Corel's Artisan, and Live Picture 2.5 or later. Even freeware image editing programs, such as NIH Image, support Photoshop-compatible plug-ins. Most compatible plug-ins also function with Adobe's consumer-oriented Photo Deluxe program. Other related graphics programs, such as Adobe PageMaker (after version 6.0), Deneba's Canvas (5.0 and

A Mac OS Tip

If you want to store but not necessarily use (right now, anyway) plug-ins, you can hide them by adding an Option-L keystroke (it looks like ¬) in front of the subfolder's (subdirectory's) name. When Adobe Photoshop loads the filters, it will skip this one. To load it, just remove the "¬."

later), Equilibrium Technologies' DeBabelizer, Macromedia's Director and Freehand, and StrataVision 3D, also work with Photoshop-compatible plug-ins. Adobe's Premier video editing program also accepts compatible plug-ins.

If you already have Photoshop installed on your hard disk, some programs, like MetaCreations' Painter, allow you to access all of the plug-ins already stored in Photoshop's plug-in folder (or directory). When you take a peek inside the Plug-in folder, you will discover that confusion reigns. Since Photoshop 3.0, Adobe's Installer creates a group of additional folders inside the Plug-ins folder. They are the Acquire/Export, Extensions, Filters, Displacement Maps, Parser, and File Format folders. When installing third-party filters, some users agonize over making sure these new filters are placed in the right sub-folder. Don't panic! As long as all of your plug-ins are placed in the overall Plug-ins folder, it does not matter which subfolder they are located in. Photoshop will make sure they appear in the correct menu. But that does not mean some kind of organization strategy is not called for.

Managing Plug-ins

I recommend you take all of your newly added special filters and place them inside a new folder located inside the Plug-ins folder. Name it something like "My Plug-ins" or whatever—make it personalized. When programs, like Painter, ask where your plug-in folder is located, you can specify "My Plug-ins"—even though it's inside your Photoshop folder. Painter will then be able to access your third-party filters without installing them a second time. For programs that do not have a default plug-in folder, create an alias of your new folder and place it inside the program's "Filters" folder. When you launch the program all of those filters will be available without having to duplicate or relocate them. Simply placing a 4K alias inside the Filters folder can give you access to 35MB of filters. Variations on either of these techniques should work with most image editing or graphics programs.

FOUR WAYS TO PLUG IN

There are four basic types of plug-ins—Acquire, Special Effects, Export, and Select—all of which allow you to customize a graphics program to fit a specific job. Within each of those basic categories there are subtypes or specialty plug-ins that are designed to work with specific hardware or with particular applications.

After installation, Acquire plug-ins appear in a submenu of the Acquire or Import portion of your program's File menu. This submenu includes all of the commands that allow you to import or "Acquire" an image for import into your graphics program. Special Effects plug-ins usually appear in the program's Filters menu, which is why these plug-ins are often called "filters." Since many Export plug-ins relate to producing color separations, they usually appear in the graphics program's Export menu. This is also the place where you will find plug-ins that can convert your original file type into another one—maybe for another platform or for use on the World Wide Web. Previous versions of Adobe Photoshop only supported these three types of plug-ins. With the introduction of version 4.0, a new type of plug-in—Select—was added. The Select menu has been part of Photoshop since the beginning, and now it, too, has been opened up, allowing plug-ins to be written for this portion of the program. Select plug-ins allow users to modify a selection or select an entire image. If you are not yet familiar with selection tools, Adobe Photoshop almost always requires that part of an image needs to be isolated, or selected, before an effect can be applied.

Image Acquisition

Most acquisition plug-ins allow you to directly scan an image into your program without leaving it, but one of the most popular Acquire plug-ins is Kodak Photo CD Acquire 2.0.1, which lets you import Photo CD images. While Adobe Photoshop allows you to import a Photo CD image through its Open dialog, the methodology and steps are anything but convenient. Kodak's plug-in makes it easy to find and open a Photo CD image and adds increased functionality. You can, for example, sharpen an image while importing the photograph. Since the first thing most users do after opening a Photo CD image is sharpen it, that saves you one step. The latest version provides access to the higher resolution (4,096 × 6,144 pixels) images found on Pro Photo CD Master discs. When you access the plug-in, you will see an attractive dialog box that includes an Edit Image button, which enables you to crop, adjust color balance, increase or decrease color saturation, and change the brightness and darkness of an image—all before it's imported. The plug-in also lets you select the image's size and resolution and change its color type to match the type of output device you plan on using. An Image Info button provides specifications on how this particular image was created, as well as relevant copyright information. Kodak has not updated this plug-in for some time, and it may be hard to find, but it's worth the search.

Many scanner manufacturers include a plug-in allowing users to provide access to their hardware. When you purchase their Coolscan slide scanner, Nikon includes a scanner plug-in along with a stand-alone scanning application. While the application is useful, you can only save a completed scan in one of two different graphics file formats. The plug-in, on the other hand, allows you to scan the item and save it in any file format that your program supports. By having the item directly accessible within a graphics program, you can perform enhancement to the image before saving it or exporting it to another application, such as desktop publishing.

Step 1. Start by inserting a mounted slide into the opening on the front of the scanner. Negatives or unmounted slides can be scanned by using a film holder that is included with the scanner. The film holder looks remarkably like a negative carrier you would use on an enlarger in a conventional darkroom.

Step 2. After choosing Nikon Scanner from the Import menu, you can select the scan's image resolution, then do a preview scan. After prescanning, you can color correct the image and crop it. In this case, the brightness was set at a maximum of 100 and the image still needs brightening.

Step 3. Once you have the preview looking the way you want, you can open it in your graphics application and make any further adjustments or cropping. In this case, Photoshop's Auto Levels com-

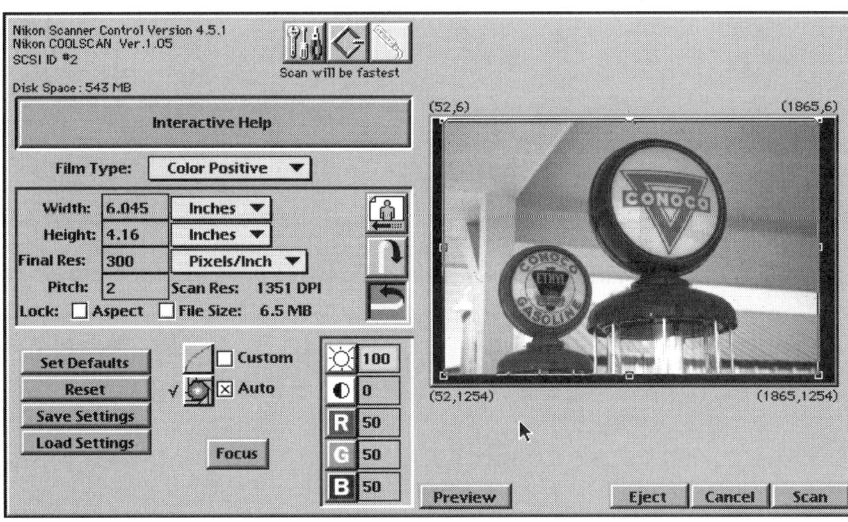

Figure 6.1 The Nikon Coolscan plug-in allows you to prescan a slide or negative. You will notice that you have to set the scanner to read whether the image is a color positive or negative, or black and white or color. Photo © Joe Farace.

Free Plug-ins?

Plug-ins are available commercially, but free ones can be found on the Internet. One source is Slab's Photoshop & Graphics Page, which can be found at http://phobos.winmail.com/~slab/photoshop.html. It's a good place to find information about books, plug-ins, and other items of interest for the digital imager.

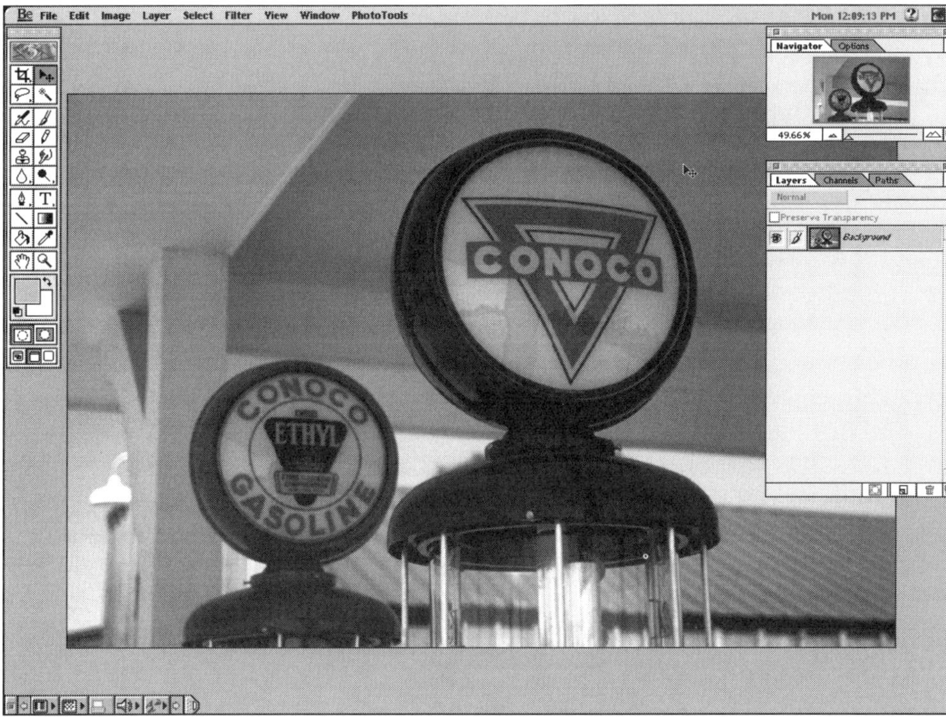

Figure 6.2 After initial tweaking, this image is opened in Adobe Photoshop for further manipulation. Photo © Joe Farace.

mand (in the Image menu) was used first. This was followed up with slight tweaking of the brightness and contrast commands.

IMAGE MANIPULATION

One of the first digital filter packages available was Gallery Effects, which is now an integral part of Adobe Photoshop. These filters remain some of my favorites, and, as was demonstrated in previous chapters, they can be used to create some interesting visual effects. There are also many third-party image manipulation plug-ins available that will help you create interesting images—easily. Let me show you a few.

Convolver

MetaCreations Convolver takes plug-ins to a new level, something you will notice as soon as you select it from the Filter menu. Its diamond-shaped 3D interface contains two windows: a small "Before" and a larger "Preview." In the upper left-hand corner are buttons that activate one of Convolver's three modes: Explore, Design, and Tweak. When one of the modes is selected, controls that affect the others are dimmed or "asleep." When Explore mode is selected, three more buttons appear, allowing you to try different filters whose results are displayed as fifteen variations or "tiles" in the Preview window. Clicking the Mutate Genes button generates fifteen new tiles. When you click on any one of the fifteen, the selected tile becomes the basis for the next round of mutations. Two other buttons control how much each tile is different from one another. The Genetic Diversity button has a pop-up menu that lets you set five different levels of diversity, from Minimum to Maximum. Gene Influences lets you vary your choice of: Blur/Sharpen, Embossing, Edge Detection, Hue, Saturation, Brightness, Contrast, and Tint. You can select any or all of them to be used in the mutations. Design Mode lets you apply two different filters at one time, and contains sliding arrows that allow you to set how much or little the effects will be implemented. Tweak Mode contains fourteen filter controls that allow you to tweak the image's color, sharpness, and contrast.

Step 1. The first step is opening a digital image. In this case, I opened a sunny Fall photograph of a Victorian house in Georgetown, Colorado. The original image was photographed on Kodak ISO 25 color negative film and transferred to Photo CD.

Step 2. In Tweak mode, I used Convolver's Sharpen command to sharpen the image 20%. (See Figure 6.4.)

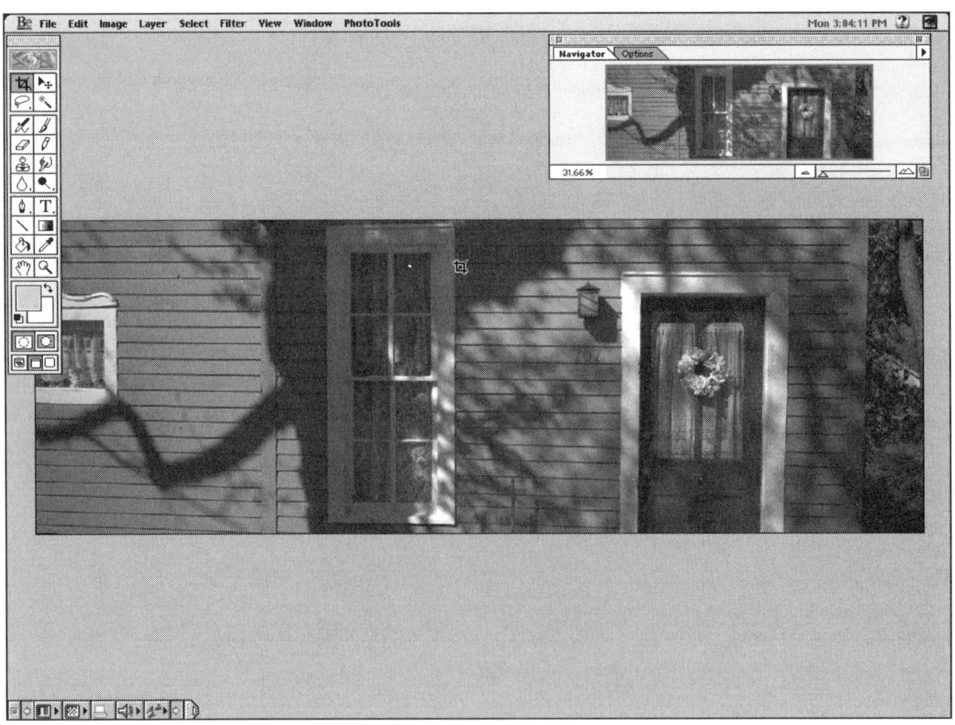

Figure 6.3 The starting point for Convolver manipulation is one of the author's panoramic photographs that had been transferred to Photo CD. Photo © Joe Farace.

Step 3. Next, I used Explore mode to work through several levels of color manipulation, ending up with one that (kind of) matched my previsualization of turning a sunny-day image into something that could be used to illustrate a Stephen King short story.

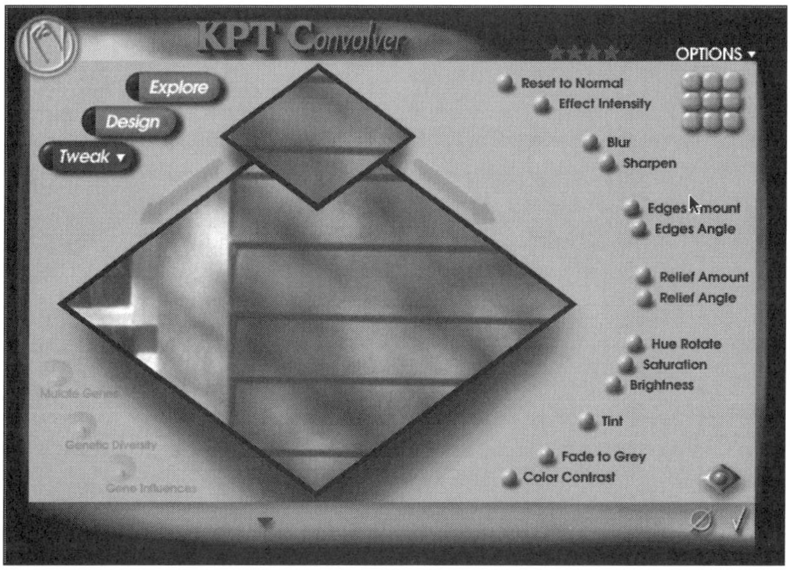

Figure 6.4 Convolver's Tweak mode was used first to sharpen the image 20%.

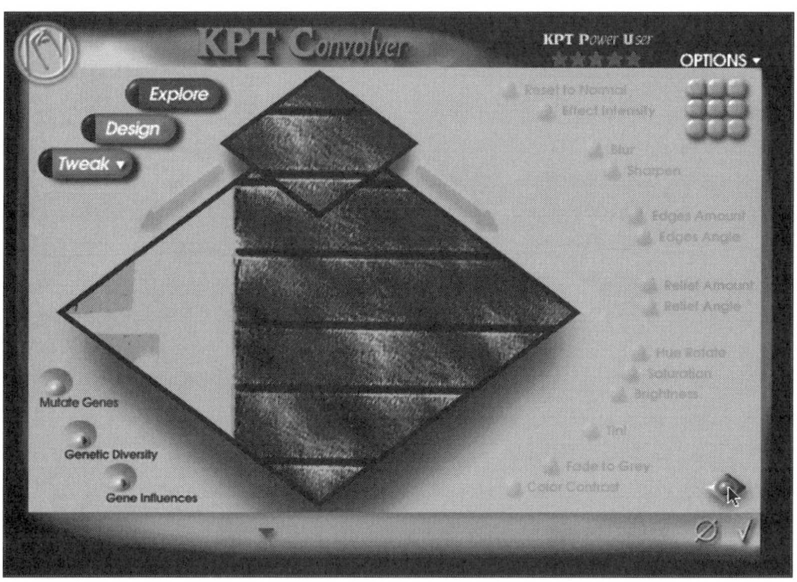

Figure 6.5 Using Convolver's Tweak mode, the author experimented with color and texture combination to arrive at something that fit his previsualization.

Step 4. While the effect was dramatic, I used Photoshop's Fade command to reduce the level of the Convolver filter effect to approximately 75% of what the raw filter accomplished.

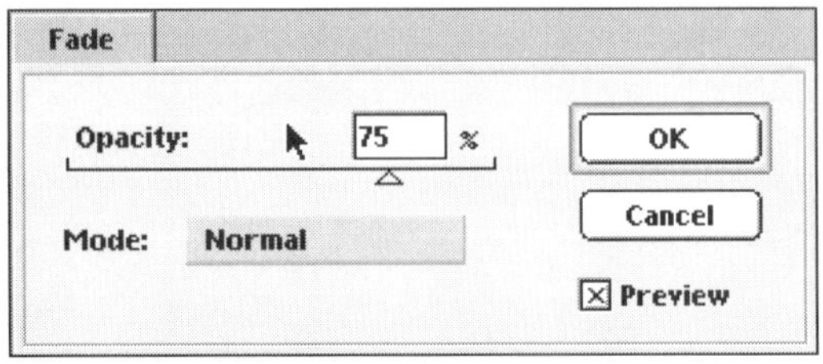

Figure 6.6 To arrive at the appropriately "Stephen King" look the author desired, Photoshop's Fade command was used to reduce Convolver's effect to 75% of the original.

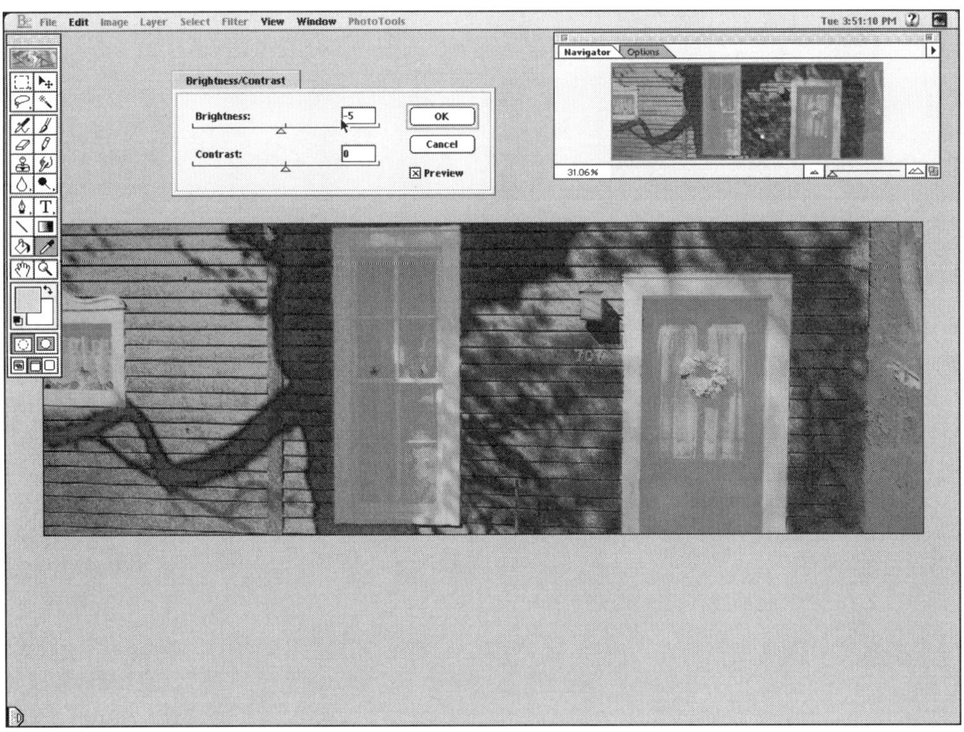

Figure 6.7 The author then used Photoshop's Brightness and Contrast controls to tweak the image just a bit more. Photo © Joe Farace.

What Are Those Stars?

Part of Convolver's design includes a star system that rewards photographers who frequently use certain features by providing enhanced versions of those features. Like a good teacher, stars are awarded for performance, and they are displayed in the upper right-middle of the Convolver dialog. You can accumulate up to five possible stars, and the awarding of each one is accompanied by a brief explanation of how to use the new feature. The first star indicates that you have passed through each of Convolver's three modes at least once. The first star does not really add any functionality but is a "feel good" award for your efforts in exploring the plug-ins interface. The second star provides side-by-side "before and after" views of the current image and its Convolver effect. To turn on the Split Screen preview mode, all you have to do is click on the sphere located in the lower right-hand corner that appears the same time the star does. The third star provides an algorithmic color wheel for the Tint control. Clicking on the Tint button (in Tweak mode) makes the wheel appear. You can navigate anywhere on its multicolored disc—it reminds me of Saturn's rings—to achieve any one of 3,600 hues to add (or subtract) the tint you want for a particular image. The fourth star adds what MetaCreations calls "Memory Dots," but they remind me more of M&M's (or maybe I'm just hungry right now). This is a 3 × 3 matrix of three-dimensional circles that allows you to save the status of the image you are currently manipulating, while allowing further explorations without having to worry that you may not find the proper combination of filters and variations to achieve that effect again. It adds a level of nine Undo's, something Adobe Photoshop sorely lacks. The fifth star, which I achieved quite by accident when working on the above example, lets you animate changes in any of the previously stored (in dots) configurations.

Why aren't these features built-in from the beginning? MetaCreations' Kai Krouse told me that the idea is to provide as simple an interface as possible and to provide only those tools a user needs as he or she requires them.

TIP: Convolver Tip

The manual recommends that you start in Explore mode, add effects in Design mode, and touch up the finished image in Tweak mode. In practice, I am comfortable doing the opposite. I start in Tweak mode by using the Sharpen control, because all Photo CD and many scanned images invariably need some sharpening. Unlike Photoshop's Sharpen command, Convolver displays a number (in percentages) in the bottom of the windows, indicating how much sharpening is being applied. Most of the percentages I put to use were smaller than the large numbers (usually over 100%) required using Photoshop's Unsharp Mask command. Then I use the Fade to Gray setting to make the color as neutral as possible and kick the Contrast up a bit before moving into Design Mode. Convolver's Tweak mode contains some controls that are available within Photoshop, but, for the first time, enables you to quantify the changes you make. The Design and Explore modes allow you to produce effects not possible with any other Photoshop add-on.

Just Goo It!

The programming wizards and interface designers at MetaCreations also produce a creative imaging tool (it's not a plug-in) that's easy and fun to use called Kai's Power Goo, or KPG. KPG's interface is completely different and removed from either the Windows or Macintosh environment the program operates under. The opening screen contains six large icons that MetaCreations calls "rooms," and clicking on one of them lets you enter it. Since the first thing you will need to do to get started is open an image, you should click the In Room screen. This screen gives you several image acquisition sources: KPG's Library, a file on your hard disk, Photo CD disc, a digital camera, or a frame from a QuickTime movie. The program also reads BMP, QuickTime, PICT, Photoshop, and TIFF image formats.

Double-clicking any In Room icon launches a standard Open dialog that allows you to import an image into KPG's workspace. The program's main controls are contained in two rainbow-hued rows of dots that are arranged in an arc shape. The first set of controls contains effects you brush onto the image; the second set applies to the entire photograph. Clicking on either toolset enlarges them to surround your photograph. These f controls are: Grow/Shrink, Move, Smear, Smudge, Nudge, Mirror, Toggle, Smooth, and Ungoo.

The best way to experience KPG's tools is to click on them and move your mouse around the image. What you will discover is the electronic equivalent of the finger-painting you did in Sunday School. The only difference is that, in this case, you are dipping your fingers (or mouse) into a liquid photograph! The

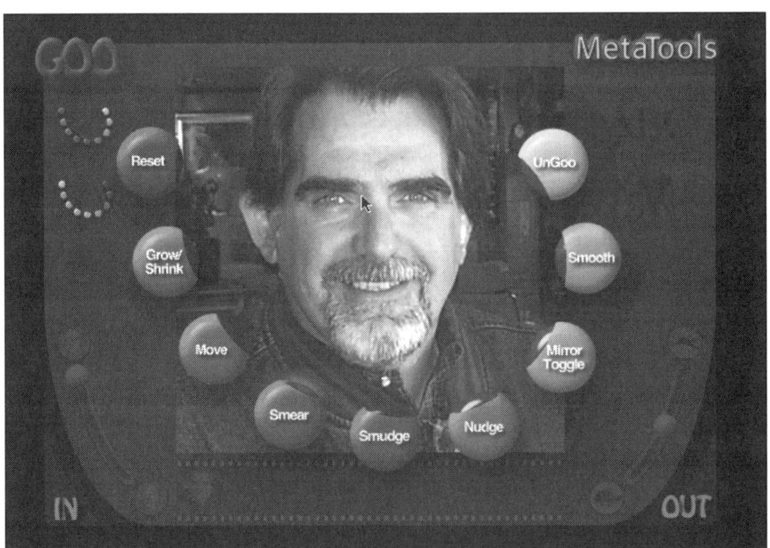

Figure 6.8 Kai's Power Goo has several uses—including just having fun—for amateur and professional photographers alike. Photo © Barry Staver.

UnGoo button provides an almost unlimited number of Undo's and allows you to step backward through the effects that you have applied. There is also a slider that lets you move back in time through the changes you have made. I had much better results with the slider than the UnGoo button, which seemed to work intermittently. The safest way to work is to occasionally click on the filmstrip at the bottom of the screen, which saves and displays the current version of the image you are working on. This allows you to experiment, but you can always find your way back to the last version of the image you liked. Think of it as a digital version of Hansel and Gretel's breadcrumbs.

One of KPG's many features is Fusion, which allows you to paint features from one image onto another. This is accomplished by importing two images, appearing on the left and right side of a large preview window in the center of the screen. There are four buttons at the bottom of each small image allowing you to Paint + (add), Paint - (subtract), Smear, or Smooth. Clicking on a feature of one image allows you to paint that feature onto the other one!

Output is controlled by the Out room, which lets you save the image as a still image or QuickTime movie or print it. Even if you work with images of modest resolution, you can output at 2,000 × 2,000 pixels to get smooth, sharp images. If you need larger resolution images, just assign more RAM to Goo. All KPG's tools and commands are intuitive, and there is no User's Guide in a form commonly understood as documentation. Instead, there is a four-page Installation Guide and a poster that, more or less, explains everything.

While Kai's Power Goo may seem to be a home- or even game-oriented product, I think many studio owners and photographers will find ways to put KPG to work right away. Here are a few ideas that immediately come to mind.

- Set up an inexpensive PC in the waiting room and let kids play with it while waiting for their parents to place orders.
- High school seniors love anything that's different. I can image a creative studio owner coming up with a "Funny Face" or "Fun House Mirror" option using KPG manipulated images as a way to cross-sell more wallet-sized photographs.
- Use images created with KPG as public relations to call attention to the studio's involvement in digital imaging.

I am sure all of you will think of others.

There are no separate versions of Kai's Power Goo for Windows and Mac users. The same CD-ROM installs the program on both kinds of computers, and I successfully installed and ran KPG on my Power Mac and 486 PC-compatible. That's the good news. The bad news is that Goo demands that the original disc be placed in your CD-ROM drive. Since the program reads Kodak Photo CD files and most users have only one CD-ROM drive, you are left with two choices: copy the Photo CD files you want to Goo around with onto your hard drive, or install a CD-ROM changer.

Chromassage

Second Glance Software's Chromassage manipulation plug-in provides Photoshop users with color table manipulation, palette rotations, as well as color "injection" into 25-bit images. Effects can range from posterizations to color effects you could not otherwise imagine. Chromassage appears under the Second Glance item in Photoshop's pull-down Filters menu. The filter's interface features an interactive preview of your image as it is being modified. Tools include current and modified color palettes and "jog wheel" type sliders that roll the color palettes back and forth (and up and down) to provide a dazzling amount of color choices. There is an "injector" that can be used to place a user-definable amount of color on the image. Over thirty optional color palettes are pre-installed, and users can supplement these by importing colors used in a favorite photograph.

Step 1. Using Chromassage is a lot of fun, so I wanted to begin with a colorful, fun photograph. In this case, a Photo CD image of the my wife at play in Disney World was selected and opened in Adobe Photoshop.

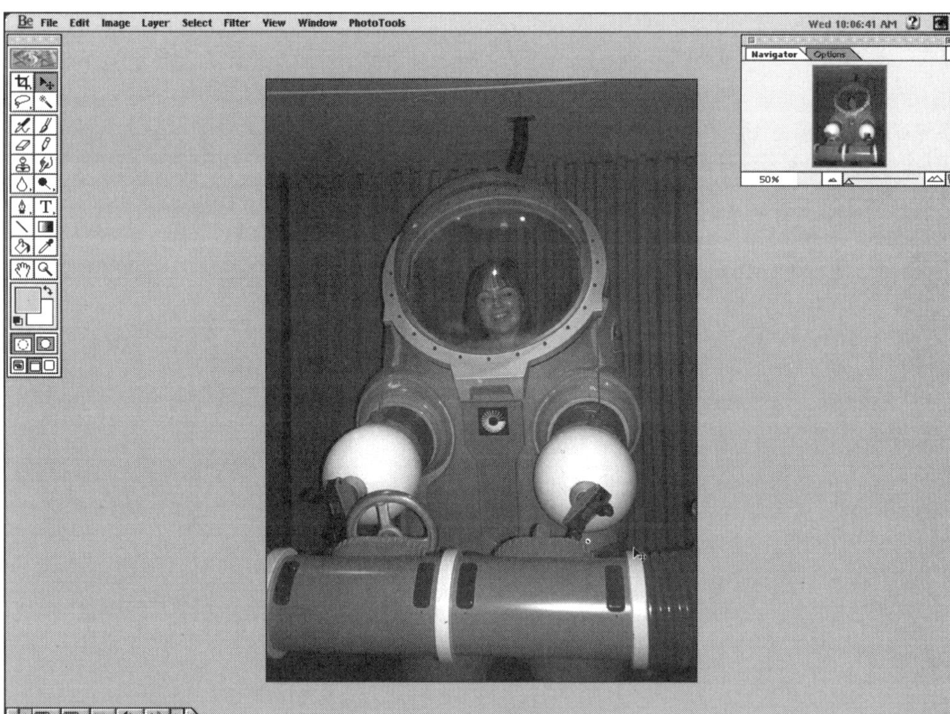

Figure 6.9 The starting point for the Chromassage manipulation was a photograph of the author's wife's—doing a Captain Nemo imitation—at Disney World. Photo © Joe Farace.

Step 2. Next, I chose Chromassage from the Second Glance submenu in Photoshop's Filter's menu. When you launch Chromassage you will see a large window with an equally large preview of your image. From the Operations pop-up menu, I selected the Super Range color palette, then used the Hand tool to drag the entire palette on top of the colors in my image's palette. This action replaces all of the photograph's colors with new ones. Next, I used the jog and shuttle wheels to experiment with further combinations and permutations of the colors.

Since results can vary from dramatic to dramatically bad, each step in the process has an Undo function to set things back the way they were before you started playing with one of Chromassage's many functions. This plug-in is a filter that only does one thing—manipulate the color palette—but the effects it produces are infinitely variable. When you find something you like, click Apply.

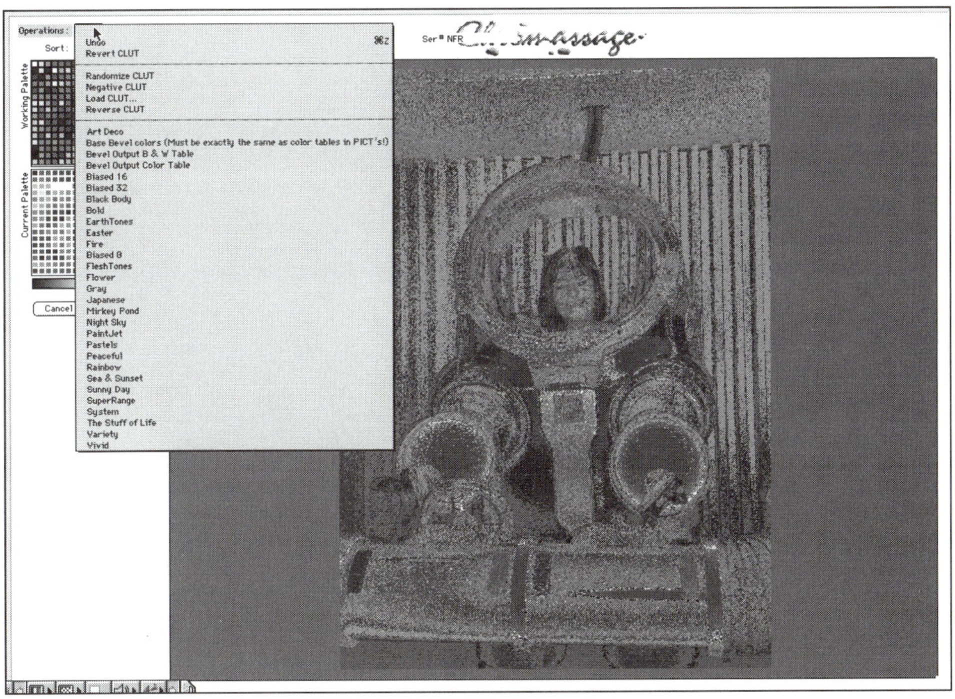

Figure 6.10 Chromassage's interface allows you to apply thirty preset color palettes, but variations are also available and, when combined with the jog and shuttle wheels, an almost infinite number of color possibilities exist.

(See Figure 6.11 on CD-ROM.)

Eye Candy

The most fun and exciting new plug-in shown at MacWorld Expo 1997 was Alien Skin Software's Eye Candy 3.0. This is a set of Photoshop-compatible plug-ins formerly know as The Black Box 2.0. In case you are wondering why, the name change was made to avoid confusion with the Black Box computer hardware catalog. Although the show may have been Mac-oriented, the company offers the plug-ins in both Mac OS and Windows versions. Eye Candy consists of a total of twenty-one filters. The ten filters carried over from The Black Box (Drop Shadow, Inner Bevel, Outer Bevel, Glow, Glass, Swirl, HSB Noise, Carve, Cutout, and Motion Trail) now have a new interface and more parameters, and they use color pickers where appropriate. The eleven new filters are Fire, Smoke, Fur, Chrome, Perspective Shadow, Star, Antimatter, Squint, Jiggle, Weave, and Water Drops. How good are they? The typical way for adding digital water drops to the surface of a photograph involves using a series of shadow and highlight masks. Eye Candy's Water Drops filter does the same thing in much less time, is much easier to accomplish, and the results are just as impressive. In the following example, I decided to have fun and selectively apply several Eye Candy filters. Here's what I did.

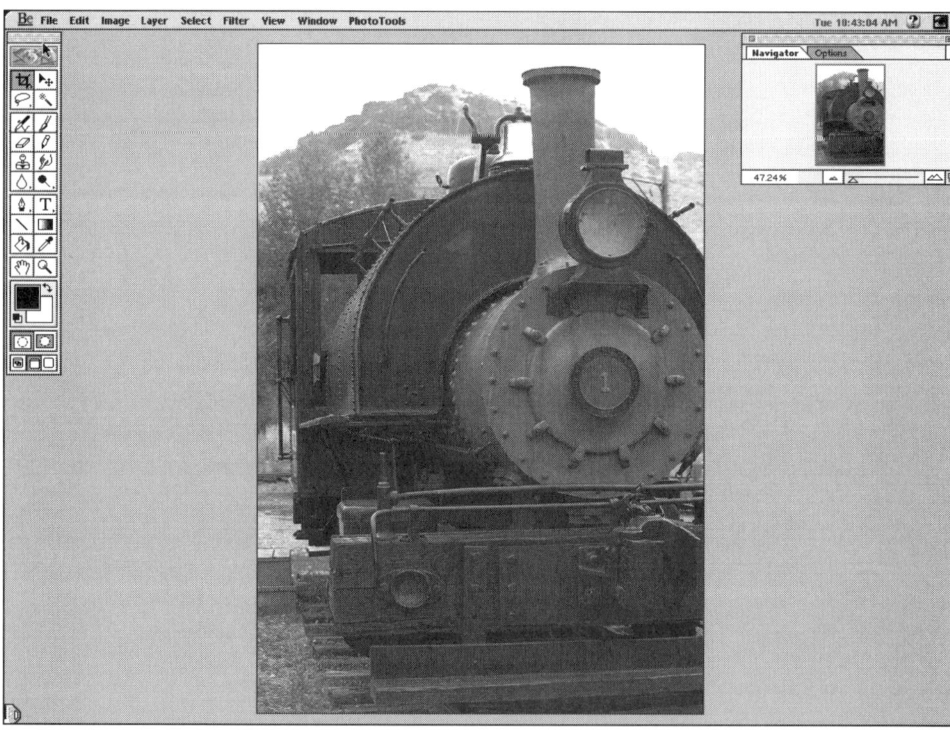

Figure 6.12 A photo CD image of a locomotive photographed on 35mm color negative film was the starting point for this exploration of Eye Candy. Photo © Joe Farace.

Step 1. I opened a Photo CD image of a vintage locomotive, adjusting the photograph's contrast and sharpness to my taste using Adobe Photoshop's built-in commands.

Step 2. Since the locomotive is a static display, I wanted to add some "life"—if only in digital form—to the photograph. I used the rectangular selection tool to select an area at the top of the smoke stack, then I chose Eye Candy's Smoke filter from the Filters menu. As with all plug-ins that use sliders, I like to move them to the opposite ends to find an effect that looks good. You need to go past the point that you are happy with, then back it off until you find an effect you like.

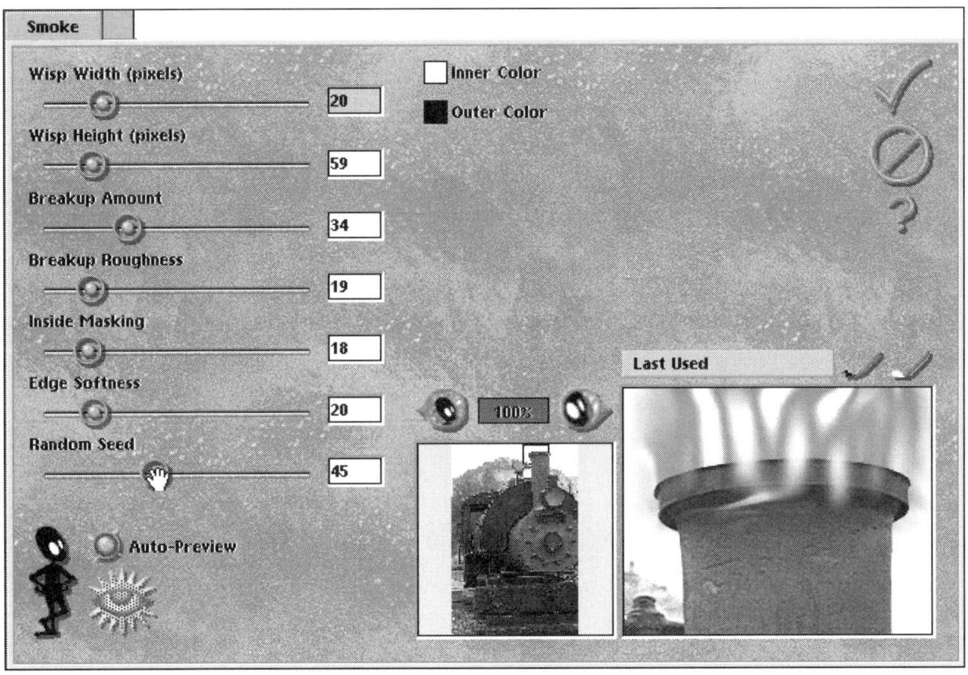

Figure 6.13 Eye Candy's Smoke filter provides sliders that let you control seven different aspects of digital smoke.

Step 3. Next, I wanted to add a little glow in the locomotive's headlight. To do this I (naturally) reached for the Glow filter that is part of Eye Candy. I used Photoshop's circular selection tool to draw a circle that fit in the headlight, then I chose the Glow filter from the Filters menu. There are only a few settings for Glow, so I experimented to provide something that might be subtle but was fun and easy to do. It also added some color to the image. (See Figure 6.14.)

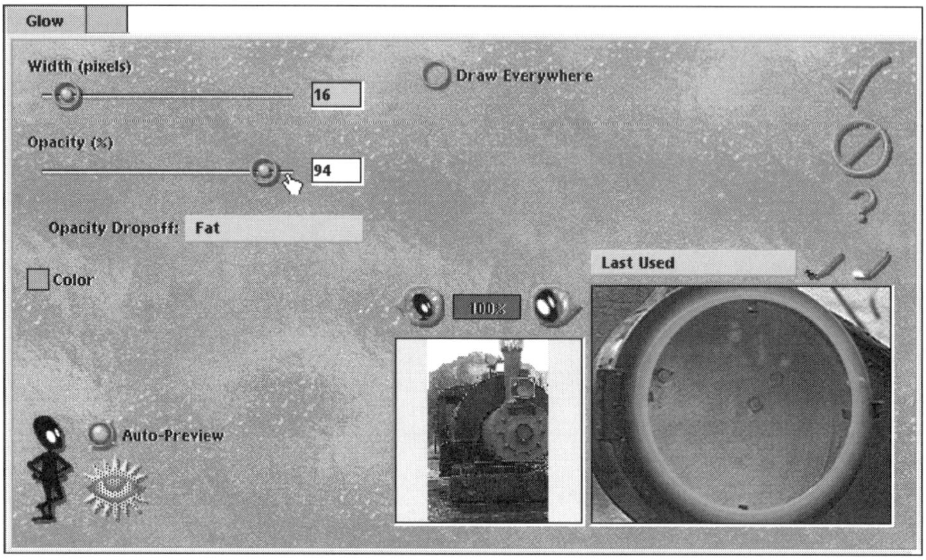

Figure 6.14 Eye Candy's Glow filter lets you apply different kinds—and colors—of glow effects to selections.

Step 4. Lastly, I used the Weave filter to create a quilt-like look to the photograph. (The idea of the hard metal image and a soft fabric look appealed to me.) The Weave filter works with five sliders, plus a Smear Threads check box that I especially like. Experiment, then apply.

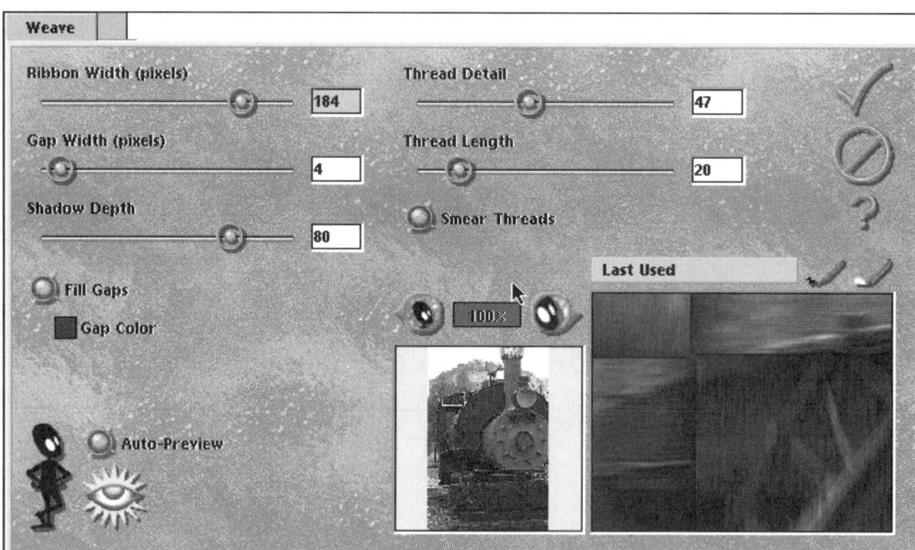

Figure 6.15 The Weave filter that is part of the Eye Candy package lets you apply a quilt-like look to your digital images.

TIP: Plug-in Slider

Eye Candy ships each filter with at least ten presets, giving a total of over 200 single-click effects — even before you begin experimenting. But when you use the techniques that I suggest, you will quickly find settings — for all of the filters in the package — that fit your taste and style. When you do, you can save these settings and be able to apply them again without going through trial-and-error experimentation. This makes it easy to consistently reproduce specific effects.

Step 5. Even though Weave provides a preview, the pattern size I chose was so large that it was difficult to properly evaluate in the Eye Candy preview window. Consequently, the effects I used seemed to be too much. No problem. I used Photoshop's Fade command to reduce the effect by 50%. Using three of Eye Candy's filters, I was able to create what was—for me—a fun image. (See Figure 6.16 on CD-ROM.)

While many Photoshop-compatible plug-ins are aimed at photographic effects, Eye Candy includes filters like Cutout, which are better suited to text or graphic effects. Cutout makes your selection appear as a hole in the image. It does this by adding a shadow and optional fill color inside the selection so that it appears recessed behind the rest of the image. Perspective Shadow is another great graphics filter. The filter creates a shadow behind the selection so that it appears to be standing up with the light coming from above and in front. You can do this in Photoshop by duplicating the object (or selection) as a new layer, selecting it, and filling it with black. Then you have to select the now-gray object, skew it at an oblique angle, apply some blur, and offset it. Or you can just use Perspective Shadow.

The interfaces for the various plug-ins that are part of Eye Candy have been redesigned and feature a contemporary—but not gimmicky—look. The previews are resizable and zoomable for magnifications from 6% to 1,600%. A thumbnail is provided to instantaneously move the preview to any part of the original image. Initially, Eye Candy 3.0 is designed to work with Photoshop 3.0.4 or later versions, and all of the filters are fully scriptable using Photoshop 4.0 Actions.

WildRiver SSK

Plug-in connoisseurs may recognize WildRiver SSK 1.0 as being derived from the Japanese package Sucking Fish. (That's why, when working through the User's Guide, you will see that a graphic of a fish is often used as an example.) Like Eye Candy, WildRiver SSK is a package of several plug-ins that include Chameleon, MagicCurtain, MagicFrame, MagicMask, TileMaker, TVSnow, and DekoBoko. Chameleon remaps a user-selected range of colors to a newly defined range. In

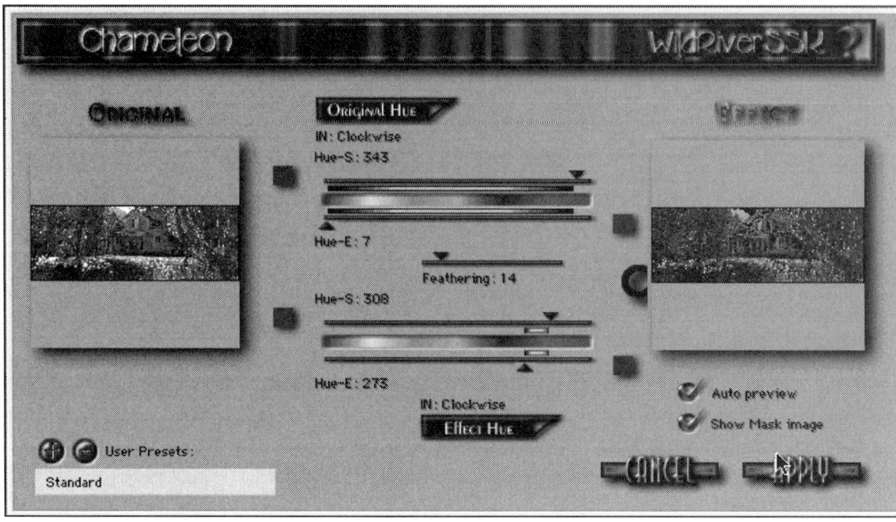

Figure 6.17 One of the WildRiver SSK Chameleon plug-in's most useful feature is the ability to select a color or color range and have it protected by an automatically created mask while you manipulate the rest of the image's colors. Photo © Joe Farace.

concept, the plug-in acts much like Second Glance Software's Chromassage, the big difference is in the interface and the ability to use an Eye Dropper to select a color or color range from the original image.

DekoBoko is Japanese for convex and concave. This filter creates 3D frames that can be used to make button shapes from rectangular selections. MagicCurtain creates gradated fills based on selected waves. The original image can be used as a texture to create a "wavy" background. By comparison, MagicFrame creates straight, gradated color frames. Both TileMaker and TVSnow do just what you would expect. The heart of WildRiverSSK is MagicMask, which provides twenty-four (count 'em) effects that revolve around lighting and color effects. Like Photoshop itself, you could spend a lot of time with this filter working with effects such as MetalShadow. To help you sort out this multi-faceted package, Datastream has provide a User's Guide that not only tells you how to use the filters, but is chock full of tips, too.

Paint Alchemy

Xaos Tools Paint Alchemy 1.0 had an interesting interface, but some digital imaging newcomers found it difficult to understand. Version 2.0 corrects this design fault and features an easy-to-use interface that's attractive to look at as well. The goal of Paint Alchemy is simple: this plug-in applies brush strokes to an image or to a selected portion of an image. This may sound uncomplicated, but an examination of the plug-in's capabilities shows that there are many, many definitions of what a "brush stroke" can be. Paint Alchemy's definition is wide and allows you to use any square PICT file as a brush, which enables you to create your own custom palette of brushes. The Styles pop-up menu contains 101 built-in styles, giving you access to a wide range of effects. Brush size and opacity may be varied by hue, saturation, or lightness of the image, allowing you to create effects that work with the natural light and shadows of the original photograph. There is even a Randomize option that creates more variations on the built-in styles. Brush strokes can be layered in a random or ordered way, and paint colors can be mixed using Blend, Over, Under, Sum, or Difference methods to provide an infinite amount of color effects. Once an effect looks the way you want, you can save its settings so you will be able to produce the identical results the next time. One of the effects that Paint Alchemy makes it easy to achieve is an artistic or painterly look. Let me show you how easy it is to do.

Step 1. I opened a photograph of a Victorian house in Georgetown, Colorado. The image was originally shot on color negative film and digitized using Kodak's Photo CD process. While I would normally add sharpness through Unsharp Mask and bump the contrast, I did not do that in this case. Since the image would be softened by the brush strokes I planned to apply, I felt that I would waste time sharpening the image—but that does not mean that you cannot try this to produce a more photorealistic painting style. (See Figure 6.18a on CD-ROM.)

Step 2. Next, I opened the Paint Alchemy filter from Photoshop's Filter menu. Its two windows provide before and after views, but you must click the Preview button to see any changes that you made.

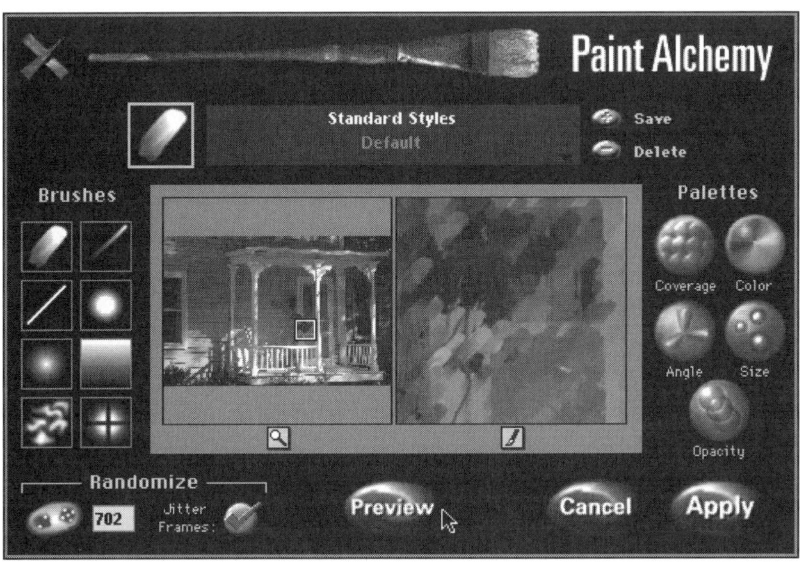

Figure 6.18b Paint Alchemy's control panel gives you access to many effects, plus the Size, Coverage, Color, Angle, and Opacity that allow you to customize any of the built-in brush strokes and effects. Photo © Joe Farace.

> I experimented with different brush styles and settled on the brad brush, but I changed the size of the brush by clicking on the Size palette that Xaos Tools provides. There are four other palettes, including Coverage, Color, Angle, and Opacity, that allow you to customize any of the built-in brush strokes and effects. When the Preview window gave me a look I liked, I clicked Apply and was finished.

(See Figure 6.18c on CD-ROM.)

Paint Alchemy can change the look of an entire image or just one section. You can, for example, use the plug-in to create an infinite number of backgrounds that can be added to any studio portrait.

IMAGE OUTPUT

Test Strip

Most photographers are already familiar with the concept of the test strip when used in conventional, wet darkrooms. Vivid Details' Test Strip is a functional plug-in designed for photographers, artists, and service bureaus that are interested in achieving accurate color reproduction. Like the classic test strips of wet darkroom days, Test Strip can make either horizontal or vertical strips to match the kind of image you are currently working on. You can also produce a series of repeating thumbnails, much like Photoshop's Variations feature. You can view Test Strip images against a black or white background, as well as an 18% gray that is produced with only black and white pixels. (See Figure 6.19 on CD-ROM.)

Where Test Strip breaks with Variations is in the manner in which you can alter the number of strips that may be displayed, and in the fact that colors can be added or subtracted. For example, colors may be altered in increments as small as 1%. The plug-in lets you interact with the correction process by clicking on the strip that displays a reduced or increased amount of color or density. If you are used to printing from transparencies, you can remove color casts by selecting the opposite color on the color wheel. Similarly, precision-minded users will find that Vivid Details provides a digital densitometer that provides precise numeric feedback. While you are tweaking away, Test Strip maintains a Task List that records and displays all of the color corrections steps you have made—as you make them. If, later on, you discover that you need to make a similar set of corrections to other images, you can save the Task List and apply it to a different image. Test Strip also lets you save one of its views as a file and print it on any output device, from a FARGO Pictura 310 to an Iris printer. The proof can be used for client approval or for a guide for making your own color management decisions.

PhotoSpot

Second Glance Software offers an Output plug-in package called PhotoSpot that lets users produce spot color separations from within Photoshop by exporting separation documents for each color in your image. You can print directly from Photoshop or import the file into programs like QuarkXPress or Aldus PageMaker to match other elements in your layout. Included in this package are three additional filter plug-ins that perform color reductions. Acetone is a fast method for color reduction and remaps the tones in the image to the colors you specify for separation. You can access the remapping process with a color bar interface that lets the user nudge a color range toward another hue. All images can be previewed and altered before finally applying this filter. Paint Thinner provides control over color reduction and posterization when making spot color separations. This filter's interface shows a preview of the image along with a palette of 256 reduced colors. To use it, all you have to do is select a range of image colors in the palette or on the preview and reassign them to a single spot color. Turpentine creates an eight-color diffusion tone image from your photographs. This technique can produce butt-registered super-color process separations that have more vibrant colors than CMYK alone can produce. PhotoSpot is only available for Macintosh, but a Windows version is planned.

On the Web

Other Output filters can be used to prepare images for use on the Internet and World Wide Web. While Photoshop reads and writes many different graphics file format, version 3.0.5 does not support PNG (Portable Network Graphics). Banana Software offers a shareware PNG plug-in for the Windows version of Photoshop and compatible programs. To install the output filter, copy it into the same directory with the other filters, then exit Photoshop and start it again. The Open and Save dialog boxes will now contain an entry for PNG file type. The plug-in will also be present in the list of filters under Help About Plug-ins.

HVS Color 1.2.6 from Digital Frontiers is another Web-oriented output plug-in that converts 24-bit images into 8-bit with no visible loss of quality. You can save realistic-looking photographs having the advantages of 25-bit but with one-third the file size. Because HVS Color achieves its effects without dithering, files compress 5 to 40 percent better, meaning less download time. Depending on the image, you can expect up to a 70 percent reduction in file size. When working with large images, be aware that the plug-in requires a Photoshop partition equal to six times the original file's size but HVS Color is compatible with virtual memory and Connectix's RAM Doubler.

7

Go Mouseless

Tired of mousing around? Maybe it's time you gave your mouse a rest and switched to a graphic tablet the next time you want to manipulate a digital image. Graphics tablets have been around since the late Sixties and are widely used in the CAD (Computer Aided Design), computer graphics, and teleconferencing industries. Long considered the province of the artist or designer, there are four reasons digital imagers should be using a graphics tablet.

First, because a stylus, or pen, is more natural to hold than a mouse, graphics tablets are one of the best ways to create original drawings, illustrations, and other nontext information. Second, because of their design, using a graphics tablet and pen is easier and faster when using an image-editing program's burning or dodging tools. Third, the human engineering aspects of graphics tablets can, for some people, reduce the pain caused by carpal tunnel syndrome. Lastly, graphics tablets are a much more accurate pointing and input device than a mouse.

WHAT IS A GRAPHICS TABLET?

Because they can convert graphics and drawings into digital information, graphics tablets are often called digitizing tablets. This now-digitized visual data can be entered into your computer for storage, analysis, modification, or archiving. While the product may be referred to as a tablet, they really have two major parts: a tablet and pen or stylus that is used to "draw" on the tablet's sensitive surface.

The tablet portion, which nowadays can be so thin that it's called a "pad," contains a mechanism for sensing where on the surface a stylus is positioned. Its bed is divided into a high-resolution matrix that can respond to active or passive actions. (Active response is when the element is drawn and passive is after it is drawn.) Digital information is represented as the X-Y coordinates of where the pen is placed. (See Figure 7.1 on CD-ROM.)

The accuracy of graphics tablets and their ultimate performance is defined by resolution, accuracy, and linearity.

Resolution

Resolution measures the number of points per inch that a tablet can recognize and how fine a distinction it can make between adjacent points. Typical resolutions vary from 25 to 1,000 points per inch, but specifications for high-end CAD markets are higher. Higher resolution devices cost more, but tablets can cost as little as $129 or more than $2,400 from the same manufacturer, depending on resolution and pad size.

Accuracy

Accuracy measures fidelity to the actual distance being measured versus what happens on screen. A tablet that resolves 100 points per inch typically has an accuracy of 0.01 inches, and units that resolve 1,000 points per inch can exceed 0.005 inches of accuracy. By comparison, a human eye resolves approximately 5,000 lines per inch at a distance of ten inches. The average user's accuracy will be plus or minus 0.01 inches, but a skilled CAD operator can usually beat this.

Linearity

Linearity tells you how much variability there is in the first two parameters across your field of work. Brochures and documentation for graphics tablets contain specifications for resolution, accuracy, and linearity, and you can use them to compare one to another.

WHAT TO LOOK FOR

When you are shopping for a graphics tablet be sure to keep in mind that the needs of a digital imager are different from an engineer designing parts for a Boeing 777.

Graphics tablets come in many configurations. The first variable is the tablet itself. Tablet size varies from 4 × 5 inches up to 44 × 60 inches, depending on the manufacturer and your specific application. When manufacturers specify size, they are referring to the active area of the tablet, that is, its usable area, and not the unit's physical size. A tablet's actual size will always be slightly larger. One of the advantages of a flexible tablet is that it can be rolled out on any surface and left in place, acting not just as a tablet but as a permanent desktop or work area. Numonics was the first company to introduce a flexible digitizing pad in 1990, and for some presenters, having a soft rather than rigid tablet may be a consideration. Their GridMaster Flexible Digitizing Mat is 1/33-inch thick, weighs twelve ounces, and is available in sizes from 12 × 12 inches to 20 × 24 inches. Presenters will prefer smaller pads, while the larger ones are used by artist, and designers. The space a tablet takes is usually less than a mousepad and can be extremely light. The 4 × 5 CalComp DrawingSlate II is 1/5-inch thick, weighs less than one pound, and can be held in the palm of your hand, placed on your lap, or plopped down onto the most crowded desk or lectern. (See Figure 7.2 on CD-ROM.)

Some graphics tablets allow an option to have either a stylus or a mouse-like device called a cursor or puck. Summagraphics offers small pads with a puck option. Their 4 × 5 SummaPad, which is an ideal size for cramped work spaces, comes equipped with your choice of a cordless 4-button pressure sensitive pen or a cordless 3-button puck.

Styluses are available in several flavors, including both corded and cordless models. Cordless models are further subdivided by having those that require batteries and those that do not. Batteryless cordless styluses are preferred over pens with batteries because—if you don't have a battery—it makes it impossible to have the pen "run dry" during a crunch deadline. Wacom's UltraPen looks like a typical stylus but contains no batteries or magnets. Instead, radio waves are sent by the pad to the stylus and are returned for position analysis—much like radar. Every twenty microseconds, a grid of wires in the pad alternates between send and receive. In send mode, the signal from the pad stimulates an oscillation in the coil and capacitor circuit in the pen. In receive mode, the pen's circuit oscillations are detected and are analyzed by Wacom's software to determine not only position but pressure too. Since the grid provides power through resonant coupling, no batteries are required. (See Figure 7.3 on CD-ROM.)

Each of these configurations has their advantages and disadvantages. Corded pens may be less convenient than cordless models, but because they're tethered to the tablet with an umbilical you will never lose a stylus. Another advantage of corded styluses is that they are always less expensive. ACECAD's ACECAT II, which has a 5 × 6-inch tablet size, has a street price of $100.

Some pens feature the latest hot-button features—erasablity and pressure sensitivity. The Wacom UltraPen, for example, features an "eraser" end that can, depending on software implementation, remove information as well as add it. CalComp's Drawing Slate II features what they call "fumble-free" erasing. To erase work, you can activate the erasing function by pressing one of the two buttons on the side of the pen instead of having to flip the pen over. Erasability may or may not be something you need. If you like this feature, make sure it is implemented in a manner you will be comfortable with, and that it cannot accidentally be activated during a presentation. A pressure sensitive stylus lets you control the width of each pen stroke. The harder you rub, the more you erase. When used with word-processing programs, like Microsoft Word, Wacom's UltraPen replaces its pressure sensitivity with one-stroke erasing of words or cells.

Anything you can do with a mouse, you can do with a stylus. And there are some things a stylus does better. Try writing your name with a mouse, and you'll see what I mean. One area of stylus superiority is cursor placement. Instead of rolling a mouse to locate a cursor, just tap the pen on the tablet and that's where the cursor appears. Don't automatically assume a graphics tablet will make a perfect mouse substitute. Make sure the manufacturer includes software controls that lets the unit emulate your favorite mouse and has a way to perform mouse clicks. ACECAD's ACECAT III, for example, features a programmable 4-button stylus giving you access to "mouse clicks" with their corded pen. Typically, a double tap of the stylus represents a double click, and Wacom's Ultra Pen has a side switch that can be set to provide a double-click. Many tablets, like Hitachi's Studio Pad, also include a series of function "keys" across the top of the pad that give you access to the commands controlled by function keys on a traditional keyboard.

If warranty requirements are important, graphics tablets typically offer a better deal than most mouse or other mouse substitutes like trackballs. CalComp's 4 × 5 Drawing Slate II offers a lifetime limited warranty. Most graphics tablets work with both Mac OS and Windows platforms as well as most popular workstations, so that the question of matching a tablet with a computer is a nonissue.

FOR PRESENTATIONS

Many photographers give presentations. It may be just to your peers, or you may give presentations to civic and professional groups to market your photographic services or products. One of the best reasons for using a graphics tablet is to improve the quality and throughput of graphics images used in presentations. The other reason for using a graphics tablet during a presentation is the control and comfort it gives the presenter. Since presentations are always fraught with some level of tension and uncertainty, anything that reduces the presenter's stress levels will increase the quality of his or her performance. That's why a graphics tablet works so well for interactive presentations, where intuitive user reactions are required.

Presentation software from third-party vendors can be used to enhance the capabilities of your new graphics tablets. For presenters working with a Windows system, Mind Path Technologies' Presentation F/X Pro includes a zoom tool that can magnify the screen's contents by up to 800%, use special effects on the fly, and add check marks on the screen—even use pink, green, or

TIP: A Long Reach

A graphics tablet does not have to tie you to a lectern during your presentation. ACECAD provides an optional 20-foot serial cable to allow presenters to move around, and a wrist strap on the back of the tablet makes it easy to hang onto.

yellow highlighter pens. Piptel's Mac OS-based software, called PaperPower, helps users of PowerPoint, Harvard Graphics, Astound, and other presentation packages work with graphics tablets. It does this by allowing you to create overlays for Wacom tablets. An overlay can be created in any size, shape, and layout, and it can contain dozens of labeled functions designed for specific presentations. A demonstration version of PaperPower can be downloaded from Wacom's home page at http://www.wacom.com. When you get there, click the "Device Drivers" button.

One of the newest uses of graphics tablets is using them to draw on top of presentations, including video. This technology is not just limited to all of the budding John Maddens out there, and it was used in the O.J. Simpson trial for on-line annotations over video images as they were being discussed. Boeckler Instruments' PVI-80 is part of the company's family of video markers that are connected between the video source, such as a VCR, and the video display, a monitor or video projector. The PVI-80 series comes with a keyboard and one of a variety of devices, including a light pen, wireless remote control, or digitizing tablet. In fact, it was Boeckeler Instruments' video annotation system, using ACECAD's ACECAT II digitizing tablet bundled as a front end, that was actually used during the O.J. Simpson trial, allowing witnesses to draw and sketch information over video and still images. In addition to being able to "draw" on top of video images, a presenter can call up a solid background and use it like a chalkboard to make a point or two or three. Depending on options, Boeckeler's hardware prices vary from $2,695 to $2,995.

Chisholm's Rainbow active LCD projection panel features a graphics tablet option. Using an overhead projector, you can place the Rainbow LCD on the projector's stage. To control the presentation you can use a pen instead of a mouse, but more importantly, you can pick up the pen and produce interactive writing or drawing on the on-screen images. You can use the pen to add notes, draw "circles and arrows," and underline key points as you talk. Prices for this package vary from $5,495 to $6,995, depending on the options.

Do not let the fact that you always use a mouse to control presentations keep you from exploring other options. Graphics tablets can increase the comfort level of your presenter while, at the same time, allowing you to add features such as annotated video to your next presentation. With the least expensive tablets costing only slightly more than a replacement mouse, the costs involved can be surprisingly small, especially when compared to possible benefits.

8

Analog to Digital to Analog

In this chapter, you will get a look at the digital imaging cycle—from Analog to Digital back to Analog. You will learn about getting your digital images into a form that can be printed using conventional analog (silver-based darkroom) techniques. This includes tips on how to work with service bureaus to produce output from your digital images and how to avoid problems along the way. This chapter's case study shows how a magazine photographer uses both digital and analog techniques to create customized portfolios. Before getting to that, let's take a look at one of the first output-related problems that face the new digital imager: making sure the color you see on the monitor matches the output.

MANAGING DESKTOP COLOR

Most desktop color management problems can be boiled down to a single statement: making sure that what looks good on your computer screen also looks good when the file is output by a printer. The problem is the same no matter if the output is handled by a desktop printer, service bureau, or printing firm. Any differences that occur between what you see on-screen and what the printer delivers to you are caused by the different ways that light and ink represent colors. That is the crux of the color management dilemma.

Color management problems are not just limited to computer-based imaging. Photographers who shoot images using color negative film will, sooner or later, also encounter difficulties managing color. If you've looked at prints delivered by a color lab and complained that they were "too light," or "that wasn't the color of the car I photographed—it was much greener," you have already experienced the need for color management. Those same problems happen with your computer imaging system—for reasons not too dissimilar to what happens when color negative film is processed and printed.

Running the Gamut

Every output device has a range of colors it can accurately reproduce. This range is called the gamut of the device. Every hardware device from every manufacturer, whether it is a monitor or printer, has a unique gamut. Each device's gamut is part of a standard area of color science called color space, and different types of devices work in different color spaces. Because of the way they are designed and constructed, monitors, for example, work in a different color space than do printers, and this creates part of the color management problem. If you find that the output of your color printer does not match what you see on screen, you are beginning to understand the need for color management. One of the reasons for this problem is that the color seen on the display is "in gamut" for the monitor, but not for the printer. The problem is compounded by the fact that the gamuts of desktop devices—not unlike film itself—is relatively small when compared to the spectrum of visible light.

The other problems endemic to precise color management has to do with the way computer peripherals communicate with one another. The predecessor to today's desktop color management systems has previously existed only in dedicated, computerized systems used by printers, called color electronic publishing systems or CEPS. Many new desktop imaging hardware and software products are manufactured by different companies, and none of them communicate in exactly the same color language. Desktop color management systems were developed to solve these problems.

Many of the devices you currently own have some degree of color management already built into them. You may discover that the first thing you need to do to minimize "out of gamut" problems is to make sure you have done all you can to maximize their color management using built-in controls.

Calibrate, Calibrate!

Calibrating your monitor is the first step in color management. Some programs force you to set up your monitor when you install them. While installing Quarterdeck's HiJaak Graphics Suite, you are presented with two dialog boxes to help the software match your monitor. This is the opposite of the approach that Adobe Systems takes by matching the monitor to the software. Photoshop has a Monitor Setup option in the Color Setting of its File menu, which lets you set the Gamma, White Point, and Phosphors for your specific monitor. If you are not familiar with these terms, here's a quick overview.

Gamma, White Point, Phosphors

Gamma. This setting measures the contrast that affects the midlevel grays of an image. Adjusting gamma lets you change the brightness of the middle range of gray tones without affecting shadows or highlights. The gamma for your particular monitor can be adjusted by the Gamma Control Panel that Adobe includes with the Mac version of Photoshop. The Windows version of the program has a Calibrate function built into the Monitor Setup dialog box.

White Point. Sometimes called Highlight Point, White Point is one of the endpoints on a curve (the Shadow Point is the other) that defines the dynamic range of a photograph.

Phosphors. This setting affects the different kinds of red, blue, and green phosphors used by different manufacturers in their monitors. Monitor Setup contains most of the common phosphors used and allows you to match your monitor's specifications.

Many different brands of monitors are built into Photoshop's Monitor Setup dialog. If you have one of the listed brands, all you have to do is select your monitor from the menu, and the data in all three of the above categories will be automatically entered. If your monitor is not one of them, call the manufacturer's customer support department and ask them to provide the data you need. Sometimes they will give you specific numeric data to enter, or provide the name of an equivalent monitor that you can use. Radius' PressView monitors include a ProSense colorimeter, which allows users to directly measure the display's phosphor color and white point.

Remember that all of this data, along with the rest of your preferences, is stored in a separate Preferences file. When you install a new version of Photoshop, it automatically writes over your "Prefs" file, destroying all the data in it. It's a good idea to back this file up onto a floppy disk so that you can reinstall it when installing any new version of Photoshop.

Managing Color

Color Management Systems software (CMS) can help you produce accurate and faithful reproduction of your original color images. A good CMS must address two major aspects—calibration and characterization—and all successful systems include both of them.

Calibration

All kinds of variables—including your working environment—can affect the way a device is calibrated. Calibration stabilizes the inevitable variables in the way a device reproduces color. To produce optimum results, all of your color reproducing devices must maintain a consistent, calibrated state. Depending on the device and manufacturer, a variety of calibration products are available.

Characterization

This establishes the relationship of your calibrated device to what is referred to as a "device-independent reference color space," or RCS. Color space describes how a device reads, displays, and stores color values.

The most popular color management system available is Apple Computer's ColorSync. Some of its features include:

Color Matching Method. CMM is a routine used by a color management system to apply transformations to color data. Apple's CMMs transmit color information between documents and have been designed to be compatible with other companies' CMMs.

ICC Compatibility. The International Color Consortium is a group of eight of the largest manufacturers in the computer and digital imaging industries. The consortium works to advance cross-platform color communications, and it has established base-level standards and protocols in the form of ICC Profile Format specifications in order to build a common foundation for communication of color information. ColorSync supports all profiles that conform to ICC profiles specifications, allowing the same device profiles to be used across multiple platforms.

Postscript Support. Postscript is a page description language used to communicate page layout information from the computer to the output device.

Support for More than Four-Color Devices. ColorSync supports devices that use more than the standard process colors, such as Hi-Fi color printing.

Other color-management engines are also supported within ColorSync. If a Kodak device profile is used, it will look for the presence of the Kodak Precision color management system. If it finds it, ColorSync uses the Kodak system for the transform.

Making Sense

One way to ensure that the colors you see on screen match the output is to look at all of the options in your Print or Page Setup dialogs that are part of the drivers supplied by the printer manufacturers. When working with a new printer, check the Print or Page Setup dialog associated with its driver. The driver for the FARGO Pictura 310 dye-sublimation printer, for example, locates its color management choices under an Expert button in the Print dialog. In addition to "None" and "Fargo," the Color Matching pop-up menu displays any other color management software that may be installed. The default is "None."

One alternative is what I call "commonsense color management," and this is a good approach for the individual user who wants to color manage the output of a single desktop printer connected to their computer system. It is based on the classic technique of test strips used in conventional, wet darkrooms. For darkroom neophytes, a test strip is a single sheet of photographic paper on which different exposures are made. This allows you to see the effects on the image of different exposures, contrast, or color filter choices. One of the best ways to calibrate your color printer is to create your own test strips and analyze the results. Here's how to do it.

Step 1. Start by evaluating an uncorrected test print. Make sure you have done the monitor and printer setups properly, then make a print of a photograph that has a wide range of colors in it. Then, critically evaluate the print for color balance.

Step 2. Use an image editing program, such as Adobe Photoshop, to open a grayscale image.

Step 3. Use the program's Mode menu to convert the grayscale image into RGB. This may sound like a backwards approach, but to apply color corrections you need to start with a "color" image.

Step 4. Use the Marquee selection tool to select a vertical strip of the photograph. Using Variations from the Image/Adjust menu, set the slider all the way to the left—the lowest setting. If my original test print showed a green bias, I would add one "click" on the slider on the Red variation. If your photograph was too magenta, you would be adding gradually increasing amounts of green—you want to add the complementary color.

Step 5. Repeat the above step by selecting another strip next to the previous one, calling up Variations, and adding two "clicks" of red. Then repeat it again, each time adding a new strip and additional red.

Step 6. Print the test image and evaluate it. The reason for using a black-and-white image will now be apparent. The colored strip you are looking for is the one that is the most neutral in color. In evaluating my test, the strips varied in color from a cyan color on the left to a deep reddish brown on the right. The most neutral area was two steps in from the original setting. In order to make any future prints on this particular desktop printer appear neutral, I have to add two "clicks" of red before printing.

Until recently, the only way to produce color test strips with your computer was to make your own. All that's changed with the introduction of a Photoshop-compatible plug-in from Vivid Details called Test Strip. Available currently for Mac OS systems, Test Strip can produce either horizontal or vertical strips that can match the shape or design of your photograph or artwork. Test Strip was covered in detail in Chapter 6.

Managing color is important if you are outputting to a printer connected to your computer or sending your work to a service bureau.

WHAT IS A SERVICE BUREAU?

One day, I received the following e-mail message: "What is a service bureau? How does it differ from a regular printer? I use a Windows-based machine and every printer I called can only use files created on a Mac. I would like to try digital imaging, but if I cannot have them printed by anyone, it doesn't seem to be worth the effort."

Let's clear up some confusion about the name "service bureau." It's a term left over from the bad old days of computing when only the high priests and their acolytes had access to computers and few "real" people could afford to own a computer. Instead, you had to take your data—in punched card form—to companies who, for a fee, would process data for you. Today's service bureau can digitize your analog photographs using scanners or Kodak's Photo CD process, or turn digital images back into analog form, producing prints, slides, or negatives, images for presentations, and camera-ready artwork. As you can see, few typical print shops could be called service bureaus, but nowadays, some commercial photo labs offer many of these capabilities.

Regarding the question of Windows versus Mac OS platforms, any competent service bureau should be able handle digital input from Windows computers as well as Mac OS computers. If the service bureau you contact cannot handle PC-based graphic files, keep looking. If you live in a small town that does not have a service bureau labs, look in the back of publications such as *MacWeek*, *PC Week*, and *ComputerUSER* for ads for those that will work via mail order.

FINDING THE BEST SERVICE BUREAU

A service bureau can take many forms. It can be a small specialized facility that only provides Kodak Photo CD service, or a large commercial facility that offers a wide range of digital input and output services. Some service bureaus cater to the prepress market and can provide four-color separations directly from your Adobe Photoshop or PageMaker digital files.

How Do You Find a Good One?

Compare. Talk to your friends and find if they are using a service bureau that provides what you need at prices you can afford. I switched Photo CD service providers when speaking with a photographer who turned me on to a supplier who did a better job at a lower price than the one I had been using. While price alone is not a major consideration, it can be used as a basis for comparing facilities that offer a standard product or service. For example, in my area, I can pay anywhere, $3.00 or 70¢, for a five-resolution Photo CD scan. Photo CD Pro scans range from $4.00 to $18.00. In each case, my experience with the lowest-cost Photo CD provider has been as good as the highest price.

Test. Take a group of representative digital files and divide them into two groups. Send one to one service bureau and one to another. When the output comes back, evaluate the entire experience, not just the quality of the output. Were they delivered when you were told? Is the delivered price the same that was quoted? After that, look at the results. One Pro Photo CD provider I tested was unable to provide the index print that slips into the cover of the CD's case. "I couldn't get the color right," he told me. If he could not get the color right on the index print, I was concerned that he would not be able to get the color right on the Photo CD scans themselves.

Evaluate. In the case of any kind of scanning services, open the files and view them on your monitor. For other forms of output, you will be able to see the quality. Is it what you expected—or better?

Once you have made a decision to use a certain service provider, stick with it—through thick and thin. People who constantly change service bureaus are never satisfied. Everyone makes mistakes. What differentiates a good service bureau from a bad one is not just the quality of their product, but how they treat you when they make a mistake. What you need to find out is how quickly they correct these mistakes and how they treat you during the process.

IMAGE DELIVERY

The next question many people ask me is, "What is the best way to deliver your images to a service bureau?" Like other questions about digital graphics, there is no simple, single answer. The simplest way to transmit large image files is to send them by modem. Fast modems are available at very modest cost, and no other method delivers your files right now. Many service bureaus even provide free software for you to upload your files. The only disadvantage of this approach is that—depending on the speed of your modem—it could take several hours to transmit your files. On the other hand, you can upload images during a weekend and they will be ready first thing Monday morning.

Don't overlook removable media (see Chapter 4). These days, one of the most popular removable formats that you will see in use at service bureaus is Iomega's Zip. With a street price for a drive around $150, Iomega's Zip drive is affordable and its cartridges are compact and inexpensive. As I write this, the street price for a 100MB cartridge is $19.95. While the Zip is a relatively new format, it has been widely embraced by service bureaus, printers, and the graphics industry. My two Zip drives have been in operation for over a year, and during that time the drives and cartridges performed nearly flawlessly. I say "nearly" because I had one cartridge go bad of the over twenty that I have been using. Another format whose removable cartridges have enjoyed a good reputation is SyQuest's now discontinued 270MB. No matter what kind of removable media you choose, be careful how you handle the cartridges. PC Guru Vern Prime advised me that he always handles all of his Iomega Zip and Jaz media as if they were "real" hard disks, and he has never had a media problem. (See Figure 8.1 on CD-ROM.)

Whatever choice you make, look at the economics, too. A modem fast enough to transmit an 18MB image in a reasonable time will be almost as expensive as an Iomega or SyQuest drive. In fact, a drive might be cheaper. If you know how to look for bargains, affordable removable media drives are readily available. What do you do when a service bureau does not support your favorite removable media drive? I asked Cies-Sexton's Kevin Elliott what they did. "If a client has a device we don't support, some of them just bring us their hard drives. We plug them in and we can transfer stuff on and off of it. As long as it doesn't take some strange driver, it's not a big deal to hook another SCSI device."

DIGITAL CHECKLIST

Communication is important in working with service bureaus, but submitting your digital information in a proper form is even more important. Especially if you do not want any surprises when you get your (often expensive) output back. A study conducted by the Graphics Arts Technical Foundation showed that 57 percent of the files submitted to service bureaus needed additional work before the file could be processed. I also conducted an informal survey of local service bureaus to discover other common problem areas. Here's a look at some of those problems and how to avoid them.

Incorrect page settings or image ratio accounts for 7.8 percent of the problem files. This can be a problem for photographers requesting 35mm slide output. A 35mm slide has an aspect ratio of 1.5:1. If your original image has a different ratio, you are forcing your service bureau to make a decision. Do they deliver the image with black borders on two edges of the slide to maintain the ratio of the image you sent, or do they enlarge the image to fill the 35mm frame? A good service bureau will call with that question, but even great labs get busy and phone calls can be forgotten. What is worse, they could call you and your response is "I want to fill the frame." At that point, something has to be cropped. Who is going to make that decision, the service bureau or you? If it's you, they will have to send the image back to you for cropping, further delaying completion of the project.

The best way to make sure that your image has the proper ratio is to use your software's Show Rulers command to actually see if your image has the proper dimensions. The next step is to look at the Image Size dialog. A typical dialog includes two data sections: one displaying data for the original image, and one to use to make changes in this data. Typical Image Size data includes length, width, and resolution. Use the cropping tool (and the ruler as a guide) to trim the photograph into a shape that has the proper ratio. By doing it at this stage, you are making sure that the image retains information and nothing important is missing. You cannot expect a service bureau to know what to keep and what to eliminate, so it's up to you to make sure your image is formatted correctly.

Missing Linked Files can be a problem when submitting an Adobe PageMaker or QuarkXPress file that contains multiple images that have not been saved as part of the original files. The GATF survey showed that 5.3 percent of problem files had missing linked graphics. Having the ability to link files instead of making them part of the original file can save hard disk space while you are working, but you have to remember to send those linked files to the service bureau. That's where a proof—if only ink-jet output—helps the service bureau and you, too. Use the proof as a checklist and check off each item—fonts and images—to make sure they are included in the package you are submitting for output. Some service bureaus require a proof print, and the lack of a proof accounts for 4.6 percent of their problems.

Kevin Elliott told me that "the next biggest problem is not receiving all the stuff a service bureau needs to create output." This problem gets worse if a file includes type. Missing or incorrect fonts account for 22.2 percent of problems. While service bureaus have many hundreds of fonts in their systems, they may not have the Hobo Bold Italic you used. I know. I use Adobe Skia for my promotional material. When working with a new service bureau, I call and ask if they have it. If not, I make sure I include a copy on disk when I submit my files. That's another reason why it's a good idea to send a proof of what you expect the output to look like. If you forget a font and the service bureau's default is Courier, the quality control people will compare what you sent with what was output, then call and ask "where's the font!"

Other more obvious problems include scans supplied in the wrong format (7.8 percent), files defined with incorrect color space (10.9 percent), and missing or incomplete trapping (11.5 percent). Believe it or not, another problem service bureaus have to deal with is clients that don't bring the most original generation of an image that they have; that situation, along with missing graphics, accounts for 4.5 percent of service bureau problems. Some users, expecting miracles from digital imaging, submit a dupe, or a dupe of a dupe, or a print rather than using the original negative or transparency. Your best results will be obtained by giving the service bureau the first generation, or the closest to the first generation you possibly have. Kevin Elliott told me that, "In probably half of the cases where we call and ask if they have something more original, they do." A service bureau cannot read your mind. They don't know what material you have in your office or studio. The quality of the material submitted will be reflected in the quality of the output. As the old computer saying goes, "garbage in, garbage out." Nowhere is this more true than working with service bureaus.

PHOTO QUALITY OUTPUT ON YOUR DESKTOP

Not so long ago, seeing a color printer on a desktop was a rare site. Now the market's reached a point where computer stores bundle inexpensive color printers with systems, or even throw them into a deal for free. Right now, the most popular desktop color printers use ink-jet or dye-sublimation technology.

Ink-Jet Color Printers

Ink-jet is are the most popular technology used in color printers. The reasons for this popularity are simple: low price and high quality. In an ink-jet printer, a print head sprays one or more colors of ink onto paper to produce output, and the type of methods used to accomplish this has an effect on output quality. Piezoelectric technology is based on the property of crystals to oscillate when subjected to electrical voltage. This mechanical vibration is used to fire ink onto paper in Epson's Stylus Color family to place uniform ink droplets on paper. This allows Epson's printers to deliver output at up to 720 dots per inch (dpi) resolution. Another approach is the drop-on-demand method. This method uses a set of independently controlled injection chambers—the newest of which use solid ink—which liquefies when heated and solidifies when it hits paper. This thermal approach is favored by Canon, Apple, and Hewlett Packard for their ink-jet printers. Another method is the continuous stream method, which produces droplets that are aimed onto the paper by electric field deflectors. The weak link of all ink-jet printers, large or small format, is fading from UV radiation and susceptibility to water damage. These limitations can be overcome by laminating the finished print.

Most color ink-jet printers use two different cartridges to produce output: one containing cyan, magenta, and yellow inks, and the other containing black ink. Some printers use a single three-color cartridge to create all colors, which usually produces a muddy black when mixing the three colors. Other low-cost printers provide a single cartridge slot and require that you switch cartridges between color and black and white—depending on what you are printing.

Dye-Sublimation Printers

Dye-sublimation printers—often called just "dye-sub" or, more correctly, thermal-dye transfer—use a printing head that heats a dye ribbon, thereby creating a gas that hardens onto special paper. The more heat that is applied, the denser the color and the image on the paper. Like most printers, it does this as "dots" of colors, but because these spots are soft-edged—instead of the hard edges created by laser and ink-jet printers—the result is smooth, continuous tones. This makes dye-sub printers work especially well with photographs, and even 300 dpi dye-sub output can be more impressive than output from higher-resolution devices.

Most dye-sublimation printers also support printing with wax thermal materials. This process uses a coarser wax-like ink in its ribbon. During printing, wax thermal-paper is pressed against each color in the ribbon as it passes the printer's heating element, transferring the ink onto the paper. The results are inferior to a dye-sublimation print, but the material is much less expensive, making it an option for proofing a layout or image.

Working with a dye-sublimation printer may take a little more care than you are used to, but following a few steps will assure the best quality output. First, to avoid creating splotches or blobs on your prints, handle the fragile ribbon by its edges. Second, after placing the paper in the tray, make sure the side and back printer guides in the paper are snug. This helps maintain registration, because in order to print an image, these printers make up to four passes of the same sheet of paper. The first is through the yellow portion of the ribbon, the second through the magenta, the third through the cyan, and finally the black layer. Keeping the paper flat makes sure that the four passes are in perfect registration.

Many companies, including FARGO, Kodak, and Sony, make dye-sublimation printers.

Epson Stylus Photo

The introduction of a 720 dpi ink-jet printer by Epson, who broke the 1440 dpi barrier with their Stylus Color 600 and 800 printers, doesn't seem too exciting, but wait till you see the output. The images coming out of the Stylus Photo exhibit smooth continuous tones and true photographic quality.

The Epson Stylus Photo is the best looking ink-jet printer they have ever made. Gone is the shoe-box styling of recent Stylus printers. The hard edges have been replaced by Porsche-like curves, and like the German sports car, it's the engineering under the hood that makes it special. The two ink cartridges hold not four but six ink colors. In addition to the cyan, magenta, yellow, and black that you might expect, there is also light cyan and light magenta ink in the color cartridge. The additional colors make it possible to better reproduce subtleties, such as flesh and metallic tones. Backing up these inks are a variation on Epson's piezoelectric-head-design technology that allows the print heads to produce a more precise and consistent dot pattern. The company tells me this new design produces dots that are 47 percent smaller than previous models. This same design also reduces the ink-drying time when compared to the thermal approach used by Canon, H-P, Apple, and other ink-jets. (See Figure 8.2 on CD-ROM.)

An important component for producing photo-realistic output from any ink-jet printer is paper. Epson's drivers work with "plain paper" or their own family of paper that includes the gorgeous, but expensive, "High Quality Glossy Paper." Digital photographers, and those for whom only the best is good enough, will want to use this paper. Epson also makes a 720 dpi paper called "Photo Quality Ink Jet" paper that produces excellent results at a lower price, but lacks the glossy surface and heavier weight of the "High Quality Glossy Paper." Epson's new Photo Paper provides the ultimate in photo-quality reproduction, and is available, for now anyway, in 4 × 7-inch sheets. The paper is heavier and has a light texture that reminds me of a fine-quality fiber-based photographic paper. There is even an "Epson" watermark on the back, echoing the Kodak imprint on the back of its photo paper. Do not confuse Epson's new paper with Kodak's Ink-jet Snapshot paper, which is also available in 4 × 7-sheets. While the output—on the Stylus Photo—from the lighter weight Kodak paper is quite good, it pales in any side-by-side comparison with Epson's paper.

Like many of Epson's other ink-jet printers, the Stylus Photo is completely cross-platform. The back of the printer features a serial port for connection to a Mac OS computer and a parallel port for connection to a Windows-based PC. If you have both kinds of computers, you can even do what I did and connect both of them to the printer. The results are like having a network without any of the overhead a network requires. I simply installed the drivers on both machines, connected the cables to both computers, and was ready to go. In the past, the Windows drivers seemed more complete and comprehensive than the Mac versions, but that seems to be changing. As far as user interface, the Mac OS driver is more intuitive, better looking, and easier to use than the Windows version. It also features what I call "smart" controls. You specify the type of paper you will use and adjust the "Quality-Speed" slider where you want it, and the driver picks the appropriate settings. You can set all of the controls manually, but 99 percent of computer users will find that letting the driver pick the settings works best.

While printing, the Windows driver automatically shows a thermometer-like gauge monitoring the quantity of ink in each of the cartridges. The Mac OS driver does this too, but you have to click a "Utilities" button to see the ink status. There are other utilities there, too, including head alignment tests and an ink-jet head clearing routine. The Epson Stylus Photo is not just for printing pretty pictures. I used it for all my business correspondence, too, and the text is sharp and black. I even feed envelopes and sheets of Avery labels through the Stylus Photo with no problems or jams. You can even produce 720 dpi output with labels, allowing me to add a digital portrait of myself on my mailing and floppy disk labels.

I have never used any computer peripheral that worked as perfectly out-of-the-box as the Epson Stylus Photo. The photo-realistic output quality belies its down-to-earth, under-$500 price. It's fast, too. While any printer lacking built-in memory performs in accordance with what computer it's connected to, the Stylus Photo seems faster than any other ink-jet printer I have used. It even seems a little quieter.

FARGO Primera Pro Elite

FARGO Electronics has carved out a niche for itself by producing low-cost, high-quality dye-sublimation printers. Their newest product is the Primera Pro

Elite, a 25-bit photorealistic dye-sublimation printer that can also produce wax thermal proofs.

The Elite produces output in standard A (letter) sizes and European A4 (8.25 × 11.7) sizes on what the company calls Extended A4 paper. This paper measures 8.5 × 15-inches, allowing the printer to output an image up to full A4 size. The paper stock—FARGO calls them receiver sheets—is thicker and has a more photographic feel than what the company has used in the past. It even feels more substantial than the high-quality stock the company uses for their large-format Pictura 310e printer. Ten sheets of paper and one of FARGO's new FotoShield ribbons is included. FotoShield uses a CMYO format that includes cyan, magenta, yellow colors, and an overlay. The overlay is a clear UV-resistant material that protects images from fading, from fingerprints, and from sticking to plastic photo pages. Having the option of using either CMYO or CMYK materials gives digital photographers the option of selecting the kind of output that is appropriate for a specific application.

The three-color plus overlay ribbon produced photographic quality images, but when I switched to a four-color (CMYK) ribbon, the results—from the same images—went from good to great. The quality of the four-color output was more subtle, with neutral shadows and better blacks, all of which produced more depth than prints made with the three-color ribbon. This is not consistent with my CMYO experience with other FARGO printers. When I ran test sheets on a Pictura, the CMYO ribbon produced better looking prints than the CMYK ribbon did. A FotoShield ribbon capable of printing fifty pages lists at $112.95, with paper costing $52.95 for fifty sheets. This yields a per-sheet cost of $3.32 for an 8 × 10, which is more than competitive for a lab-produced print. And there are no rush charges.

To get the most out of the Elite, you will need some form of color management software. Using no color management produces output with a slight green or cyan cast. When you install the printer drive, you have the option of installing FARGO's color matching system, which was developed for them by Candela. Some photographers may be more comfortable using Vivid Details' Test Strip Photoshop-compatible plug-in for color management. The plug-in mimics a traditional darkroom-produced test strip, enabling you to print a single image showing different percentages of color and density ranges—all labeled and easy to read. I ran a Test Strip test print and found that a plus 10% magenta gave me natural colors and skin tones. This is consistent with other FARGO printers (FotoFun and Pictura) that I have used. FARGO's color management system, however, produced excellent results after spending time to tweak the density adjustment in the printer driver. With the other FARGO printers, I produced excellent results with the density set at the default 50%. The Elite produced better results at 25%.

The printer has two printing modes: Regular quality at 300 × 300 dpi, and Highest quality at 600 × 300 dpi. I tried both settings and could barely see a difference between them. FARGO suggests the 600 × 300 mode for business graphics and the 300 × 300 mode for photographs. Some software programs, FARGO told me, may have problems in the 600 × 300 mode and will print a stretched and distorted version of your original file. You should not have that problem with popular programs like Adobe Photoshop and PageMaker or QuarkXPress. With ink-jet printers besting these dpi specs, you need to evaluate the differences between how a dye-sublimation printer actually produces images in order to evaluate the Elite's output. A dye-sub printer's head heats a dye ribbon creating a gas that hardens onto special paper. The more heat that's applied, the denser the color and the image on the paper. Like most printers, the Elite does this as "dots" of colors, but because these spots are soft-edged, instead of the hard edges created by laser and ink-jet printers, the result is smooth continuous tones. This makes dye-sub printers work especially well with photographs, and even 300 dpi dye-sub output is more impressive than output from higher resolution ink-jet and laser printers. Unlike other inexpensive dye-sub printers, including FARGO's previous models, the Elite is fast. It can print an 8 1/2 × 11-inch on A/A5-sized paper in 4.5 minutes. My actual printing times varied a bit from these specifications. For example, a 10MB photographic (TIFF) file took a little over five minutes to first spool, then print.

The Elite, like most dye-sublimation printers, also supports printing with wax thermal materials. This process uses a coarser wax-like ink in its ribbon. During printing, wax thermal-paper is pressed against each color in the ribbon as it passes the printer's heating element, transferring the ink onto the paper. The results are inferior to a dye-sublimation print, but the material is much less expensive, making it an option for proofing a layout or image.

The printer is compact—even small. It has a smaller desktop footprint than the Epson Stylus Photo, although the Elite cheats a bit by having the power supply as a separate external unit. The Elite has a serial port for connecting to Mac OS computers and a parallel connection for Windows-based computers. Software for both kinds of machines is included in the box. Having both kinds of connections available is great news for those photographers working with both Windows and Mac OS computers. You can connect the printer to both computers at the same time, install drivers for both systems, and be able to print images from both computers. This setup provides all the advantages of a networked printer without any additional cost or hassles.

The Primera Pro Elite dye-sublimation printer is not cheap. It has a list price of $2,195. But it is easy to use and fast to set up and lets you produce true photographic quality output within minutes of unpacking the box.

CASE STUDY: BUILDING A DIGITAL/ANALOG PORTFOLIO

You remember how it goes: the Art Director says, "I know you can photograph right-handed baseball players, but can you photograph left-handed ones?" An unfortunate reality of this business is that you have to constantly prove to potential photo buyers that you can produce—or have already made—images just like the one they need right now.

Your key marketing tool during this aspect of the sales process is the portfolio. Yet the traditional laminated, custom-print portfolios can be so expensive to produce that many photographers find it difficult to create additional portfolios for specific market segments. But not any more. In this case study, I would like to introduce you to the digital/analog portfolio: a method of using digital prints with off-the-shelf packaging originally designed for wedding photographers. The concept and brains behind this idea belongs to photographer Barry Staver, who graciously shared this idea with me so that I could share it with you.

The Portfolio Binder

Staver's key to making his concept work is Art Leather Company's PK Preview album. The leather-like Aristohyde album covers are available in nine different colors and can be imprinted with your studio name or logo in gold. Page inserts are available in four colors, but Staver prefers to use black, which he feels is the best choice to show off commercial photographs. Each page measures approximately 7 1/2 × 9 1/2 inches, and the cover is slightly larger than that. Inserts are available with gold embossing on one side to outline your prints. Standard formats are 3 1/2 × 5 and 4 × 5 in either Horizontal or Vertical orientation as well as and 5 × 5 square. Plain, unembossed pages are also available. An album can hold up to fifteen inserts, providing a thirty-print capacity—if you use both sides—and the plastic comb binding allows for easy removal of inserts. The base price for covers is $8.53 each, with bulk discounts at 10, 100, and 1,000. Inserts cost $0.74 each with bulk discounts at 100, 1,000, and 10,000 lots.

Digital Portfolio Prints

Prints for the portfolio are created using standard digital imaging tools and techniques. Staver uses Photo CD as an image acquisition method for his 35mm and 120 negatives and transparencies. For his digital darkroom, he uses a Power Macintosh 8100/80 and Adobe Photoshop software to tweak each image's color, brightness, and contrast and occasionally perform a subtle manipulation. Images are sized to fit the blank album pages he prefers to use. He prefers to vary the print size slightly within the portfolio and uses a maximum image size of 6 1/2 × 9 inches. Depending on the portfolio, Staver usually places a single image on a page but this is not a hard-and-fast rule for him and should not be for you either.

When enough images are prepared for the portfolio he is assembling, he uses QuarkXPress to combine as many photographs as will fit on a 12 × 20-inch page and outputs them using a FARGO Pictura 310 dye-sublimation printer. Typically, he can print up to four different images on a single sheet of paper.

Staver has discovered, as have I, that the output quality of this four-color printer is equal to many purely photographic processes and is more than acceptable to clients for portfolio presentation. After the sheet of images is printed, he trims them, leaving a thin white boarder around each photograph to separate the images from the black page. Prints are attached to the inserts using the same double-sticky HermaFix tabs that Art Leather sells for fastening wedding prints to their albums. When he is finished, he has a fifteen-page bound portfolio, with his studio name imprinted in gold, that cost him just under $40—less than the cost of a single laminated custom color print.

Variations on a Theme

None of the techniques that Staver uses to create a portfolio are unusual. What is unusual is that he has crafted an idea that combines off-the-shelf hardware and software along with Art Leather's albums to produce an inexpensive and impressive portfolio. When fine arts photographer Bill Craig was shown Staver's prototype album, he was immediately struck by the marketing potential for the art world. Like their commercial cousins, fine art photographers need to produce portfolios for gallery directors and show organizers. The digital/analog portfolio provides a low-cost way for the photographer/artist to produce many portfolios without the high cost associated with printing and archival mounting. Craig suggested that he would like to place a small photo of himself along with a biographic sketch on the first page of the portfolio. I think that's also a good idca for commercial shooters who may be mailing their portfolio to potential out-of-state clients.

While Staver uses the $3,400 FARGO Pictura 310 to produce his prints, there are less expensive alternatives available. The low-cost (around $400) FARGO FotoFun! can produce dye-sublimation prints you can use to create your own digital/analog portfolio. As in everything else in the world of computing, using a lower-cost output device involves compromises. The first is print size. The FotoFun! is limited to a maximum size of 4 × 7-inches, slightly smaller than the prints Barry uses in his portfolio, but a size that fits the Art Leather inserts well. The second compromise is that while the Pictura 310 produces four-color (cyan, yellow, magenta, and black) prints, the FotoFun! lacks the black dye layer. In its place, the FotoFun's fourth ribbon layer contains a UV protection coating that reduces the danger of fading and protects prints from finger marks. This can be a big help in dealing with those clients who seem to love sticking their fingers all over your portfolio prints. FARGO recently announced that they are making this same type of three-color plus UV protectant ribbon available to users of the larger format Pictura printer.

Considering the low cost per portfolio, you can now create portfolios for specific groups of potential clients. Staver intends to create additional portfolios for all of the market segments that he services—and so can you.

Tool: The FARGO FotoFun!

While dye-sublimation printers provide the most photorealistic output, they are also the most expensive. With a street price of $399, FARGO Electronics FotoFun! breaks the dye-sublimation price barrier. One of the ways it does it is by limiting the maximum print to a snapshot-sized 4 × 6 inches. FotoFun! is a compact printer with a footprint measuring only 7 × 9.5 inches. It uses a three-color (CMY) ribbon that has a fourth component that applies a clear UV coating to protect finished prints from finger prints and moisture. The printer comes with a 37-print ribbon and 36 sheets of paper.

Connecting the printer is also simple: you plug a cable (on the Macintosh version) into the serial port on the back of the computer and the printer. If you already have a modem and want to have more than one printer connected, you should consider an A-B box to let you switch between the FotoFun! and your "regular" printer. The only false note in setup is the chunky external power supply that takes up a lot of space on your floor. The upside is that the power supply is designed to work in any country, from the United States to Japan, Europe, and Australia.

Printing could not be easier. Open a digital image with your favorite image processing program, then chose Page Setup from the File menu. The information shown in Page Setup gives you control over how the image will be printed. You can set the page orientation, paper size, ribbon type, and color density. After that, choose Print, click the Print button, and FotoFun! starts to work. The first step is a rasterization process that converts the file into printable form then saves it to disk. I thought that this would take longer with bigger files, but both 1MB and 6MB files took about the same time. While this is going on, a dialog displays what percentage of the rasterization is complete. When the printer's internal rollers start to spin, insert a sheet of paper—glossy side down—and wait. It takes just a minute for the completed print to roll out.

In addition to snapshots (you can also print two 2 × 4-inch wallet sized photos on the same sheet of paper), FARGO offers an optional photo postcard kit ($39.95 for 36 prints) that uses heavier-weight media preprinted with the address and postage indictors on the nonimage side. When 6MB Photo CD files were sized to 4 × 6 inches, the quality of the output was superb. Some of the 72 dpi GIF images that I printed were acceptable but far below the quality from Photo CD.

9

Fine Art Printing

One of the newest trends in photography is applying fine art printing techniques to the production of digital images. Some of the techniques—such as working with watercolor and other papers—can be tried with your own in-house printers. Other approaches require the use of high-end ink-jet printers and allow photographers to create limited editions of their digital fine art work. While others, such as the creation of digital art for use in the traditional silk screening process, are also possible.

DIGITAL SILK SCREENS

The road from original design to finished art can take many twists and turns in the journey from the art to the print shop. In the example that follows, the original photograph will have its number of colors reduced, a mechanical dual blend created, and separations made for each color. The black-and-white artwork that comes off your printer can be delivered to a silk screen facility to be transferred onto a screen ready for inking the final product.

Getting on Track

The photograph of a steam locomotive that is used as the basis for this design was made with a 35mm camera and color negative film. In this case, the negative was digitized using Kodak's Photo CD process. The software tools used to create the final image and separations are Adobe Photoshop supplemented with plug-ins from Auto F/X and Second Glance Software.

Step 1. Open the photograph in Adobe Photoshop. When working with Photo CD images, I use the largest resolution file to maintain image quality. In this case, it is (what Kodak calls) "16 Base," which has a resolution of 2,048 × 3,072 pixels and a file size of 18MB. (See Figure 9.1.)

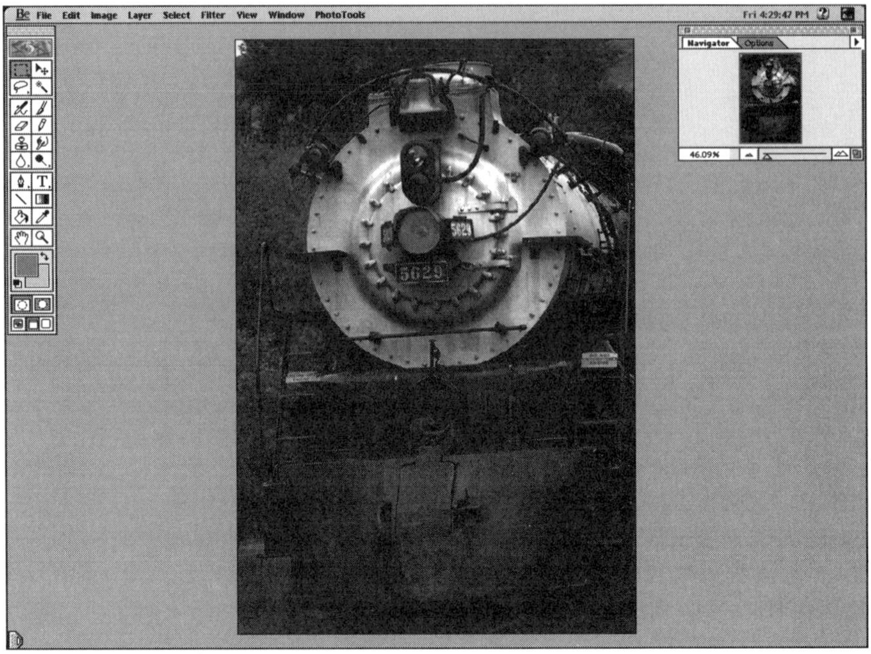

Figure 9.1 The original photograph was made by the author using a conventional camera and film, then digitized with Kodak's Photo CD process. The resulting image was opened in Adobe Photoshop. Photo © Joe Farace.

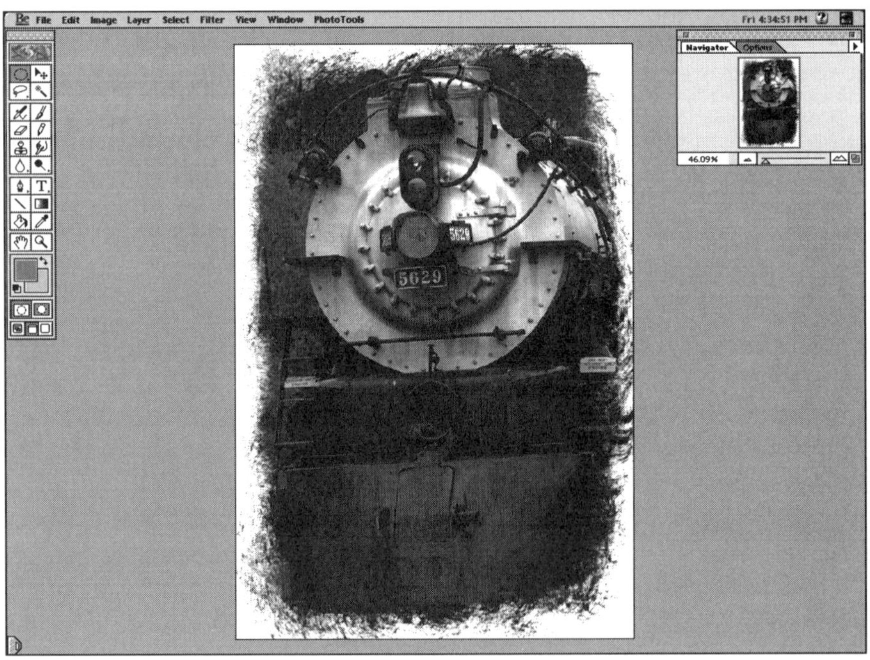

Figure 9.2 Auto F/X's Photo/Graphic Edges plug-in is so simple to use that even a beginning computer user can produce the effect shown here in less time than it takes to read this. Photo © Joe Farace.

Step 2. I wanted the image to have rough, irregular edges, so I used Auto F/X's Photo/Graphic Edges plug-in to create the effect I desired. The use of Photo/Graphic Edges was covered in a previous chapter, so I will not repeat it here. (See Figure 9.2.)

Posterizing the Photo

Since any photograph, including this locomotive image, contains millions of colors, I need to reduce the number of colors and create a more graphic and, I hope, more dramatic image of the locomotive. The goal is to produce a manageable number of separations—and screens—that any print shop can handle. The next step, and all that follow, will be created using a Photoshop-compatible plug-in called PhotoSpot produced by Second Glance Software. The product is actually a collection of four plug-ins that includes Paint Thinner, Acetone, Turpentine, and PhotoSpot—all of which are designed to produce spot color separations.

Step 3. Open Acetone, which is found in the Second Glance sub-menu of the Filter's menu. Before the plug-in does anything, it asks how many colors you want to use. I chose six. You can choose any number based on how many colors your budget or your press can handle for this particular project.

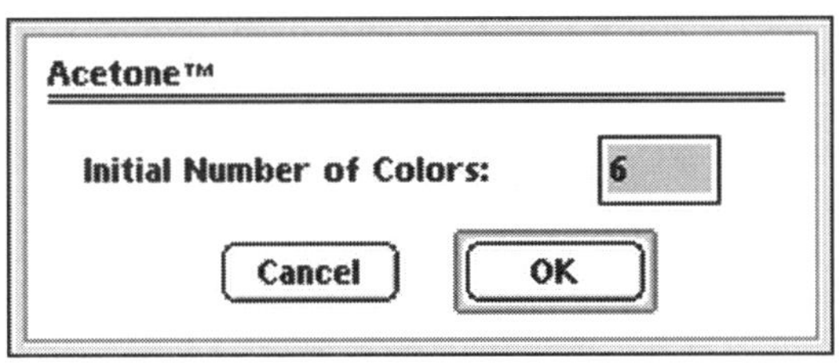

Figure 9.3 The first thing that the Acetone plug-in does is ask how many colors you want the image to contain.

Step 4. Work with Acetone's dialog box to delete any colors Acetone has selected, or add your own by clicking on the "spectrum" area at the top of the screen. To keep the process simple, I used the colors that the plug-in selected. (See Figure 9.4.)

Step 5. Click the Apply button to produce the effect. When back in Photoshop's working window, I used the program's selection tools along with the brightness and contrast commands to "punch up" the color of the red areas and to increase the image's overall brightness and contrast. (See Figure 9.5.)

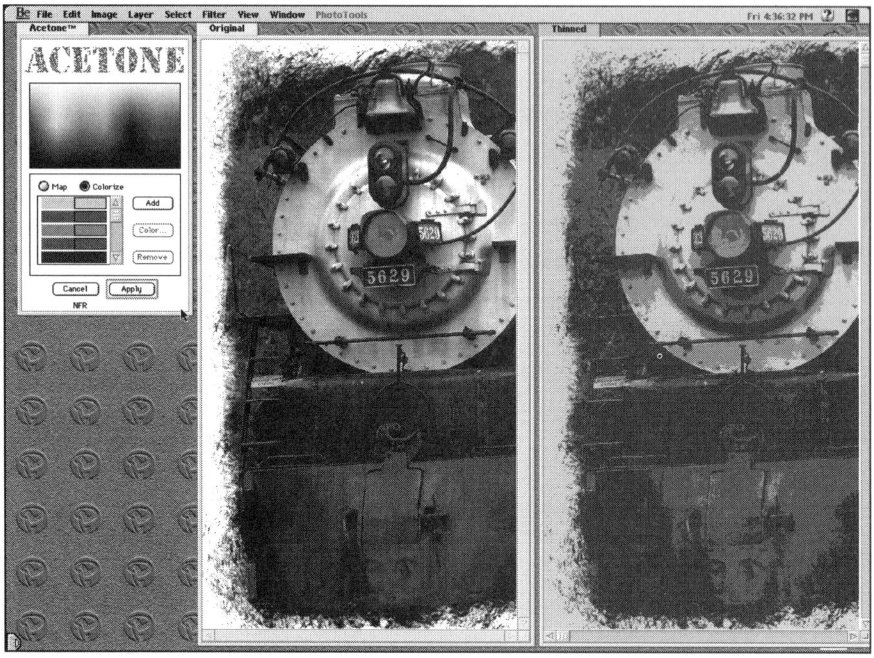

Figure 9.4 The Acetone plug-in lets you keep, delete, and or add colors to the posterized image that it creates. Photo © Joe Farace.

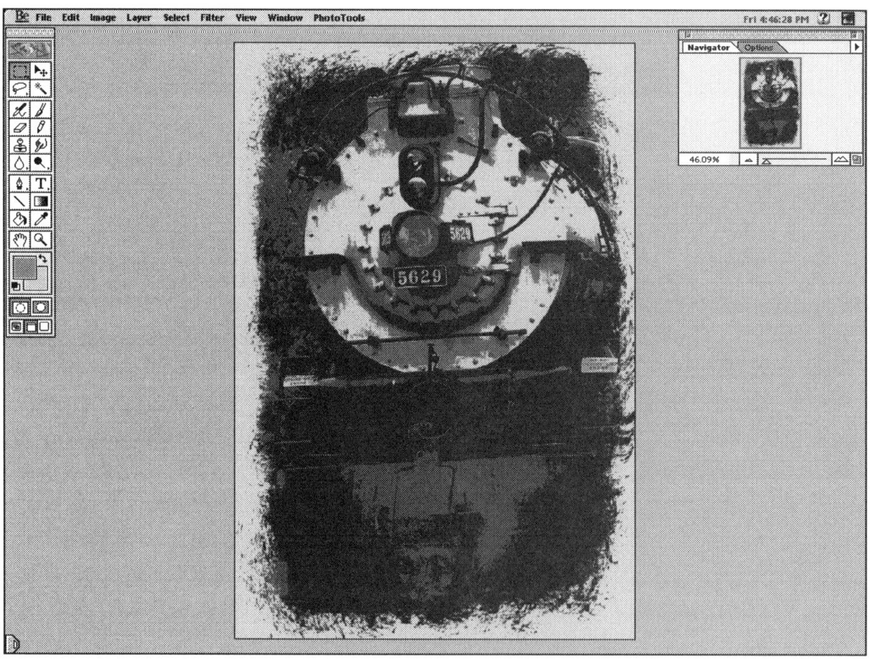

Figure 9.5 In this example, the author uses Photoshop's selection of brightness and contrast controls to improve the visual impact of the posterized image. Photo © Joe Farace.

Making Separations

Now that the total number of colors is reduced to six, it's time to create black and white separations that will be used to produce the actual screens used for the design. That's where the PhotoSpot plug-in goes to work.

Step 6. Choose PhotoSpot from the Export menu. PhotoSpot begins the separation process by extracting all of the colors in the image. When the operation is complete, you will see a PhotoSpot dialog box listing the colors found in the file. It can assign a color name to them, or, if you prefer, you can list them by number, as in this example.

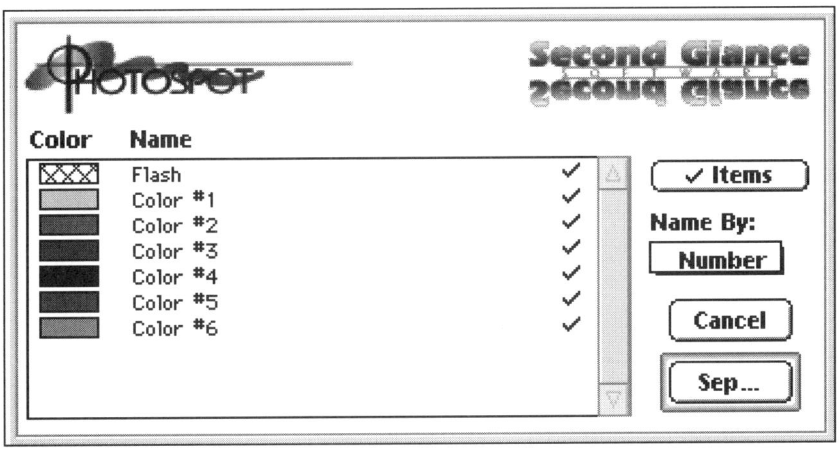

Figure 9.6 After digitally separating the images, PhotoSpot displays the name and numbers of the separation files that will be created. Click the "Sep..." button to make the separations files.

Step 7. To make the separations files, click the "Sep..." button. When you do, you will see an Open/Save dialog that lets you save the files in either TIFF or Photoshop format. (See Figure 9.7.)

TIP: Which Way to Go?

If you plan to import the separations into a graphics program, such as QuarkXPress or Adobe PageMaker, you should use the TIFF format. The Photoshop option creates multiple 1-bit files in Adobe Photoshop's native format. Use this one to print separations from within Photoshop — which is the option most photographers will use.

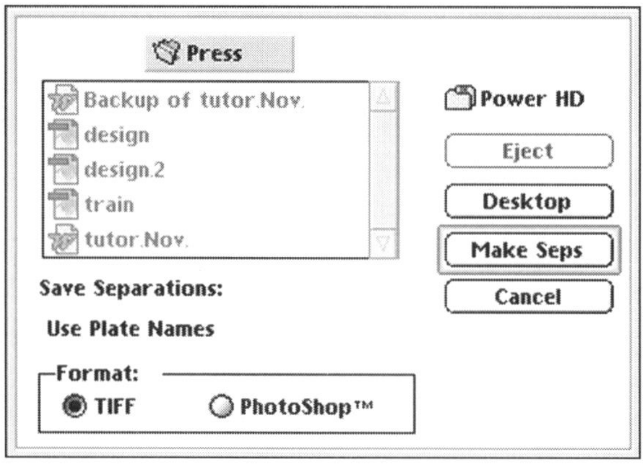

Figure 9.7 This dialog lets you save separations in either Adobe Photoshop or TIFF format.

Mechanical Dual Blend

If you like, you can quit with Step 7, and still have a useful Image. If you would like to add a little more interest—and only one more color—to the final design, consider adding a dual color blend to one of the separations. This next phase takes one of the separations and converts it into two, providing gradation from one color to another one. That's why you can consider the following steps optional.

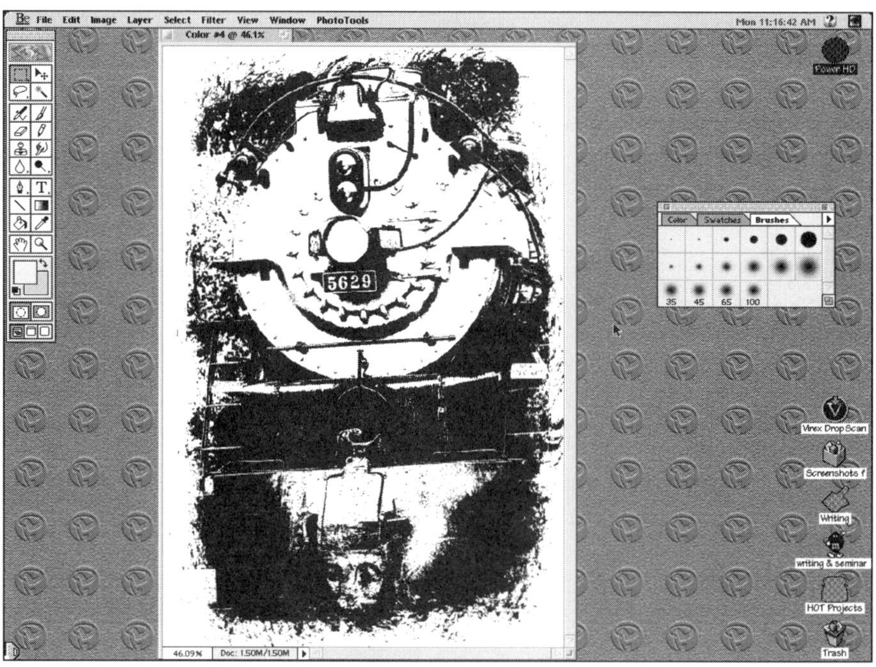

Figure 9.8 The first step in making a dual blend is to open one of the separation files. Here, separation #4 is opened in Adobe Photoshop.

Step 1. Open the Color #4 (black) separation. You could, of course, use any one of the six separations. I picked this one because it had the largest black area that would work better when trying to create blended colors. (See Figure 9.8.)

Step 2. Convert the separation file to grayscale by using that command in the Mode menu. Since all of the files and modifications you will create in the next several steps must keep the file the same size, be sure to leave the Size Ratio in the dialog box set at one.

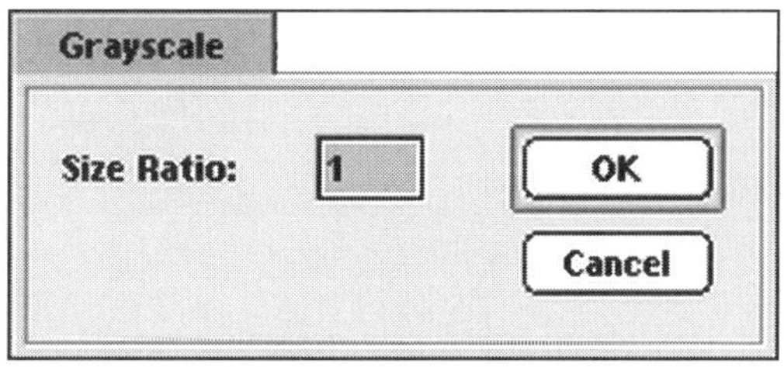

Figure 9.9 When converting to grayscale, leave the Size Ratio in the dialog box set at one.

Step 3. Use Photoshop's Blend tool to apply a gradation across the entire image. With the Foreground Color set at white and the Background

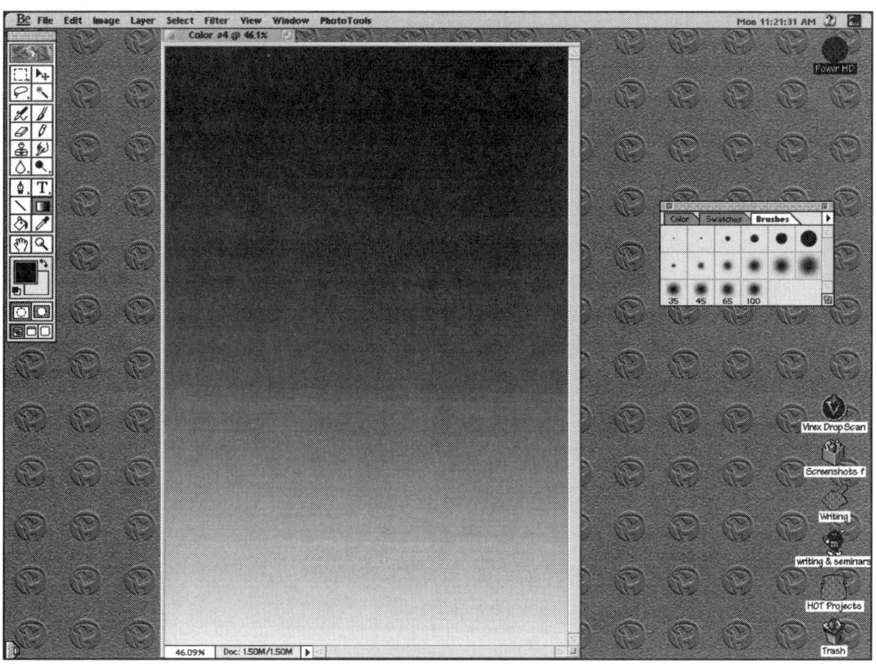

Figure 9.10 The Blend tool is used to cover the entire image with a gradation from black to white.

set at black, the blend will cover the entire image. Don't let this step worry you—it will be fixed later.

Step 4. Use the Bitmap command (found in the Mode menu) to convert the blended image into a bitmap. Then, select "Halftone Screen" as the method for converting the file.

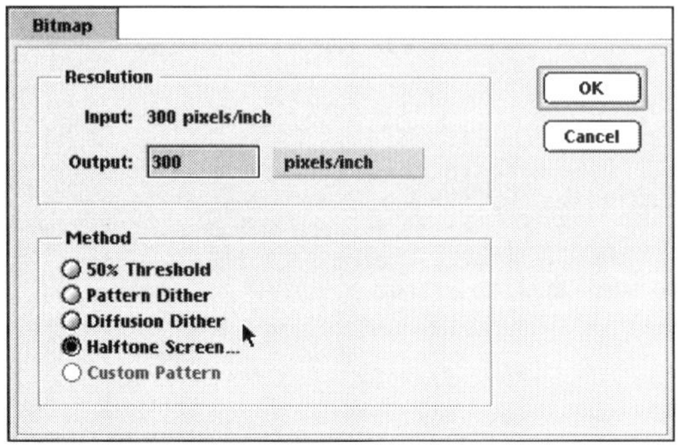

Figure 9.11 Convert the resulting image to Bitmap using a halftone screen.

Step 5. Select the desired method for screening the image.

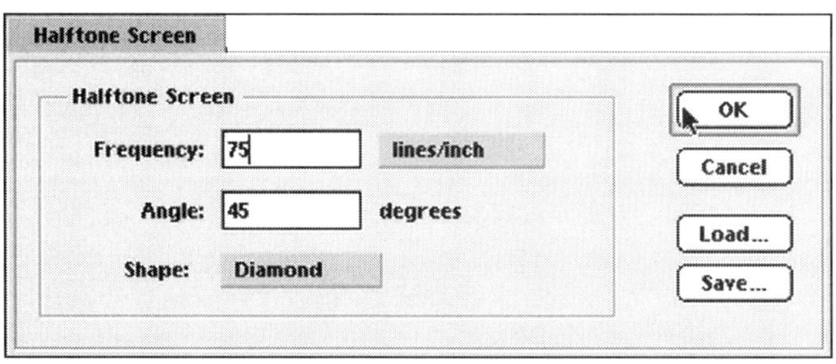

Figure 9.12 Select the desired method for screening the image. If you are not familiar with these functions, they are covered in detail in the Photoshop manual.

Step 6. Convert that file back to Grayscale, then covert it to RGB. Unfortunately, Photoshop will not let you go directly from Bitmap to RGB. Converting to Grayscale is a required intermediate step. (See Figure 9.13.)

Step 7. Reassign the black and white portions of the image with new colors. The easiest way to do this is first to convert the file to Indexed Color Mode and use Photoshop's Color Table command (it's in the Mode menu, at the bottom) to reassign colors. Click on the first box in the color table, then use the Color Picker to assign the color to black. Next, I clicked on the second box to assign a

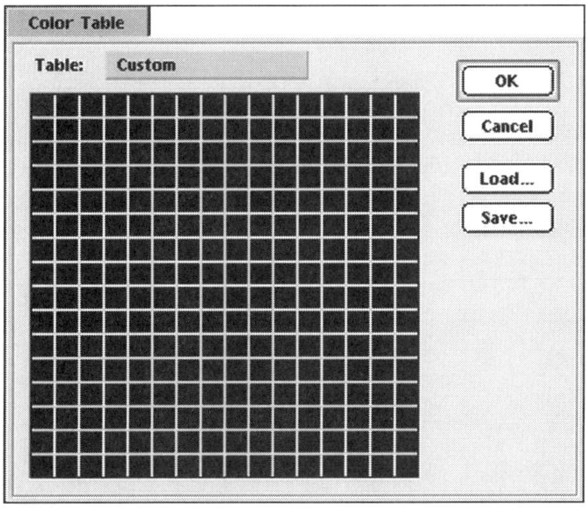

Figure 9.13 Use the Color Table to reassign the black and white portions of the image with your new, desired colors.

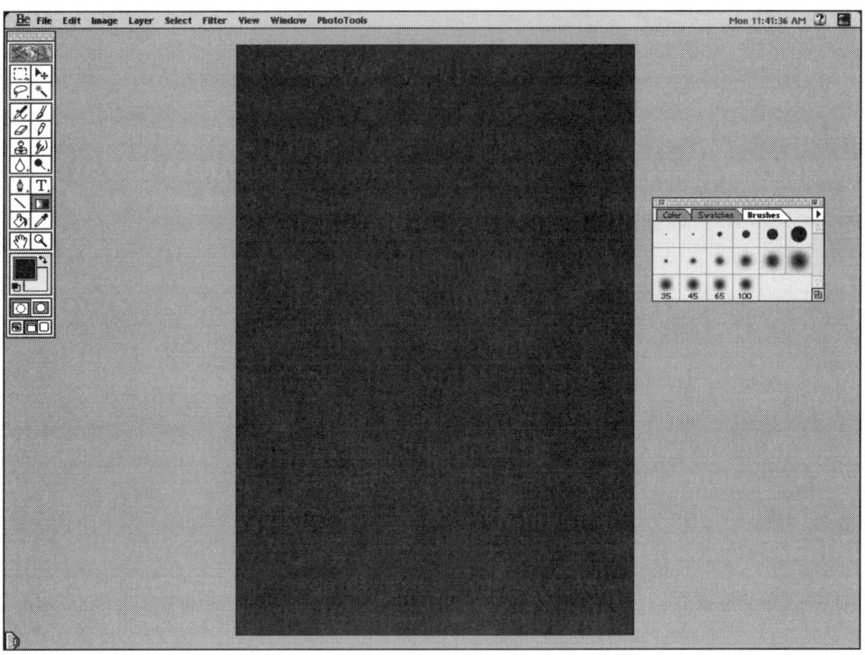

Figure 9.14 To wrap up the gradient creation part of the project, save the document under a new name as an RGB file in native Photoshop format.

color to the white pixels. In this case, I used blue—but you could have done it vice versa.

Step 8. Save the document under a new name as an RGB file in native Photoshop format.

End of the Line

At this point, your head may be spinning due to conversions from one color mode into the next, but have faith, you are almost to the end of the line.

Step 9. Re-open the separation file.

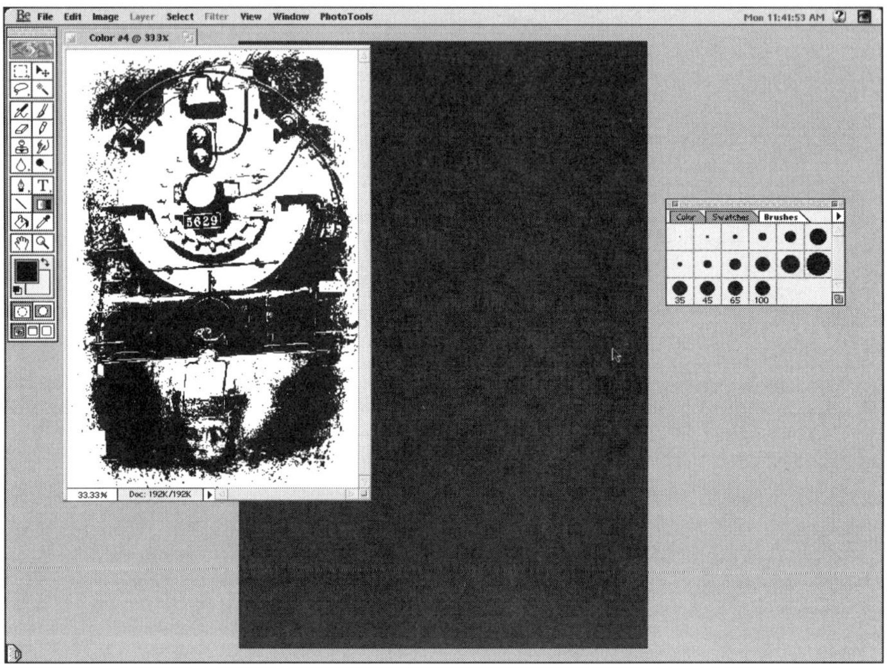

Figure 9.15 To enter into the final step, you need to re-open the original black-and-white separation file.

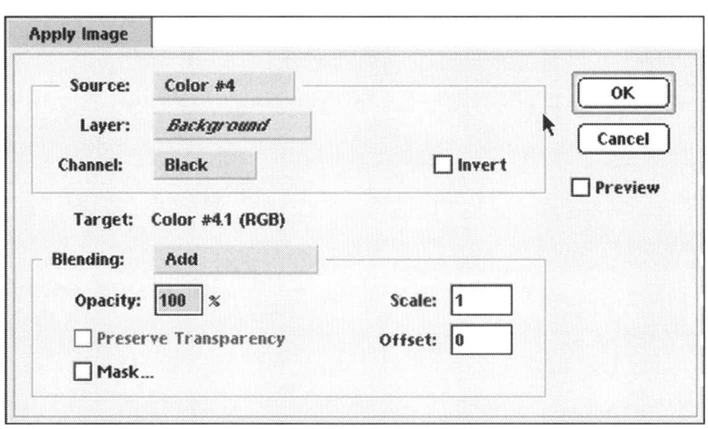

Figure 9.16 The Apply Image dialog box is used to knock out the image from the gradient blend file.

Step 10. Make sure the gradient blend file is the active window, then choose Apply Image from the Image menu. Make sure that the Color #4 file is selected as your Source document, and select Add under the blending menu. (See Figure 9.16.)

Step 11. The final image includes a gradual transition from black to dark blue. You are not quite finished. In order to make these two colors work together, you need to run PhotoSpot again to create two separations—one for the blue ink and one for the black ink.

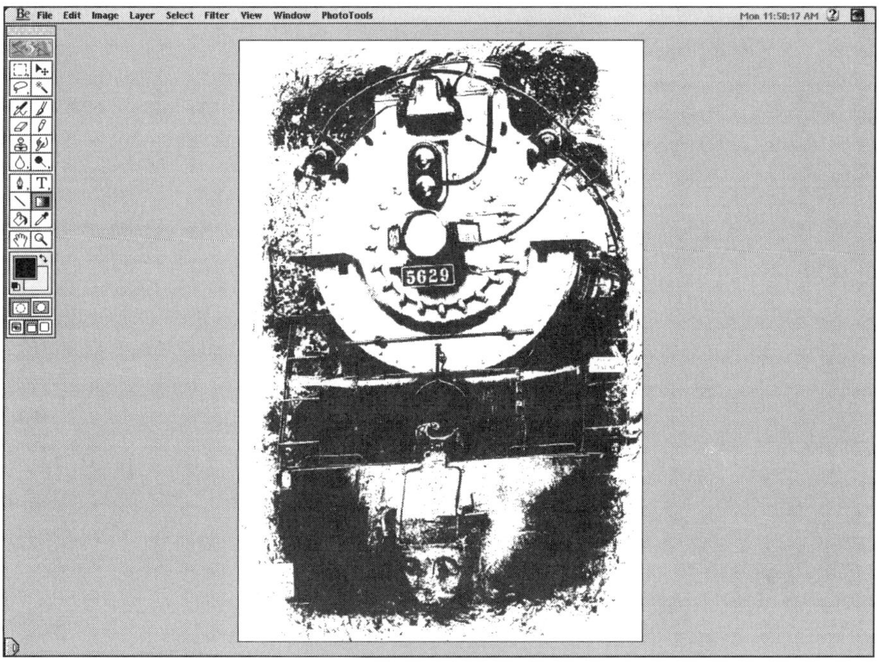

Figure 9.17 The original separation now includes a gradated blend from black to dark blue.

The final image, originally created as a continuous tone photograph, has now been separated into seven colors that can be used to create screens to produce the finished work of art.

At this point you have two options: you can submit the digital separations to a print shop and have them print them, or you can print them yourself to deliver to the print shop—or print them yourself if you already have silk screen experience and a press.

THE IRIS PRINTER

One of the most popular printers that service bureaus use to produce fine art prints is the IRIS ink-jet printer. IRIS Graphics Inc. was formed in April 1984 and became a wholly owned subsidiary of Scitex Corporation, Ltd. in 1990. Since its founding, IRIS has developed and manufactured continuous ink-jet printers for a variety of high-fidelity color applications. Their products are used in color-intensive, quality-sensitive design and production environments by operations that require fast turnaround of cost-effective, high-quality color output.

IRIS products are designed for both the graphics arts industry and visualization/presentation applications in many other industries. IRIS printers offers photographic-quality characteristics from ink-jet printing systems through the use of leading-edge variable-dot printing technology. This technology, packaged in various forms and formats for differing industries, has kept IRIS clients and partners at the forefront in quality and price/performance applications.

IRIS Graphics, Inc. designs, manufactures, sells, and supports a line of continuous ink-jet color printers. These include: the IRIS 3047, the IRIS 3047HS, the IRIS Realist 5015, and the IRIS Realist 5030 printers. Service bureaus use these printers to produce high-resolution color images of digital data files. IRIS employs a unique printer technology that forms images from precisely controlled, variable-sized dots of ink. As a result, their printers produce documents that achieve the visual characteristics of a continuous-tone photograph. Printing at an addressable resolution of 300 dots per inch (dpi), IRIS printers actually produce images with an apparent (perceived) resolution of 1,500 to 1,800 dpi. To achieve a comparable resolution, a color printer that creates images from uniform-sized dots would need to deposit from 1,500 to 1,800 of those dots per inch. So far, no other digital printer can create dots small enough to achieve that standard or to produce images with a resolution comparable to IRIS printing.

IRIS SERVICE BUREAUS

IRIS printers are too expensive for the average photographer to own, but many service bureaus—some of which specialize in the creation of fine art images—offer services allowing the average photographer to take advantage of this technology. By no means are these service bureaus the only ones offering fine art imaging. Check your local commercial photo labs and service bureaus or use the World Wide Web to search for others. That's how I found the companies listed

TIP: How Big?

Iris printers can handle different sized media, depending on the model. Here's a quick look at the maximum print size of the most common models:

Model	Size
3047	34 × 46.3
3047HS	34 × 46.3
Realist 5015	14 × 21
Realist 5030	21 × 28
3024	24 × 24
SmartJet 4012	10.6 × 17.2

here. During several searches, I found six service bureaus that produce IRIS prints; the ones that were interested enough to respond are listed below.

Grayphics Digital Imaging

Grayphics is a full-service prepress bureau. They advertise that they offer the best available equipment, particularly in scanning, image setting, and color printing using the IRIS Realist 5015. They print IRISes in three size categories, from 8.5 × 11 to 14 × 21-inches, with prices ranging from $30 to under $60. Additional prints from the same image cost $9 less. Duplicates must be ordered at the same time as the initial print.

The IRIS printer can output on almost any material that can be smoothly wrapped around its drum. They have printed all kinds of media for their customers, but by far the most popular choice of output media is watercolor paper. Grayphics carries a specially coated type that is especially suitable for IRIS printing, in 14 × 20-inch sheets and for $15 on top of the imaging charge. They do not charge a mounting fee for this paper. They have printed on a wide range of media for customers, but because they need to specially mount other media, there is a $10 charge for mounting customer-supplied stock. The only additional charges a customer might see would be time-based charges if they needed to modify the customer's file to get it to print. Like any good service bureau, they notify customers and ask permission before spending billable time.

Imagineworks

Imagineworks was founded by Robert Kato and Roland Dumas. Robert Kato serves as the master Iris printmaker. He is a photographer who attended The Art Center in Los Angeles and apprenticed under some of the San Francisco Bay Area's prominent portrait photographers. Creative Director Roland Dumas, the General Manager for Imagineworks, is accountable for the technical services and Web-site design process. He is a physiological psychologist by training and a management consultant by profession; he focuses on customer service quality systems for large companies. His background includes research on color perception and software design.

Imagineworks offers a full range of digital services to photographers, fine artists, and retail customers. They differ from traditional service bureaus in that the technical staff are all professional photographers with extensive digital imaging training and experience. Customers deal directly with an artist and collaborate on the appropriate enhancements and standards for their images. Imagineworks executes photographic restorations for retail customers as well as for professional photographers. The restorations are IRIS printed for a fine art finish. Family composites and commemorative montages are the most common retail service purchased at Imagineworks. Imagineworks maintains a gallery featuring resident artists' work and client samples. Portions of the gallery are on-line at Imagineworks' Website (http://www.imagineworks.com/art/).

Imagineworks' IRIS printmaking service is strictly defined as a fine art process. The company does not accept prepress orders because the inks, substrates, and calibrations appropriate for prepress proofing is not compatible with fine art printmaking. At Imagineworks, the Iris printmaking process includes one or more of the following steps. The particular instruments and methods used change over time and are a function of the customer's objectives.

When a new customer comes into Imagineworks, a meeting with the creative director is scheduled so that the company can best understand the photographer's business and imaging preferences and objectives. The client is often given advice on how to bring his or her specific images into the Imagineworks system to control expenses and to optimize quality. Chromes, negatives, or print art are digitized by the appropriate calibrated scanning device. Scanning imbalances are corrected (particularly if they receive a file scanned outside of their system) and adjusted to meet the customer's requirements. The master printmaker collaborates with the photographer to introduce enhancements that will contribute to the artist's objectives. The collaboration process helps define requirements and opportunities that the artist may not have understood initially. Enhancements are sometimes subtle, sometimes significant transformations of images. RGB files are converted to CMYK using profiles that will meet output objectives. Enhancements and color adjustments can be introduced to the CMYK image. One or more prints are created for the photographer, and the approved image file is archived for later reprints. Imagineworks does not accept direct electronic submissions, as file sizes are typically too large.

At Imagineworks, Iris print pricing currently ranges from $50 for a first 8 × 10 print to $150 for a 24 × 24-inch print. Prices are proportional to image size. Multiple prints, when ordered with the original print, are discounted 20 percent. Color correction and image processing (including scanning) are charged at a rate of $100/hour, and creative time (design, interpretation, etc.) at $150/hour.

TIP: Image Stability

Image stability is determined by ink set, substrate, and the environment. The ink sets that are typically used in prepress Iris prints are very short-lived and are not used by Imagineworks. The inks they use are those that have been tested as having the longest expected life span, currently rated at twenty years under normal lighting conditions. If an Iris print is placed in direct sunlight, it will fade faster. The current ink sets and substrates are permanent enough that internationally recognized galleries are accepting them in permanent exhibitions.

Preparing Files for IRIS Printing

As I discussed in the last chapter, the best way to get quality results from a service bureau is to provide them with digital files in a form and format that they know—from experience—will produce the best output. In discussing the production of IRIS prints with various service bureaus, I obtained the following suggestions on how to submit files that will produce the best results.

Color Space. Photographers should submit files in either CMYK or Lab Color format. While the IRIS is capable of printing RGB images, the results are not predictable. Any printing process involving ink on paper must inherently be converted into a reflective color model such as CMYK, but most service bureaus have seen excellent results printing files in Lab color. Since the IRIS uses special inks, it can produce colors well outside of the common CMYK gamut, producing some very compelling prints. Do not use both Lab and CMYK images in the same document.

Keep it Simple. Files with extra channels and compression can cause problems during printing. These files are rejected by the RIP (Raster Image Processor) with PostScript errors. Any extra channels must be removed before submission. Additionally, files should not be compressed; the service bureau will, most likely, have to decompress them before they print the files, but it may discover the fact that the file is compressed afterwards, creating an expensive ruined print.

Media. For submitting files, most services bureaus accept jobs on Iomega Zip and Jaz, SyQuest 44/88/200/105/270, floppy, 128M and 650M/1.3G MO, CD-ROM, Bernoulli, and, of course, via the Internet.

File Types Accepted. Most service bureaus accept a lot of different file types, including QuarkXPress, Adobe PageMaker, Illustrator, and Photoshop, Macromedia Freehand, and others. From a photographer's perspective, a TIFF or EPS file proba-

TIP: CIELAB or just Lab?

This color system was created by the Committee Internationale d'Eclairage to produce a color space that consists of all visible colors. The CIELAB system, sometimes shortened to just LAB, forms the basis for most contemporary color matching systems (see Chapter 8 for more details) and lets you convert, for example, RGB images to LAB to CMYK in order to produce accurate color matching. Because it offers the largest possible color gamut and is the only format delivering device-independent color, some digital stock companies scan their images in LAB mode.

bly makes the most sense, if all they wish to print is the image. Since Photoshop's RGB to Lab conversion is not the greatest, the photographer should submit RGB files as CMYK.

Image Resolution. Resolution should be 300 dpi. A higher resolution does nothing, but a lower one may result in visible pixelization.

FAUX IRIS OR INK-JET ART ON THE DESKTOP

If you would like to try making smaller prints—IRIS-based services bureaus can make large prints for you of up to 34 × 47 inches—you should experiment with the ink-jet printer that's already sitting on your desktop.

The first step is to visit an art supply store in your area and ask to see their selection of watercolor papers. Take a look at their selection, but keep in mind that, unlike an IRIS printer, a desktop ink-jet printer has limited paper thickness capabilities. Most printers, like the Epson Stylus Photo, have a "thick paper" handling option. This feature is traditionally designed so that you can print on #10 envelopes or labels without causing any problems with the thicker media, but you can use this feature to your advantage when experimenting with fine art output. The heaviest watercolor paper that I have found that works in the Epson Stylus Photo—in envelope mode—is ninety-pound stock. Also, be wary of paper that is too heavily textured.

While at the art supply store, try to get samples of the various watercolor papers that they have available. Pick those that have an interesting texture, but not too deep. Deeply textured papers will be harder to print on than slightly textured papers. Sometimes, these sheets are only available in larger sizes that will be too big for the typical desktop printer. Not to worry. These large sheets can always be trimmed down to fit whatever size paper your printer can handle.

When running your test prints, you should be aware that the printer driver decides on how much ink to spray based on the paper that you choose. Since art paper—and watercolor paper in particular—is not one of the paper choices, you are going to have to experiment with the available choices to find one that works. You may find that none of them will work with the porous watercolor paper. If that's the case, it's time to go deeper inside your driver and look for sliders that allow you to control the amount of ink or saturation that you can apply.

When making your test prints, slide up the paper into 4 × 7-inch (or so) sized bits. It will take less time to make small test prints than large ones. This will save time and money while you are experimenting. Do not reduce the size of your test image to 4 × 6 inches. Instead, carve out a 4 × 6 section and print that. In this way, you will be able to better evaluate the grain structure of the paper with your photographs.

TOOL: Large Format Ink-Jet

While not designed specifically for fine arts use, Epson offers two larger format ink-jet printers that are excellent candidates for such applications. Like the IRIS printer, the Epson Stylus Color 3000 has been designed for the graphic arts industry but has features that will appeal to photographers no matter what applications they may have in mind. The Stylus Color 3000 uses a Micro Piezo ink-jet print head design that is capable of producing ink droplets that are smaller and more consistent in shape and volume than other kinds of head design. The printer uses QuickDry inks that are rich in dye-based color and dry immediately on contact with most surfaces. This provides vibrant color, dark blacks, and resistance to bleeding and smudging on all media types — including plain paper. The printer features AcuPhoto halftoning, a method of determining how ink droplets should be applied to a page for the best quality results. This is built into the Stylus Color 3000 printer driver software. Using advanced half-toning algorithms, the AcuPhoto half-toning module examines each page's contents, resolution, and media type and then determines the best pattern in which to apply dots to a page. This provides the absolute best print quality possible, whether printing text, graphics, or photographs. The Stylus Color 3000 allows you to present full bleed, 13 × 19-inch prints at 1,440 × 720 dpi. The printer has Adobe PostScript Level 2 and PANTONE Calibrated approved colors, along with networking options. Slightly less expensive, the Stylus Color 1520 also delivers 1,440 dpi print quality. This printer uses Epson's Micro Piezo print head technology, Quick-Dry inks, and AcuPhoto halftoning. Like the 3000, this printer can also handle media up to 17 × 22 inches. The printer can output at six pages per minute in monochrome, and up to five pages per minute in color.

CASE STUDY: DIGITAL ART

There was a time when I was a co-owner of an art gallery. During that time, I used digital imaging technology to create what I felt was fine art.

My initial fine art prints were made on the FARGO Pictura 310 dye-sublimation printer. The Pictura 310 has 300 × 300dpi resolution and delivers continuous tone, photorealistic 25-bit color or 257-level black-and-white prints as well as fast wax-thermal color proofs. The printer can print photographs as large as 12 inches wide by 20 inches long. The original Pictura plugs into the Centronics parallel port of Windows computers, and FARGO supplies a NuBus interface board for Macs. The 310e will connect to Mac OS computer's serial port. At $4,995, the price tag may seem a little high, until you realize that dye-sublimation printers capable of this size have typically cost $15,000. FARGO sells the 12 × 20-inch dye-sublimation material as a kit containing 100 sheets of paper and a thermal ribbon, which works out to $6.59 per print. In an age when everything seems to be made offshore, the print engine for the Pictura 310 is made in the good old U.S.A.

TIP: Wearable Art?

The Pictura prints faster in wax thermal mode, but the quality of the output suffers when compared to the dye-sub mode. Since the material is less expensive and the process faster, wax thermal is great for a quick proof. You can also use wax thermal to make transfers for T-shirts or ceramic coffee mugs. This is one area where the Pictura really shines, since it can print up to 12 x18-inch T-shirt transfers.

Installation of driver software takes only a few seconds, and while the instructions on setting up the printer leave something to be desired in clarity, there are two important tips. First, to avoid creating splotches or blobs on your prints later on, handle the ribbon by the edges. Second, after placing the paper in the tray, make sure the side and back printer guides are snug. This is especially important to maintain registration, because the Pictura makes four passes of the paper when it prints an image. The first is through the yellow portion of the ribbon, the second through the magenta, the third through the cyan, and finally the black layer. Keeping the paper flat makes sure that the four passes are in perfect registration; during the time I had the printer, I never had registration problems.

Here's what I found out about using the Pictura: I seldom worry about compressing images for printing on the Pictura, because it's been my experience that the printer will produce great output from photographs made at almost any resolution or dpi.

Mini-Posters

I began making mini-posters with the FARGO Pictura using the largest print area I could. FARGO's 12 × 20-inch paper has a 1-inch area around the edges that is unprintable. To determine how large the printable area really was, I ran a test print that should have filled the entire page, then measured the area that was not printed. To save expense, I used wax thermal materials for this test. This turned out to be a false economy, because when I ran my first mini-poster using dye-sublimation materials, I discovered that the two different printing materials cover slightly differently from one another: the dye-sub ribbon produces a slightly smaller printable area.

I used these tests to produce a template in Adobe PageMaker to set the limits on the image area for the poster. In the illustration, you will notice that the poster is shown horizontally. I did this to provide the maximum screen size for the 12 × 20-inch paper. The posters can be created in small numbers for an out-of-pocket material cost under $7 each—and you can even change the images from time to time to target specific kinds of buyers. My most recent posters showcase black-and-white images shot on 4 × 5 sheet film and digitized with Photo CD. Instead of placing a Base*64 (4,096 × 6,144 pixels) Photo CD images,

TIP: But Is It Archival?

How does the output of dye sublimation and the newer ink-jet printers compare in image quality and permanence with conventional prints?

When assessing the quality of printer output, most photographers seem to be divided into two groups. The first is looking for an inexpensive printer that can deliver quality results. At this time, the FARGO Primera Pro Elite and Pictura printers are the best available solution. The second group is composed of photographers who want to be able to include "acceptable" looking photographs in their correspondence and newsletters. This second group will love the Epson Stylus Photo ink-jet printer.

Remember, the dye-sublimation process was originally designed as a proofing media, not to be the final product. According to FARGO Electronics, dye-sublimation prints will not last as long as a properly processed color print, but other than dye-transfer prints, most conventional color prints have a limited life, too. Dye-sublimation prints have a long life, but like video tape, no one has yet done a definitive archival study. Deterioration is mostly caused by exposure to UV radiation. My own tests showed fading of the Cyan dye layer when exposed to direct sunlight for over four months. I am not sure how a conventional C print would have done under similar circumstances. The best advice for making sure that a dye-sub prints lasts as long as possible is to store the print properly (cool, no direct light) and place it under UV protective glass. This glass, available at many framing shops, can reduce 99% of UV emissions. Also be sure to save a backup of the digital image using Photo CD or similar storage media. As far as prices go, until FARGO came along, dye-sublimation printers cost $10,000 or more. Now their lowest-priced printer costs less than $1,000. All three FARGO models produce excellent prints, and the best test of whether they are "exhibition" quality will be to compare a conventionally processed image against the output of the printer.

which can run about 80MB, I select the smaller Base*16 (2,048 × 3,072) photo and use Adobe PageMaker's sizing tool to drag the image up to 9 1/3 × 13 1/2 inches in size. For my current series of posters, I am using a large vertical image with my name and some copy beneath it. Keep in mind that, when using the Fargo Pictura, it can take twenty minutes to print a poster, so get it started and go to lunch or run an errand. The poster will be waiting when you get back. How do they look? Even though the Fargo printer has a stated resolution of 300 dpi, many photo editors and researchers who see my posters mistake them for original photographs. (See Figure 9.18 on CD-ROM.)

I used the Place command to place the image in PageMaker, then rotated it horizontally. I resized it so it would be as wide as possible to fill up the maximum printable width. I used the space left over at the bottom for text. I used the same Adobe Skia font on the poster that appears on my letterhead and even my Website. I made my name red and the rest of the text black. For your own

TIP: Save File Space

Desktop publishing programs, like Adobe PageMaker, usually give you two options when placing an image into them. You can save the image file as part of the desktop publishing (dtp) document, or you can create a link to the image file that the program will use when printing the file. There are advantages and disadvantages to both methods. When saving the image as part of the file, the on-screen depiction of the photographs is exactly what the image looks like. The downside is that the dtp file size includes the photograph, which can produce a large file. Linking the image creates a smaller file size, but the photograph often looks pixelized on screen — although it will print just fine. Because I am always battling an ever-shrinking hard disk, I typically use the second option. If you do and have the image printed by a service bureau, you have to make sure you provide them with both files: the dtp document and the image file.

Text from Certificate of Authenticity

Dye-sublimation prints can be treated similarly to commercially produced color prints, but like all photographs, should not be displayed where they will receive direct sunlight or intense fluorescent illuminations. While framing this print, the best protection will be provided by using ultra violet (UV) protectant glass. UV glass reduces 99% of harmful ultra violet radiation. And like a conventional color print, do not place the surface of the print in direct contact with glass. Place the print in a mat to provide additional air space between the print's surface and the glass in the frame.

posters, feel free to use whatever colors you want, but take a look at the trends in fine art posters before creating rainbow-hued text.

The posters were placed in a clear plastic bag designed for use in galleries and a certificate of authenticity enclosed. The purpose of the certificate is twofold: the first part states that this is a limited edition of a certain number of prints and the number of this particular print. This was also written on the front of the print and signed using a Sanford Sharpie with metallic ink. The second part of the form tells how purchasers should care for the image. The entire text of that section appears in a sidebar.

Mounting a dye-sub print is not tricky, but you cannot use the traditional heat presses and dry mount tissue. Instead, you can use archival-type hinges or vacuum-mounting with spray adhesive. The latter approach is one that my custom framer does, and the prints and posters always come out looking flat with no ripples or imbedded dirt.

Appendix A

Glossary of Terms Used

ALIASING. When a graphic is displayed on a monitor, you will sometimes see jagged edges around certain objects. These extra pixels surrounding hard edges—especially diagonal lines—are caused by an effect called aliasing. Techniques that smooth out these "jaggies" are called anti-aliasing.

ALPHA CHANNEL. This is a separate image channel that is tagged onto the traditional red, green, and blue channels; it containins a value that indicates the amount of transparency for each pixel. The alpha channel is where Adobe Photoshop stores transparency information.

ANALOG. Information presented in continuous form, corresponding to a representation of the "real world." A traditional photographic print is an analog form, but when this same image is scanned and converted into digital form, it is made up of bits.

ARCHIVE. To copy any kind of data from the media it is currently stored on (typically a hard disk) onto a removable media cartridge or tape for back-up purposes. Archive and back-up software often compress the data to maximize the capacity of that storage media.

ASCII. American Standard Code for Information Interchange. ASCII is a standardized computer code for representing text data. The code has ninety-six displayed characters (characters you see on the screen) and thirty-two nondisplayed characters (some of which you can see, others that you cannot).

BINARY. A mathematical system based on the numbers one and zero. This is ideal for computers, because electrical signals can be represented by electrical current being positive and negative, on and off.

BIT. Binary digit. The smallest unit of information with which a computer can work. Computers are digital devices because they represent all data—including photographs—using numbers, or digits, that are measured in bits.

BITMAP. There are three classes of graphic files: bitmap, metafile, and vector. A bitmap (sometimes known as a "raster") is any graphic image composed of a collection of tiny individual dots or pixels—one for every point or dot on a computer screen. The simplest bitmapped files are monochrome images composed of only black and white pixels. Monochrome bitmaps have a single color against a background, while images displaying more shades of color or gray need more than one bit to define the colors.

BYTE. Each electronic signal is one bit, but to represent more complex numbers or images, computers combine these signals into larger 9-bit groups called bytes. When 1,024 (*not* one thousand) bytes are combined, you get a kilobyte, often called K.

CAD. Webster's defines a cad as a contemptible ill-bred person, but it's really an acronym for Computer-Aided Design. CAD is the use of computers to produce designs and drawings for engineering and scientific applications.

CALIBRATION. A term used in Color Management Systems (CMS). Calibration stabilizes the inevitable variables in the way devices reproduce color. To produce optimum results, all color-reproducing devices must maintain a consistent, calibrated state. A variety of calibration products are available, depending on the device and manufacturer. Some monitors, such as the Radius PressView includes the necessary hardware and software to maintain color calibration.

CCD. A Charged Coupled Device is the kind of light-gathering device used in flatbed scanners, digital cameras, and video camcorders to convert the light passing through a lens into the electronic equivalent of the original image. Some small format digital cameras use a full-frame 24 × 36mm CCD imager to deliver 37-bit color (12 bits per RGB color) digital images. The Sinar/Leaf CatchLight large-format back uses a 1.2 × 1.3-inch (3 × 3 cm) CCD chip to capture color images at 14 bits per pixel or 43-bit color. For pixel counters, this generates an image containing 4 million pixels at a resolution of 2,048 × 2,048 pixels.

CIELAB. This color system was created by the Committee Internationale d'Eclairage to produce a color space that consists of all visible colors. The CIELAB system, sometimes shortened to just LAB, forms the basis for most contemporary color matching systems (see Chapter 8 for more details) and lets you convert, for example, RGB images to LAB and to CMYK to produce accurate color matching. Because it offers the largest possible color gamut and is the only format delivering device-independent color, some digital stock companies scan their images in LAB mode.

CLUT. Color Look-Up Table. A table—it can be in hardware or software form—that contains information on the mixing of red, green, and blue color intensities in a palette.

CMYK. Cyan, Magenta, Yellow, and Black. Blame this acronym on the same printing industry that saddled us with "picas." When added together, the primary additive colors of red, blue, and green produce white light. In the areas in which they overlap, red and blue form magenta, green and red produce yellow, and green and blue create cyan. These resulting colors are the *subtractive*, filters used when making Type C prints from color negatives. When the subtractive colors are added together they don't form black but a dark brown. That's why black must be added for accurate photographic reproduction. For reproduction, an image must be separated into varying percentages of cyan, magenta, yellow, and black, which is why CMYK film output is called *separations*.

COMPRESSION. Compression is a method of removing unneeded data to make a file smaller without losing any data or, in the case of a photographic file, image quality. There are many techniques and technologies for compressing graphics, and how well each works depends on what is more important to you: file size or image quality. JPEG was designed to discard information the eye cannot normally see and is what the techies call a "lossy" method. By comparison, LZW compression is lossless—meaning, no data is discarded during the compression process.

CPU. Central Processing Unit. There are two basic families of CPUs: Intel and Motorola. Intel and similar chips are used in IBM-compatible PCs, while Motorola makes the chips for Mac OS machines. How well a chip processes data is determined by how many bits of information it can process at one time. The larger the number of bits a chip can process simultaneously, the faster it can process. Think of it as a highway. The more lanes you provide, the more cars can travel on it at one time. A 33-bit CPU, for example, processes data twice as fast as a 17-bit model. The next most important aspect of the CPU is how fast it processes data. This is measured by the CPU's clock speed. If the path defines the number of lanes on the highways, the clock speed defines how fast the cars can travel on those lanes.

DEVICE RESOLUTION. Refers to the number of dots per inch (dpi) that a device, such as a monitor or printer, can produce. Device resolution for computer monitors varies from 60 to 120 dpi. Do not confuse this with screen resolution, which refers to the number of dots per inch in the line screen used by printers to reproduce a photograph. Screen resolution is measured in lines per inch (lpi). Image Resolution refers to the amount of information stored in a photograph and is expressed in pixels per inch (ppi). The image resolution of a photograph determines how big the file is. The higher the image resolution, the more disk space it takes and the longer it will take to output.

DITHERING. A graphics display or printing process that uses a combination of dots or textures to create the impression of a continuous-tone grayscale or color image.

DYNAMIC RANGE. One key feature to look for in a scanner or digital camera is its *dynamic range*. A scanner's dynamic range depends on the maximum optical density that can be achieved and the number of bits captured. In simple terms, the greater the density range the better the scanner. Until recently, only expensive slide scanners offered a density range over 2.5, but now more affordable scanners perform at 3.0 or higher. By comparison, a Photo CD scan has a dynamic range of 2.8.

EMF. Electromagnetic Field. If you spend more than a few hours at your computer a day you should be aware of the potential problems caused by the Electromagnetic Fields that computer monitors produce. All monitors emit some kind of very low frequency (VLF) and extremely low frequency (ELF) radiation, and color monitors emit more than monochromatic ones. A cathode-ray tube releases most of its radiation from the sides and back of the monitor. That's why it's a good idea to sit four or five feet away from your monitor. For most people, that's not possible, but you should at least keep it at arms' length. You will sometimes see screen filters that purport to block radiation from computer monitors, but even lead cannot stop some ELF and VLF waves.

FILM RECORDER. Color film recorder, sometimes called CFR. A desktop film recorder is essentially a camera enclosed in a small box and focused on a very high-resolution black-and-white monitor. The CFR makes three exposures of the image through separate red, blue, and green filters to produce the final image. If this sounds slow, it can be.

FITS. The Functional Interpolating Transformational System technology that is used by Live Picture. Advantages include the ability to make multiple changes to color, brightness, and contrast on individual layers without affecting the entire composition.

GAMMA. All photographs have a characteristic called gamma. The amount of gamma present in an image is measured as the contrast that affects the midlevel grays (the midtones) of an image. The good news for digital imagers is that this gamma is adjustable by most image-enhancement programs, and you are not stuck with the gamma that is present in the original negative or print.

GIF. (Pronounced like the peanut butter.) The Graphics Interchange Format developed by CompuServe is completely platform-independent: the same bitmapped file created on a Macintosh is readable by a Windows graphics program. A 257-color GIF file is automatically compressed, making it ideal for use on the World Wide Web.

GIGABYTE. A billion bytes or (more correctly) 1,024 megabytes.

GRAYSCALE. Refers to a series of gray tones ranging from white to pure black. The more shades or levels of gray, the more accurately an image will look like a full-tone black and white photograph. Most scanners will scan from 16 to 256 gray tones. A grayscale image file is one-third the size of a color one.

GUI. Graphic User Interface.

HALO. When using a selection tool in an image-enhancement program to select certain kinds of objects, a halo can appear around part of that selection. These extra pixels are created by the program's anti-aliasing feature. Most image enhancement programs have a built-in anti-aliasing function that partially blurs pixels on the fringe of a selection and causes additional pixels to be pulled into the selection.

H&D CURVE. Hurter and Driffield Curve shows the density of grams of silver per a logarithm of the exposure given to the photograph's exposure.

INDEXED COLOR. There are two kinds of indexed color images: those with a limited number of colors, and pseudocolor images. The number of colors for the first type is usually 256 or less. Pseudocolor images are grayscale images that display the variations in gray levels in colors rather than shades of gray, and are used for scientific and technical work. CompuServe's GIF format uses an indexed color scheme; before image enhancement programs like Adobe Photoshop can use GIF files, they have to be converted into RGB.

INK-JET. In an ink-jet printer, a print head sprays one or more colors of ink onto paper to produce output, and the type of methods used to accomplish this has an effect on output quality. Piezoelectric technology is based on the property of crystals to oscillate when subjected to electrical voltage. This allows printers using this technology, such as Epson's Stylus Color family of printers, to place uniform ink droplets on paper and deliver output at a resolution of up to 1,440 dots per inch (dpi) or higher. The drop-on-demand method uses a set of independently controlled injection chambers—the newest of which use solid ink—which liquefies when heated and solidifies when it hits paper. This thermal approach is favored by Canon, Apple, and H-P. Another method is the continuous stream method, which produces droplets aimed onto the paper by electric field deflectors. The weak link of all ink-jet printers, large or small format, is fading from UV radiation and susceptibility to water damage. These limitations can be overcome by laminating the finished print.

IVUE. The name of Live Picture's IVUE proprietary image manipulation file format. It lets you display, scale, zoom, and pan images so quickly that working with a 100+ MB image takes the same amount of time as a 1MB file.

JPEG. Is an acronym for a compressed graphics format created by the Joint Photographic Experts Group, within the International Standards Organization. Unlike other compression schemes, JPEG is what the techies call a "lossy" method. By comparison, LZW compression used in file formats such as GIF is lossless—meaning no data is discarded during compression. JPEG achieves compression by breaking an image into discrete blocks of pixels, which are then divided in half until a compression ratio of from 10:1 to 100:1 is achieved. The greater the compression ratio, the greater the loss of sharpness you can expect.

K. In the computer world, K stands for two to the 10th power, or 1,024. A Kilobyte (or KB) is, therefore, not 1000 bytes but is 1,024 bytes.

LANDSCAPE (MODE). An image orientation that places a photograph across the wider (horizontal) side of the monitor or printer. A photographer would call this a horizontal image, but a computer user would say "landscape." Antonym: Portrait or vertical. Most computer screens are horizontal, but Radius makes a monitor called the Pivot that uses a mercury switch, which changes the orientation as the user physically rotates it from portrait to landscape.

LAYER. In image enhancement programs, like Adobe Photoshop, layers are any one of several on-screen independent levels for creating separate—but cumulative—effects for an individual photograph. Layers can be manipulated independently, and the sum of all the individual effects on each layer make up what you see as the final image.

LZW. Lempel-Ziv-Welch. A compression algorithm currently "owned" by UNISYS.

MASK. Many image enhancement programs have the ability to create masks—or stencils—that are placed over the original image to protect parts of it and allow other sections to be edited or enhanced. Cutouts or openings in the mask make the unmasked portions of the image accessible for manipulation while the mask protects the rest.

MEGABYTE. When you combine 1,024 kilobytes, you have a megabyte (MB) or "meg."

MOIRÉ. (Pronounced "mwah-RAY.") Moiré patterns are an optical illusion caused by a conflict with the way the dots in an image are scanned and then printed. When scanning an original photograph or artwork, a single pass scanner is all most people require, but when scanning material that has previously been printed, a three-pass scan (one each for red, green, and blue) will almost always remove the inevitable moiré or dot pattern.

NANO. A prefix that means one-billionth.

ONE-OFF. A CD-ROM disc that is made one at a time instead of being stamped from a glass master disc the way discs are usually made in volume. When a new CD-ROM disc is in production, a test disc—or one-off—is created for approval purposes. CD-ROM recorders (CD-R) are sometimes called one-off machines because they write a single disc—one at a time.

PHOTO CD. Kodak's proprietary process that places digitized files of photographs onto a CD-ROM disc. Photo CD facilities can digitize images from color slides and black-and-white or color negatives. A Photo CD Transfer Station converts your analog images into digital form by using a high-resolution film scanner, a computer, image processing software, a disc writer, and a color thermal printer. Each image is adjusted for color and density, compressed to 4.5MB using Kodak's Photo YCC format image, and written to a CD-ROM. A thermal printer creates an index sheet showing the images transferred to disc and is inserted into the cover of the CD's jewel case. Initially, there were six different kinds of Photo CDs, now there are two: the Photo CD Master disc and the Photo CD Portfolio II disc. The Photo CD Master Disc format holds 100 high-resolution images. The discwriter writes five different file sizes (and five different resolutions), which Kodak calls Image Pac, onto the CD:

Base/16 — 128 × 192 pixels
Base/4 — 256 × 348 pixels
Base — 512 × 768 pixels
Base*4 — 1024 × 1536 pixels
Base*16 — 2048 × 3072 pixels

A subset of this disc type is the Pro Photo CD Master Disc that accepts images from 120mm and 70mm rolls and from 4 × 5-sheet film. The Pro disc includes built-in copyright protection and offers a sixth, Base*64 resolution image that yields a size of 4,096 × 6,144 pixels.

PIEZOELECTRIC. The property of some crystals that oscillate when subjected to electrical voltage. A form of print head design that is used by Epson in their Stylus Color family of ink-jet printers. On the other hand, *piezo-electric* (with a hyphen) technology generates electricity when mechanical stress is applied.

PIXEL. Pixel is an acronym for picture element. A computer's screen is made up of thousands of these colored dots of light that, when combined, can produce a photographic image. A digital photograph's resolution, or visual quality, is measured by the width and height of the image measured in pixels. When a slide or negative is converted from silver grain into pixels, the resulting image can be produced at different resolutions.

POSTSCRIPT. A programming language created by Adobe Inc. that defines all shapes in a file as outlines, and interprets these outlines by mathematical formulae called *Bezier* (Bez-e-ay) curves. Any PostScript-compatible output device, whether it's a film recorder or laser printer, uses these definitions to reproduce the image on your computer screen.

QIC. Quarter-Inch Cassette. For some reason, tape is more popular with Windows and DOS users than with Mac-OS users. This is changing as multi-GB drives become less expensive and the thought of backing up these huge drives sinks in. Cartridges come in different designations: there are QIC (Quarter-Inch Cassette), XL (long), and QW (wide-long) models, and variations on these names that sound more like the latest model BMW. Data is stored on the tape in serial form instead of the random method used by all other forms of removable media. This produces inherently slower access times, which prevents magnetic tape from getting the respect it deserves.

RAM. Random Access Memory. RAM is that part of your computer that temporarily stores all data while you are working on it. Unlike a floppy disk or hard drive, this data is volatile—if you lose power or turn off your computer, the information disappears. Most contemporary computer motherboards feature several raised metal and plastic slots that hold RAM in the form of SIMMs (Single Inline Memory Modules).

RESOLUTION. A digital photograph's resolution—or image quality—is defined as an image's width and height as measured in pixels. When a slide or negative is converted from silver grain into pixels, the resulting digital image can be made at different resolutions. The higher the resolution of an image—the more pixels it has—the better the visual quality. An image with a resolution of 2,048 × 3,072 pixels has better resolution and more photographic quality than the same image digitized at 128 × 192 pixels. Unfortunately, a rule of thumb is that as the resolution of a device increases, so does its cost.

RGB. Red, Green, Blue. Color monitors use red, blue, and green signals to produce all of the colors that you see on the screen. If you have ever made Type R prints from slides in your darkroom, you are familiar with working with the additive color filters of red, blue, and green.

RIP. Raster Image Processor. RIP is a process that prepares image data for the screen or printer. Before dye-sublimation printers print images, they first save a temporary RIP file to disk—which is then used to print the final output. RIP files rasterize specific types of data, such as PostScript or vector graphics images, as well as different kinds of bitmapped data.

SATURATION. Saturation, often referred to as Chroma by show-offs, is a measurement of the amount of gray present in a color.

THERMAL DYE-TRANSFER. Often called dye-sublimation. A printer type utilizing a head that heats a dye ribbon to create a gas that hardens into a deposit on the special paper used by the printer. Like most printers, it forms "dots" of colors, but because these spots are soft-edged (as opposed to the hard edges created by laser and ink-jet printers) the result is smooth continuous tones.

UNSHARP MASK. This oddly named function is a digital implementation of a traditional darkroom and prepress technique in which a blurred film negative is combined with the original to highlight the photograph's edges. In digital form, it's a more controllable method for sharpening an image.

VECTOR. Images saved in this format are stored as points, lines, and mathematical formulae that describe the shapes that make up that image. When vector files are viewed on your computer screen or printed, the formulae are converted into a dot or pixel pattern. Since these pixels are not part of the file itself, the image can be resized without losing any quality. Photographs are not typically saved in this format. Some computer users, especially Mac OS users, call vector-format files object-oriented, and you will often see that term used on graphic drawing programs. Vector files use the same technology that Adobe uses with its PostScript fonts and has the same advantages—you can make any image as big as you want, and it will retain its quality. Vector graphics are displayed as bitmapped graphics on your monitor.

WAX THERMAL. Most dye-sublimation printers also support printing with wax thermal materials. This process uses a coarser wax-like ink in its ribbon. During printing, wax thermal paper is pressed against each color in the ribbon as it passes the printer's heating element, transferring the ink onto the paper. The results are inferior to a dye-sublimation print, but the material is much less expensive, making it an option for proofing a layout or image.

WINDOWS. More properly called Microsoft Windows, it was an attempt to make the DOS (Disc Operating System) command-line interface more user-friendly by providing a graphical user interface (GUI). The original Windows was announced in 1985, but this operating environment did not become the de facto standard for IBM-compatible computers until the creation of Windows 3.0 in 1990. Unlike the Macintosh GUI, Windows is more accurately an operating *environment* instead of an operating system, since it required that users have Microsoft's DOS installed. This requirement vanished with the introduction of Windows 95, which no longer requires DOS (after installation), but it does provide access to a DOS-like environment for the use of older non-Windows applications.

WYSIWYG. (Pronounced "wissy-wig.") What You See Is What You Get. This term refers to the ability to view text and graphics on screen in the same manner as they will appear when printed. While most text- and image-editing programs have WYSIWYG capabilities, not all do. Read the fine print when you think about purchasing any program. A graphics user interface (GUI) is useless unless the applications that run under it are fully WYSIWYG.

XGA. A type of video adapter developed by IBM for its PS/2 computers. XGA displays a resolution of 1,024 × 768 pixels with 17-bit colors, allowing it to display 65,000 colors.

YCC. The color model used by Kodak's Photo CD process. This is the translation of RGB data into *one* part of what scientists call "luminance" but the rest of us call brightness. This is the Y component that is added to two parts—the CC—of chrominance or color and hue. This system keeps file size under control while maintaining Photo CD's "photographic" look. Sony uses a similar system in its professional Betacam video system.

ZIP. Iomega's Zip removable media drive has a street price around $150, and uses a combination of conventional hard disk read/write heads with flexible disks and produces an average seek time of 29ms. Pocketable Zip cartridges, scarcely larger than a floppy disk, are less expensive than other removable media.

Appendix B

Index of Products, Companies, and Contacts

Adobe Systems Inc., 345 Park Avenue, San Jose, CA 95110-2704. 408/536-6000; fax: 408/537-6000; Internet: http://www.adobe.com.

Alien Skin Software, 100 Wake Forest Road, Suite 101, Raleigh, NC 27604. 919/832-4124; fax: 919/832-4065.

Apple Computer, 1 Infinite Loop, Cupertino, CA 95014. 408/996-1010.

Art Leather, Elmhurst, NY 11373-2824. 718/699-6300; fax: 718/699-9339.

Auto F/X Corporation, Black Point HCR 73, Box 689, Alton Bay, NH 03810. 603/569-8800; fax: 603/569-9702; Internet: http://www.autofx.com.

Boeckeler Instruments, 3280 East Hemispheres Loop, Building 114, Tucson, AZ 85706-5024. 520/573-7100; fax: 520/573-7101.

BoxTop Software, Inc., P.O. Box 2347, Starkville, MS 39760. 601/324-1800; fax: 601/324-7352; Internet: http://208.137.150.133/company.html.

CalComp Digitizer Division, 2411 W. LaPalma Avenue, Anaheim, CA 92801-9808. 800/932-1212; fax: 714/821-2832.

Chisholm, 910 Campisi Way, Campbell, CA 95008. 408/559-1111; fax: 408/559-0444.

Cies-Sexton, Inc., 1247 Santa Fe Drive, Denver, CO, 80204. 303/534-4000; fax: 303/534-4064; Internet: http://www.cies.com.

DataViz, Inc., 55 Corporate Dr., Trumbull, CT 06611. 800/733-0030, 203/268-0030; fax: 203/268-4345; Internet: http://www.dataviz.com.

Deneba Software, 7400 Southwest 87th Avenue, Miami, FL 33173. 800/622-6827, 305/596-5644; fax: 305/273-9069; Internet: http://www.deneba.com.

Eastman Kodak Company, 901 Elmgrove Road, Rochester, NY 14653-5200. 800/235-6325; Internet: http://www.kodak.com.

Extensis Corporation, 1800 SW First, Suite 500, Portland, OR 97201. 503/274-2020; fax: 503/274-0530; Internet: http://www.extensis.com.

FARGO Electronics, Inc., 7901 Flying Cloud Drive, Eden Prairie, MN 55344. 800/327-4622, 612/941-9470; fax: 612/941-7836; Internet: http://www.fargo.com.

Grayphics Digital Imaging, 10 East Figueroa Street, Suite 2, Santa Barbara, CA 93101. 805/899-2387; Internet: http://www.grayphics.com.

Hitachi Digital Graphics, 250 East Caribbean Drive, Sunnyvale, CA 94089-1007. 408/747-0777; fax: 408/746-2323.

The Human Software Company, 19925 Stevens Creek Blvd., Cupertino, CA 95014-2358. 408/399-0057; fax: 408/399-1057; Internet: http://www.humansoftware.com.

Imagineworks, 15 N. Ellsworth Avenue, Suite 201, San Mateo CA 94401. 650/696-9165; Internet: http://www.imagineworks.com.

Inforite Corp., 1670 Amphlett Blvd., Suite 100, San Mateo, CA 94402. 800/366-4635.

IRIS Graphics, Six Crosby Drive, Bedford, MA 01730. 617/275-8777; fax: 617/275-8590; Internet: http://www.hcgrp.com/products.htm.

Kurta Corp., 3007 East Chambers Street, Phoenix, AZ 85040. 800/445-8782.

Live Picture, 5617 Scotts Valley Drive, Suite 16, Soquel, CA 95073. 408/464-4200; fax: 408/464-4202; Internet: http://www.livepicture.com.

Macromedia, Inc., 600 Townsend Street, Suite 180, San Francisco, CA 94103-4945. 800/326-2128, 415/252-2000; fax: 415/626-1502; Internet: http://www.macromedia.com.

MetaCreations, Inc., 6303 Carpinteria Avenue, Carpinteria, CA 93013. Internet: http://www.metatools.com.

Microfield Graphics, 503/626-9393; fax: 503/641-9333.

Mind Path Technologies, 12700 Park Central Drive, Suite 1700, Dallas, TX 75251. 800/736-6830, 214/233-9296; fax: 214/233-9308.

Nomai, 4301 Oak Circle, Suite 20, Boca Raton, FL 33431. 800/55-NOMAI, 407/367-1216; fax: 407/391-8675; Internet: http://www.nomai.com.

Numonics Corp., 101 Commerce Drive, Box 1005, Montgomeryville, PA 18936. 800/247-4517; fax: 215/361-0167.

Olympus Image Systems, Inc., Two Corporate Center Drive, Melville, NY 11747-3157. 800/347-4027, 516/844-5000; fax: 516/844-5339; Internet: http://www.olympusamerica.com.

Photoflex, 333 Encinal Street, Santa Cruz, CA 95060. 800/486-2674; fax: 408/454-9600; Internet: http://www.photoflex.com.

Piptel, 3430 S. Dixie Drive, Suite 301, Dayton, OH 45439-2316. 513/294-6566; fax: 513/294-4390.

Quark, Inc., 1800 Grant Street, Denver, CO 80203. 800/788-7835, 303/894-8888; fax: 303/894-3399; Internet: http://www.quark.com.

Seagate Technology, Inc., 920 Disc Drive, Scotts Valley, CA 95066-4544. 408/438-6550; fax: 408/438-7852; Internet: http://www.seagate.com.

Seattle FilmWorks, 1260 16th Avenue West, Seattle, WA 98119. 800/FILMWORKS; Internet: http://www.filmworks.com.

Second Glance Software, 7248 Sunset Avenue NE, Bremerton, WA 98311. 306/692-3694; fax: 306/692-9241; Internet: http://www.secondglance.com.

Softkey International, Inc., 6943 Kaiser Drive, Fremont, CA 94555. 510/792-2101; fax: 510/792-9268.

Summagraphics, 8500 Cameron Road, Austin, TX 78754-3999. 512/835-0900.

SyQuest Technology, Inc., 47071 Bayside Pkwy., Fremont, CA 94538. 800/245-CART, 510/226-4000; fax: 510/226-4100; Internet: http://www.syquest.com.

Vivid Details, 8228 Sulphur Mountain Road, Ojai, CA 93023. 805/646-0217; fax: 805/646-0021; Internet: http://www.vividdetails.com.

Wacom Technology Corp., 501 SE Columbia Shores Blvd., Suite 300, Vancouver, WA 98661. 800/922-6613; fax: 360/750-8924; Internet: http://www.wacom.com.

Index

About the Author

Joe Farace is a Colorado-based writer/photographer. He is a graduate of Johns Hopkins University and received his formal photographic education at the Maryland Institute, College of Art in Baltimore. Joe has published over 700 magazine articles about graphics, photography, and digital imaging. He is the author, co-author, or contributor to sixteen books, including Focal Press' upcoming book, *Adventures in Available Light Photography*. He is an instructor at Photoflex's On-line School of Photography (www.photoflex.com) and maintains his own website at www.hyperzine.com/writers/joef.html.

Joe is Contributing Editor for *Photo>Electronic Imaging* and *ComputerUSER* magazines. His monthly column called "Graphics" appears in the Puget Sound ComputerUSER. Joe is also Technical Editor of *Professional Photographer Storyteller* magazine, where his monthly column on digital imaging called "Pixography" appears. He is Editor-at-Large for *The Press*, a screen printing industry publication. Joe is a regular contributor to *Shutterbug* and *HyperZine* magazines. He lives in Northeastern Colorado with his wife Mary.

Contents for the CD-ROM

CHAPTER 1

Figure 1.1. Kodak's Photo CD Acquire Module is a free Photoshop-compatible plug-in that allows you to acquire Photo CD images. Image © Joe Farace.

Figure 1.2a. Using Seattle FilmWorks free PhotoWorks program, you can work with the digital images created as Pictures On Disk. Photo © Joe Farace.

Figure 1.2b. The Add Images dialog box lets you select which images you would like to appear in an album.

Figure 1.3. Live Pix is an entry-level image manipulation and composting program that has surprising capabilities, despite its modest price. Image © Joe Farace.

Figure 1.4a. PhotoWorks Plus lets you improve or enhance your favorite photographs.

Figure 1.4b. Soap uses a "rooms" analogy, in which you move back and forth between the rooms using a Map. Here's a look at the Color room. Photo © Joe Farace.

Figure 1.4c. A FlashPix file opened and placed in a LivePix "project" window. Photo © Joe Farace.

CHAPTER 2

Figure 2.1. Adobe Photoshop is the Big Kahuna of image editing programs and is one of the most important components of your digital imaging toolkit. Image © Joe Farace.

Figure 2.2. Using Kodak's Photo CD Acquire Module, the author converted the original photograph to grayscale and selected the image resolution he wanted. © Joe Farace.

Figure 2.3. The next step in the process was selecting the entire image with the Select All command. Image © Joe Farace.

Figure 2.4. Chalk and Charcoal filters let users experiment with different settings and view their effects in the Preview window. Image © Joe Farace.

Figure 2.5. The Fade command allows you to apply the effect in varying degrees. Here the author cut the effect in half.

Figure 2.6. After tweaking the Fade command, the overall effect is that of a hand-drawn image. Image © Joe Farace.

Figure 2.7. Photoshop's Actions palette provides one-button control over any scriptable function—and writing scripts isn't too hard.

Figure 2.8. A FlashPix image of an old building was opened in Adobe Photoshop 4.0, then the Actions palette was selected from the Windows menu.

Figure 2.9. To get out of "Button Mode," the author clicked on Action's side-mounted menu, then deselected Button Mode.

Figure 2.10. The New Action dialog box lets you name it, assign a function key, and give a color to the new button.

Figure 2.11. The final action includes Change Mode to CMYK. Change Image size to 350 dpi, then Save as a TIFF file.

Figure 2.12. KPT Actions expands on the few basic Actions supplied by Adobe and allows users to create dramatic text and border effects.

Figure 2.13. After opening the author's photograph of a clock tower, clicking on the Partial Opacity Frame Action button created this effect.

Figure 2.14. Using Photoshop's Text tool to place the name of an on-line photography magazine, I applied KPT Actions Gold (text) Action—with this result.

Figure 2.15. Photoshop 4.0's Navigator function can be added with a free plug-in from Extensis. The red rectangle shows the area of the on-screen image.

Figure 2.16. Watermark was used with a setting of 15 (the default) to place a single, subtle copyright symbol across this image.

Figure 2.17. Selecting the Open command from the Converter menu is the first step in converting an image into an IVUE file.

Figure 2.18. After opening, a TIFF format image appears in Live Picture's Converter window.

Figure 2.19. The Save As dialog box—from the Converter menu—is used to convert the file into IVUE format.

Figure 2.20. For Mac OS users who want the power of Live Picture but might be intimidated by its purchase price, Live Picture Overdrive provides a less expensive alternative. Photo © Joe Farace.

Figure 2.21. DeBabelizer Toolbox's Open dialog has such a large preview window that the program could easily be considered a file viewing program, too. Photo © Joe Farace.

Figure 2.22. DeBabelizer's working window shows the image full size as well as its specification. Here, the image is shown at 928 x 617 pixels, with 17 million colors and a resolution of 150 dpi. Photo © Joe Farace.

Figure 2.23. One of the strongest parts of DeBabelizer Toolbox is the Save dialog, which lets you save your image file in many Mac OS and Windows file formats.

Figure 2.24. John Blake at work in his office. (Photographed by Joe Farace with Polaroid PDC-2000 digital camera.)

Figure 2.25. The starting point for John Blake's "A Crowded Day at the Mall" was the Erechtheum, which is part of the Acropolis in Athens, Greece.

Figure 2.26. The second part of Blake's composite image was a stock photograph of an elderly couple that he photographed in Switzerland.

Figure 2.27. The final "A Crowded Day at the Mall" is a tribute to John Blake's skill as a photographer—and a pixographer.

CHAPTER 3

Figure 3.1. Epson America also makes a Zip drive. Their compact size makes them so portable you can take the drive to a service bureau that dosen't have one. Photo courtesy Epson America.

Figure 3.2. One of the most popular and long-lived removable media drives is the SyQuest 200MB drive. The drive can also read cartridges from the older 44 and 88MB formats. Photo courtesy SyQuest Corporation.

Figure 3.3. One of the most popular MO (magneto-optical) drives for pixographers is Olympus' inexpensive and portable Sys.230 drive. Photo courtesy of Olympus Corporation.

Figure 3.4. Olympus CD-R2X6 CD-R drive reads CD-ROM discs at 6X speed and writes them at 2X. Photo courtesy Olympus Corporation.

Figure 3.5. Iomega also makes tape drives for backup and off-line storage of images. While not as glamorous as their disk and disc-based siblings, tape drives provide an inexpensive storage option. Photo courtesy Iomega Corporation.

Figure 3.6. DataViz's MacLink Plus allows you to convert many different Mac OS files into equivalent Windows-compatible form.

Figure 3.7. PageMaker's Document Setup dialog box lets you specify how big the page will be and what the margins are like. Since I plan to print on a 300 dpi printer, the resolution was set at that number.

Figure 3.8. Using Adobe PageMaker's Place command, I placed the text of my name that had been enhanced using Adobe Photoshop and KPT Actions from MetaCreations.

Figure 3.9. Adobe Photoshop is used first to tweak the sharpness of images to be used on the final sell sheet. Photo © Joe Farace.

Figure 3.10. PageMaker's Place Document command is used to select the image and place it in the sell sheet.

Figure 3.11. The stock image is now part of the desktop publishing document. Photo © Joe Farace.

Figure 3.12. There are no rules for placing images on sell sheets. Place them and resize them according to the overall design of the piece, or the importance of certain topics to your target market. Photos © Joe Farace.

Figure 3.13. The best way to draw borders around photographs is to view the images at 2X and 4X the normal screen view. This will make it possible to see the real edges of the images so that no gaps appear. Photos © Joe Farace.

Figure 3.14. With the cloud background pasted in, the sell sheet is ready to be printed. Total time to create it from start to finish—less than two hours. Photos © Joe Farace.

CHAPTER 4

Figure 4.1. Here the Layers Palette shows the layers used in the Junkyard Art image that will be explained at the end of the next chapter. It consists of three layers plus the background. Two layers are photographs and one is text.

Figure 4.2. The process starts with opening an image. This Photo CD scan was opened using Kodak's Photo CD Acquire Module plug-in. Photo © Joe Farace.

Figure 4.3. The New Adjustment Layer is found in Photoshop's Layers pop-up menu.

Figure 4.4. The Adjustment Layer dialog box lets you name the layer and choose what kind of adjustment you want to make.

Figure 4.5. The last dialog you see after creating an Adjustment Layer is the Levels dialog, which allows you to adjust an images' brightness and contrast by manipulating the newly created layer.

Figure 4.6. The first step to creating a Mosaic is opening up the image. As you can see, the Painter interface is dramatically different from other image editing programs. Photo © Joe Farace.

Figure 4.7. Painter's Crop tool was used to crop the black border and simplify the image's composition. Photo © Joe Farace.

Figure 4.8. Choosing Clone from the file menu created a duplicate copy of the original image. Photo © Joe Farace.

Figure 4.9. The Make Mosaic dialog box controls all of the aspects from tile shape to grout in the mosaic process.

Figure 4.10. To check your progress, turn the Use Tracing Paper off and on during the process. Photo © Joe Farace.

Figure 4.11. Experimenting with the grout color allowed the author to find the look he wanted for the final image. Photo © Joe Farace.

Figure 4.12. The completed mosaic provides the stained glass look that the author was trying to achieve. Photo © Joe Farace.

Figure 4.13. Just like everything else in Painter, the interface on the F.List palette looks different from what you might see in another image editing program. Nevertheless, MetaCreations has packed a lot of power and control into this toolbox.

Figure 4.14. This flower from MetaCreations Power Photos IV stock photo disc was opened and converted into a floater using the Float command. Photo courtesy MetaCreations.

Figure 4.15. Painter's Drop Shadow dialog lets you control the offset and distance the shadow is from a floater, along with its opacity.

Figure 4.16. Creating a drop shadow with a floater, as you will discover, takes less time to do than it does to read about it—and the effect is attractive. Photo courtesy of MetaCreations.

Figure 4.17. The starting image is shown alongside Adobe Photoshop's Channels palette Photograph. Photo © PhotoSphere Images Ltd.

Figure 4.18. Split the image into separate documents using the Split Channels command in Adobe Photoshop's Channels palette.

Figure 4.19. After splitting the documents into three parts, your workspace will look like this. Photo © PhotoSphere Images Ltd.

Figure 4.20. When converting the split files into Bitmap images, you will see this dialog that allows you to specify the method of dithering that the image will use.

Figure 4.21. After converting the images into Bitmap, this is what they will look like. Photograph © PhotoSphere Images Ltd.

Figure 4.22. Using channels, the original RGB photograph was converted into a dramatic mezzotint image. Photograph © PhotoSphere Images Ltd.

Figure 4.23. Kodak's Photo CD Acquire plug-in was used to import the 2,048 x 3,072 pixel image and automatically converted the image into grayscale. Photo © Joe Farace.

Figure 4.24. In the Image menu, I used the Rotate Canvas command to turn the image 90 degrees counter-clockwise. Photo © Joe Farace.

Figure 4.25. The black edges surrounding the slide mount were removed using Photoshop's Crop tool. Photo © Joe Farace.

Figure 4.26. All Photo CD images need to be sharpened, especially this one that was not too sharp to begin with. Using a 200% factor with Photoshop's Unsharp Mask command made the image as sharp as it was ever going to be. Photo © Joe Farace.

Figure 4.27. Using Photoshop 4.0's new Fade command, the Render/Clouds effect can be varied to suit your own tastes. Photo © Joe Farace.

Figure 4.28. The Graphic Pen filter was formerly part of the Adobe Gallery Effects package but is now integrated into Photoshop 4.0. Here it was used with black selected as a foreground color to apply bromoil-like brush strokes. Photo © Joe Farace.

Figure 4.29. Selecting Duotone from the Image/Mode menus causes the Duotone Options dialog box to be displayed. This is your gateway to the sepia presets.

Figure 4.30. The completed digital bromoil image. Photo © Joe Farace.

Figure 4.31. The starting point for the creative edges process was the last step in the digital bromoil process. Photo © Joe Farace.

Figure 4.32. The Photo/Graphic Edges dialog box contains all the controls needed to add inset or outset creative edges to your photographs.

Figure 4.33. A standard Open dialog is used to locate and access the selected edge file.

Figure 4.34. The finished image, complete with creative edging. Photo © Joe Farace.

CHAPTER 5

Figure 5.1. This Photo CD image of the front of an old streetcar was opened in Adobe Photoshop. The Magic Wand tool was used to select the yellow background area. Photo © Joe Farace.

Figure 5.2. The Magic Wand, with Tolerance set at 32, was used to Click-Select as much of the yellow area as possible. Photo © Joe Farace.

Figure 5.3. After clicking the Quick mask button, the nonprotected (nonselected) area of your image is covered in a Rubylith-like mask. Photo © Joe Farace.

Figure 5.4. Using the eraser, the author removed portions on the Quick Mask that he wanted to expose. Photo © Joe Farace.

Figure 5.5. After cleaning up the mask, the author clicked the Standard Mode button, converting the mask into a selection. Photo © Joe Farace.

Figure 5.6. Using the Selective Color command, the author manipulated the original color of the streetcar.

Figure 5.7. The final image created with Quick Mask has a bolder yellow color suited to the author's vision for the photograph. Photo © Joe Farace.

Figure 5.8. The photograph of a streetcar was opened in Adobe Photoshop. The Channels Palette is also open, showing the RGB plus individual color layers of the image. Photo © Joe Farace.

Figure 5.9. To create a new alpha channel, simply choose New Channel from the Channels Palette.

Figure 5.10. The mask channel looks similar to the Quick Mask, only it is part of the original image.

Figure 5.11. A Photo CD image of a tender, made at the Colorado railroad museum. Photo © Joe Farace.

Figure 5.12. The New Layer dialog lets you name and control the function of layers that are added to your background image.

Figure 5.13. A second Photo CD image was opened, copied onto the Clipboard, and pasted into the new Layer. Photo © Joe Farace.

Figure 5.14. You can select the Layer Mask for modification by Option-clicking (Mac OS) or Alt-clicking (Windows) on its icon in the Layers palette.

Figure 5.15. The final image uses two Photoshop layers and a layer mask to allow a portion of one of the images to show through.

Figure 5.16. This portrait was used as the foreground image in the composite. Photograph ©1997 Ralph Portillo.

Figure 5.17. The background was the author's photograph of a Brachiasaurus made at the Utah Field House in Vernal, Utah. Photo © 1995 Joe Farace.

Figure 5.18. The first Primatte dialog asks you to assign foreground and background images. Always assign the background image first.

Figure 5.19. The simple act of dragging the mouse across the background created this mask, but a little more work needed to be done to make the black areas blacker and the clear areas clearer.

Figure 5.20. At this point you are almost done. Photos © Ralph Portillo and Joe Farace.

Figure 5.21. The finished result is an image the author calls "Dinos are a girl's best friend." Photos © Ralph Portillo and Joe Farace.

Figure 5.22. Mask Pro offers digital masking capabilities that match and surpass features found on high-end prepress workstations. Users can control the process of defining colors to be kept or dropped, determining the characteristics of the final selection and maintaining the integrity of the image for output. Mask Pro provides numerous complementary tools to efficiently accomplish the growing number of masking projects. The primary tool is the Magic Paint Brush, which paints over the image, but only removes the user-defined drop colors. Other features include an improved Magic Wand, brush tool, airbrush, bucket fill, magic fill (a tool for patching small holes in the mask), unlimited undo/paint-back functions, zooming and panning capabilities, and an efficient clipping path generation system. Photo © 1998 Len Kaltman.

Figure 5.23. Nothing says junkyard like a stack of crushed cars. This image was taken from MetaCreations, KPT Power Photos III, volume 13, and it was opened in Adobe Photoshop. Image © MetaCreations.

Figure 5.24. Using an "edge" file from Auto F/X's Photo/Graphic Edges CD-ROM, I changed the rectangular edges of the stock photograph to something more irregular and, I hope, more interesting.

Figure 5.25. Using a plug-in called Acetone, I posterized the crushed car's image. Acetone is part of the Second Glance Software package that was designed for screen printers—the kinds of people who would create actual T-shirt designs.

Figure 5.26. A junkyard dog was selected from the disc and was reduced in size using Photoshop's Image Size dialog. This put the dog in scale with the background. Then the dog's image was selected and rotated. Image © MetaCreations.

Figure 5.27. Using Photoshop's Skew and Perspective controls, I rotated a junkyard warning sign and placed it in the upper right-hand corner to balance the dog in the opposite corner. Image © MetaCreations.

Figure 5.28. Every T-shirt design needs some kind of type. The Typeface used for this design is just a large Times Roman font, colored a bright red to stand out against the complex photographs making up the design.

Figure 5.29. The final Junkyard Art is ready to be separated or silk-screened for transfer to a T-shirt. Images © MetaCreations.

CHAPTER 6

Figure 6.1. The Nikon Coolscan plug-in allows you to prescan a slide or negative. You will notice that you have to set the scanner to read whether the image is a color positive or negative, or black and white or color. Photo © Joe Farace.

Figure 6.2. After initial tweaking, this image is opened in Adobe Photoshop for further manipulation. Photo © Joe Farace.

Figure 6.3. The starting point for Convolver manipulation is one of the author's panoramic photographs that had been transferred to Photo CD. Photo © Joe Farace.

Figure 6.4. Convolver's Tweak mode was used first to sharpen the image 20%.

Figure 6.5. Using Convolver's Tweak mode, the author experimented with color and texture combination to arrive at something that fit his previsualization.

Figure 6.6. To arrive at the appropriately "Stephen King" look the author desired, Photoshop's Fade command was used to reduce Convolver's effect to 43% of the original.

Figure 6.7. The author then used Photoshop's Brightness and Contrast controls to tweak the image just a bit more. Photo © Joe Farace.

Figure 6.8. Kai's Power Goo has several uses—including just having fun—for amateur and professional photographers alike. Photo © Barry Staver.

Figure 6.9. The starting point for the Chromassage manipulation was a photograph of the author's wife's—doing a Captain Nemo imitation—at Disney World. Photo © Joe Farace.

Figure 6.10. Chromassage's interface allows you to apply thirty preset color palettes, but variations are also available and, when combined with the jog and shuttle wheels, an almost infinite number of color possibilities exist.

Figure 6.11. The "After" picture showing the colors changed by Chromassage.

Figure 6.12. A photo CD image of a locomotive photographed on 35mm color negative film was the starting point for this exploration of Eye Candy. Photo © Joe Farace.

Figure 6.13. Eye Candy's Smoke filter provides sliders that let you control seven different aspects of digital smoke.

Figure 6.14. Eye Candy's Glow filter lets you apply different kinds—and colors—of glow effects to selections.

Figure 6.15. The Weave filter that is part of the Eye Candy package lets you apply a quilt-like look to your digital images.

Figure 6.16. The finial image uses three Eye Candy filters and was tempered by using Photoshop's Fade command. Photo © Joe Farace.

Figure 6.17. One of the WildRiver SSK Chameleon plug-in's most useful feature is the ability to select a color or color range and have it protected by an automatically created mask while you manipulate the rest of the image's colors. Photo © Joe Farace.

Figure 6.18a. A Photo CD image of a Victorian home is opened in Adobe Photoshop. Photo © Joe Farace.

Figure 6.18b. Paint Alchemy's control panel gives you access to many effects, plus the Size, Coverage, Color, Angle, and Opacity that allow you to customize any of the built-in brush strokes and effects. Photo © Joe Farace.

Figure 6.18c. The finished image combines elements of photography and painting that were produced by Xaos Tools' Paint Alchemy plug-in. Photo © Joe Farace.

Figure 6.19. Vivid Details Test Strip plug-in lets you both save the entire test strip as a file and print it. When evaluating the output, you will be able to tell if the image needs color correction for your specific output device. Photo © Joe Farace.

CHAPTER 7

Figure 7.1. A Summagraphics Expressions graphics tablet and cordless pen. Photo courtesy Summagraphics.

Figure 7.2. CalComp, like most manufacturers, offers graphics tablets in many different sizes. Photo courtesy CalComp.

Figure 7.3. Wacom's UltraPen is a cordless model that also has erasing capabilities. Photo courtesy Wacom.

CHAPTER 8

Figure 8.1. Epson America also makes a Zip drive. Their compact size makes them so portable you can take the drive to a service bureau that doesn't have one. Photo courtesy Epson America.

Figure 8.2. The inexpensive Epson Stylus Photo produces photo-quality output at a modest price. Photo courtesy of Epson America.

CHAPTER 9

Figure 9.1. The original photograph was made by the author using a conventional camera and film, then digitized with Kodak's Photo CD process. The resulting image was opened in Adobe Photoshop. Photo © Joe Farace.

Figure 9.2. Auto F/X's Photo/Graphic Edges plug-in is so simple to use that even a beginning computer user can produce the effect shown here in less time than it takes to read this. Photo © Joe Farace.

Figure 9.3. The first thing that the Acetone plug-in does is ask how many colors you want the image to contain.

Figure 9.4. The Acetone plug-in lets you keep, delete, and or add colors to the posterized image that it creates. Photo © Joe Farace.

Figure 9.5. In this example, the author uses Photoshop's selection of brightness and contrast controls to improve the visual impact of the posterized image. Photo © Joe Farace.

Figure 9.6. After digitally separating the images, PhotoSpot displays the name and numbers of the separation files that will be created. Click the "Sep..." button to make the separations files.

Figure 9.7. This dialog lets you save separations in either Adobe Photoshop or TIFF format.

Figure 9.8. The first step in making a dual blend is to open one of the separation files. Here, separation #4 is opened in Adobe Photoshop.

Figure 9.9. When converting to grayscale, leave the Size Ratio in the dialog box set at one.

Figure 9.10. The Blend tool is used to cover the entire image with a gradation from black to white.

Figure 9.11. Convert the resulting image to Bitmap using a halftone screen.

Figure 9.12. Select the desired method for screening the image. If you are not familiar with these functions, they are covered in detail in the Photoshop manual.

Figure 9.13. Use the Color Table to reassign the black and white portions of the image with your new, desired colors.

Figure 9.14. To wrap up the gradient creation part of the project, save the document under a new name as an RGB file in native Photoshop format.

Figure 9.15. To enter into the final step, you need to re-open the original black-and-white separation file.

Figure 9.16. The Apply Image dialog box is used to knock out the image from the gradient blend file.

Figure 9.17. The original separation now includes a gradated blend from black to dark blue.

Figure 9.18. Adobe PageMaker can create a mini-poster for promotional purposes as well as sales in a photographic arts gallery. Notice the low-resolution image. It appears this way because the image used was linked to the PageMaker file instead of being saved as part of it. Photo © Joe Farace.